SAVAGE
CENTURY
BACK TO BARBARISM

SAVAGE CENTURY

BACK TO BARBARISM

THÉRÈSE DELPECH

TRANSLATED BY GEORGE HOLOCH

CARNEGIE ENDOWMENT

FOR INTERNATIONAL PEACE

Published in French as L'Ensauvagement: Le retour de la barbarie au XXIe siècle, by Thérèse Delpech, © 2005 Les Editions Grasset & Fasquelle.

Carnegie Endowment for International Peace
1779 Massachusetts Avenue, N.W.
Washington, D.C. 20036
202-483-7600, Fax 202-483-1840
www.CarnegieEndowment.org

Typesetting by Naylor Design, Inc.
Printed by United Book Press

Ouvrage publié avec le concours de Ministère français chargé de la culture—Centre National du Livre.

This work is published with support from the French Ministry of Culture/Centre National du Livre.

Library of Congress Cataloging-in-Publication Data

Delpech, Thérèse.
[Ensauvagement. English]
Savage century : back to barbarism / Thérèse Delpech ; translated by George Holoch.
    p. cm.
Translation of: Ensauvagement : le retour de la barbarie au XXIe siècle.
Includes bibliographical references.
ISBN 978-0-87003-233-2
1. Security, International—Forecasting. 2. World politics—21st century. 3. Geopolitics. I. Title.

JZ5588.D4513 2008
327.101'12—dc22   2006101741

12 11 10 09 08 07   1 2 3 4 5   1st Printing 2007

I WOULD LIKE TO THANK

Jessica T. Mathews, George Perkovich, and Carrie Mullen for their support, encouragement, and friendship. I am also grateful to George Holoch for the care and dedication he brought to the translation of this book and to my friends Jack Flam and Catherine Bernard for their careful reading of and valuable suggestions about the final text.

Contents

PROLOGUE

*Modern history is like a deaf man
replying to questions that no one has
put to him.*

—TOLSTOY, *War and Peace*

The acceleration of history that we now sense so vividly began a little more than two centuries ago. Since then, humanity seems to have been launched on a wild epic journey whose trajectory is ever more obscure. Tolstoy, with characteristic Russian skill in the depiction of historical tragedy, is the writer who has presented the most gripping picture of that journey. Describing Napoleon's campaigns sixty years after the fact, he does not display any of the romanticism with which other Russians like to speak of the Emperor. Of the fantastic cavalcade through Europe that has fascinated so many great minds, he evokes only a frightful slaughter:

> For various reasons known and unknown, the French set about butchering and destroying one another. And with the event comes a corresponding justification in the expressed will of certain men who believe it to be necessary for the good of France, or in the interests of freedom or equality. The butchery stops, and along comes a corresponding justification in terms of the need to centralize power, resist Europe, and so on. Men march from west to east, murdering their fellow creatures, and this event is accompanied by fine words about the glory of France, the vileness of England, and so on. History shows that these forms of justification are no less contradictory than, for instance, murdering somebody as a declaration of his human rights, or murdering millions in Russia to take England down a peg or two.[1]

Tolstoy had no way of envisioning the massacres that would be committed after his death, whether in his own country or in distant lands. Nor would he hear the lunatic explanations that would be offered to account for them. If he had, one can imagine the feelings of horror that would have seized him. What is surprising is that he sees the French Revolution and Napoleon's ensuing campaigns as bringing about a transformation that most historians trace back only to the First World War: the transformation of Europeans into barbarians.[2]

In his narrative of the historical upheavals of early nineteenth-century Europe, there is no doubt that Tolstoy was also thinking of a much larger tragedy, encompassing not only the barbarity of warfare, the power of ideology, and the advent of the masses, but also the opposition between man and history, events and our understanding of them, and politics and ethics. He offers testimony to the fact that more often than not, all that can be discerned in history is frightful confusion—even from the perspective granted by the lapse of a half century. There is barely enough time to observe what is happening or to recall the past—men kill each other, then cease to do so; masses of people move, and more massacres take place—while events just keep following one another like painful reminders of the misunderstanding that prevails between mankind and history. Every period in history provides examples of this very same gap between what humanity predicts, anticipates, or expects and the mass of facts that no one would have thought of but that history constantly deposits in its wake. History seems to answer questions that we have had no time to put to it while we scurry about trying to understand the course of events. The justifications on offer may serve specific causes—the pleasure of princes, reasons of state, the grandeur of liberty—but what do they really tell us about "History with its great axe?"[3] Aren't they, rather, attempts to organize in one way or another something that eludes us, while simultaneously exercising the most powerful influence over the course of our existence?

There is nothing specific to the modern world in all this—it is part of the enigma of history. History, real history, is unforeseeable, and that explains the attraction of diplomatic services to *stability*—a key word in international relations, particularly in times when events foster fear of the unexpected. And while the meaning of the enigma eludes us, recognition of its existence is important in itself. If human thought did not question the meaning of a human presence in history and humans' responsibility in history's unfolding, it would lose one of its greatest subjects. But while the enigma is common to all stages of human history, modernity has drastically altered some essential phenomena—Tolstoy already understood something of that when he wrote his most important book. The pulse of time has changed, and its tempo sometimes accelerates to such a degree that the two interlocutors—man and history—are increasingly *out of phase* with each other. That gap has today become so striking that it could serve as one of the definitions for the spirit of our age. And we now have also to reckon with a scale so vast that it encompasses the entire planet and echoes from the most distant shores.

With such complexity added to the enigma, it is not surprising that the dialogue between man and history is full of inconsistencies. How is it possible to contain the consequences of what one undertakes? How can we avoid having the whole world intervene in what we decide on our own territory? Is it strange that man has lost the ability to understand what is happening around him, when everything seems inextricably tangled? And should we be indignant, seeing him fall prey to a kind of mental and moral confusion, to a chaos in ideas and behavior that seems even worse than the chaos of events?[4]

The conviction that it is increasingly difficult for human thought to grasp the meaning of the clamor of history—closer as it is to deafening cacophony than to a melody recognizable to the human ear—finds a troubling echo in the judgment of a mind very different from that of Tolstoy, but equally disturbed by the disorder of the world. In a classic passage, Paul Valéry observed:

> The unforeseen itself is in the process of transformation, and what is unforeseen in the modern world has become almost unlimited. The imagination fails in the face of it. . . . Instead of, as in the past, playing an honest card game with fate, knowing the rules, knowing the number of cards and face cards, we are now in the position of a player who is astonished to discover that his adversary's hand contains face cards never seen before and that the rules of the game change with each hand.[5]

History does not progress in a continuous fashion, nor does it even move forward in spurts. It seems to have abandoned any intelligible pattern and to have literally gone off the rails. Valéry's words might well be adopted by the generation that lived through September 11, 2001, a generation inclined to believe that events display a complexity that exceeds their imagination. Spectacular upheavals and sudden reversals are the defining characteristics of our time.[6]

Our forebears in the early twentieth century were also aware of a dangerous rift between humanity and historical reality. The possibility of sudden storms was not unknown to them. They were surprised by them as we are, and suffered as we do from their effects. How can we fail to understand them? Only an almost unthinkable series of absurdities, in Vienna, Saint Petersburg, Berlin, and finally in Paris, could have set ablaze all Europe as well as a large part of the rest of the world, after the assassination of the nephew of the Austrian Emperor by a Serb nationalist. There had been so many other political assassinations![7] What the "Great War" revealed for the first time—and this is the reason it has retained that name in some history books—was that the great powers now found it impossible to contain the most important political decision, the decision to initiate a conflict, within the confines of only two or three nations; they could not stop its engulfing an entire continent. And once the machine had been set in motion, there was no question of holding it back: all continents would be affected.[8]

We have seen that globalization of violence develop in unprecedented ways. Nearly a century later, at a time when interconnections among men and things have never been greater, those who still believe that a good fairy will protect them from a major conflict in far-off Asia, if one were unfortunately to break out, should consider 1914. We Europeans dragged the world into our wars; others will drag us into theirs.

The unforeseen has become our element, the distinctive sign of the strategic relations of our time, along with the velocity of our missiles, the firepower of our arsenals, the development of new technologies, the instantaneous spread of information, and new forms of terrorism. Recent history, punctuated by terrible explosions, natural catastrophes, and great massacres, has shown just how devastating surprises can be.[9] Such eruptions may serve to recall historical tragedies that we would like to forget. The mixture of violence and suddenness, of instability and disorder, affects our souls as well as our minds.

For that reason, the growing rift between man and history carries with it an ontological risk: it endangers the relationship between human consciousness and time. Roots in the past, the transmission of values, continuity between the generations, whatever links men to one another—all are threatened by the immediacy in which we live and by the chaos surrounding us. Our present impatience, as much as the devitalization of the past, has transformed time into a vector for agitation and anxiety. That the changes introduced by technological revolutions have been much too rapid for the human mind to absorb only exaggerates the effect. The mind is often reduced to a spectator who no longer expects anything from history, except that it will keep happening.

When we ask of history nothing other than that it go on, we cannot complain if it sometimes provides brutal answers. The fault is also in the human actor. That is precisely the way Valéry's observation concludes: "He cannot even throw the cards in his opponent's face. Why? The fact is that the more he looks at him the more he recognizes himself! . . . The modern world is shaped in the image of the mind of man."[10] The deafness of history is shared by mankind; only spectacular explosions shake it.

What is truly horrifying about the cycle of gratuitous cruelty presented on television screens, with hostages slaughtered like animals and the dead desecrated in cemeteries, is that the images express a kind of visualized "norm" of the extreme violence that prevails in the world. We wonder where it may be leading.[11] It troubles us that only great crimes now manage to move us. The return of crime as spectacle has awakened an unease that is all the greater because the spectacle no longer takes place in public, as in the time of Voltaire, but in the comfort of our living rooms. The gap is unbearable, as is the routinization of violence. Thucydides, the most essential reference for anyone meditating on history, claims that some periods express an exasperation with human passions. If that is the case, then our era, like the 1930s, is of the type that gives rise to such exasperation with passions that have run amok, and in which humanism and intellectualism are often condemned because they stand for civilized norms that attempt to restrain passions.

It has been claimed, as the character Jean-Baptiste Clamence in Camus's La Chute might have done, that there is scarcely any difference between the murderers who kill innocent victims while filming their torments and the helpless spectators who witness the scenes on their home television screens.[12] In this view, the ideological and social violence that characterize the contemporary world are ubiquitous. That is a comforting way of justifying and excusing crime, recalling once-fashionable slogans that should have been retired long ago. But we must recognize that if indeed the world has recently been reshaped primarily by terrorism and the reactions terrorism provoked, it is probably because the values that might have contained terrorism before it spread so spectacularly have been greatly weakened, or are completely powerless.

Certainly the world has assumed its present form partly because no political community has attempted to take up the formidable challenge represented by the end of a ferocious century. Memory and imagination were not up to the task. And after forty years of a war that never actually broke out, there was a lack of will as well. Of Raymond Aron's well-known formulation, "improbable war, impossible peace," we chose to consider only the first half and did not ponder the meaning of the second, which suggested the degree to which, in essence, peace was an illusion. At the conclusion of the Cold War, the elites of the countries of Eastern Europe understood better than their counterparts in the West that the continent had to be reconstructed along more radical lines than those set out in the criteria for membership in the European Union promulgated in Copenhagen in 1993. They sometimes wrote eloquently about the meaning of Europe, and it was in their writings that "European values," when invoked after the fall of the iron curtain, seemed still to have some power and some truth.[13] But power was not on their side.

It was thought possible to resume the grand march toward peace, collective security, and the harmonious development of society after an aberrant interruption attributed to a combination of totalitarian crimes, the cowardice of the free world, and the confrontation between the two blocs. But the "interruption" in question was part of our shared history and could not be disposed of by those who preferred to "take blood for wine."[14] One had only to read a few lines by Varlam Shalamov or Andrei Sinyavsky to understand that we could not get off so lightly, because the century had carried human suffering and the destruction of humanity too far. For example:

> I was told a tale in the camp about how Soviet zeks communicated news about themselves and thereby for the first time revealed the secrets of Stalin's labor camps . . . Shortly after the war, somewhere in the depths of the taiga, not far from the ocean, a number of desperate prisoners cut off their hands to free themselves from inhuman labor. They put the severed fingers and hands in

between the planks in loads of excellent building lumber bound in wire and intended for export. Eager to exchange the valuable wood for currency, the authorities paid no attention. And the precious cargo sailed to Great Britain . . . And when the cargo was unloaded, what did they find? Severed hands. They took apart a second, a third load: over and over human flesh between the planks . . . The fact was that they had really cut off their hands. Out of despair.[15]

After the First and Second World Wars, the magnitude of the destruction and the upheaval in international relations required that the great powers take radical steps to put the world back on its feet. Margaret MacMillan's account of the 1919 Paris Conference is an essential source on the enormous amount of time, energy, and intelligence the victors of the Great War devoted to the reconstruction of Europe.[16] That the effort ultimately failed and that a second conflict, even more terrible than the first, was unleashed twenty years later, should not erode the admiration we feel for the three great protagonists of the conference: Wilson, Lloyd George, and Clemenceau. After the Second World War came the important Geneva Conventions on the laws of war, and it was in the name of the "conscience of mankind" that the Nuremberg tribunal rendered its judgments.

Nothing like those monumental measures was undertaken after the peaceful collapse of the Soviet Union, largely because the Cold War had been carried on by spies and experts, not by the people. The novels of John Le Carré thus provide some of the best accounts of this confrontation. As Peter Hennessy has pointed out, the Cold War reversed the process Clausewitz observed in the nineteenth century, by which wars ceased to be a matter for professionals and became a matter for the people.[17] The principal participants in the Cold War were nuclear strategists and intelligence specialists.[18] Policy papers on mutual assured destruction, gradual escalation, and extended deterrence, and encounters at Checkpoint Charlie and in prisoner exchanges on the bridge in Potsdam were what punctuated the Cold War. It was in no way a Third World War. Anyone who makes that claim has completely lost sight of what occurred during the 1914–1918 and 1939–1945 wars and is peculiarly lacking in information on Cold War capabilities and propensities. The declassification in recent decades of numerous secret documents from the 1960s and 1970s gives one some idea of the limitless violence that an authentic world war during the period would have unleashed.

Since a third global war did not take place, it could not help forge a new consciousness among people at large comparable to the one that had played a major role in the reconstruction of international affairs after the two world wars. At the end of the 1980s, the flood of refugees and the destruction of the notorious Berlin Wall awakened strong feelings, particularly in the countries that had suffered most from the division of Europe. But those events did not touch the depths of the human conscience, as had the discovery of the camps and the ruins across Europe forty years before. To be sure, on the other side of what was called the iron curtain, public and private misfortunes had been too numerous and harsh for people to forget very easily. The devastation and the crimes of forty years of cold war, even though spoken of publicly only by associations with a limited audience, such as Memorial in Russia,[19] remain present to every household. Nor are the effects limited to the widespread criminalization in Russian, Belarusian, and Ukrainian society[20] and in the former republics of Central Asia, to the savage conduct of Moscow in Chechnya, or to the massive corruption of the Chinese bureaucracy. Yet the traumatic experience of those crimes in the most directly brutalized societies, as was also true in societies that merely learned of them, had the effect of accustoming the public to the infliction of overwhelming violence and cruelty. What the 1914–1918 war began in the trenches was continued with deportations, prison camps, and the massacre of civilian populations. Once those destructive forces were unleashed in all their savagery, they could not simply be repressed at the end of the Cold War. They will continue to affect people and international relations in coming decades, like the aftershocks of a major earthquake.

In France it took the entire nineteenth century to recover from the French Revolution, but the violent events of the revolutionary period bear no comparison to what Russian, Chinese, or Cambodian society suffered in the twentieth century. And because there was no catharsis anywhere at the end of the 1980s, that past continues to fester in all our minds. The work of memory and of mourning has never been done for the tens of millions of victims of state violence, and the ghosts of those who disappeared have not left us.[21] That is equally true for Western nations, because we are speaking of a collective tragedy of mankind; moreover, the West often participated directly in the crimes. That was already the case before the onset of the Cold War, when Russians who had joined the German army,

often out of despair, were turned over to Stalin by the Allies, in the knowledge that they would be sent to camps or killed. Support for appalling
dictatorships and support of apartheid in the name of the struggle against
communism can be included in the same category. Western civil society
also shares responsibility: In France, for example, *Les Habits neufs du président Mao* by Simon Leys, one of the first books to denounce Maoist barbarity, was burned at the University of Vincennes in 1968.

In fact, the world as a whole is still disoriented by the storms of the
twentieth century. One of the principal signs of the internal disorder is the
sheer skepticism about the capacity of the human mind to influence events
that has succeeded the great period of historical *experiments*, in the Faustian sense of the term. We often speak of the decline of courage in contemporary societies, but it would be more accurate to say that the era is *discouraged*. The intellectual and spiritual chaos visible everywhere spring
from the feverishness of societies that have lost their way, in the resulting
boredom, in the destruction of hope for the future, but above all in the
decline of confidence in the human spirit.[22] That is a worldwide phenomenon, which affects former communist societies, where nationalism is
attempting to take the place of Marxism-Leninism or Maoism, as much as
Western societies, where hedonism is beginning to come up against its
limitations. The only clear message delivered by the huge, diverse crowd
that traveled to Rome in April 2005 for the funeral of John Paul II was a
message of spiritual hunger. The pope had grasped the distinctive characteristic of humanity at the dawn of the twenty-first century, in all the
regions of the world, and it allowed him to touch a string in the human
spirit that was waiting only to be plucked.

On October 26, 1932, in the house of Maxim Gorky, who lent himself
to many of Stalin's staged performances, Stalin told the assembled writers:
"Even more than machines, tanks, aeroplanes, we need human souls."[23]
It might be objected that the engineering of human souls is the heart of
totalitarianism, and that in liberal regimes there can by definition be no
question of any such enterprise. That may well be true, but is that a reason
to reduce politics, as has been true since the end of the ideological confrontation between East and West, to the treatment of economic and social
problems alone? Despite all the speeches about the *values* of Europe, now
enshrined in the preamble to the 2005 draft European Constitution, whom
do we see in the airplanes of heads of state when they travel abroad but the

representatives of stock market values? How else is the success of an official trip measured but by the financial value of the contracts signed? This
limitation of politics, which has made most of our leaders into traveling
salesmen, says a good deal about the degradation of an activity that must
nonetheless take on ever more burdensome responsibilities. Of course,
political figures are merely reflecting a broader development in society, but
they have shown themselves unable to rise above a mass trend, as those
who count in history are required to do.

In these circumstances, it is not surprising that the struggle that best
reveals the weaknesses of Western societies in opposition to their enemies
involves neither the military nor the police nor the judiciary, but intellectual and moral questions. The specific strength that comes from conviction
is on the other side. Nor is it an accident that the fact that one can die for
an idea has returned in the monstrous form of suicide attacks against civilians throughout the world. Such attacks pose crucial questions to the societies that are their targets. Which ideas do our post-heroic societies find
worth defending? How can we make judgments about the affairs of a
world in which everything is relative? Where tragedy and death are eliminated from the field of consciousness? Suicide attacks are striking not only
because death has come back to us *in that form*, but also simply because it
has come back at all.

As early as 1915, in his "Reflections upon War and Death," Freud
explained how European societies had eliminated death before it came
back to them wearing the terrifying mask of the First World War. The
anger of soldiers on leave discovering that life continues as though the hell
of the trenches did not exist showed just how powerful the denial of reality was at the time. These are the pictures that passed through their heads
when they found themselves in drawing rooms or country houses:

> We see men living with their skulls blown open; we see soldiers run with their
> two feet cut off, they stagger on their splintered stumps into the next shell-hole;
> a lance-corporal crawls a mile and a half on his hands dragging his smashed knee
> after him; another goes to the dressing station and over his clasped hands bulge
> his intestines; we see men without mouths, without jaws, without faces; we
> find one man who has held the artery of his arm in his teeth for two hours in
> order not to bleed to death. The sun goes down, night comes, the shells whine,
> life is at an end.[24]

Still, today, the eradication of death from the awareness of Western societies is what their fiercest adversaries perceive most clearly. "You who love life, be warned that we do not fear death." Such is the message, they believe, that gives them the decisive advantage. They may be right.

The conclusion to these preliminary remarks is simple: if it is not possible to follow the thread of the dialogue between man and history, it is because the two participants are not only out of phase but deeply unsettled. It is a dialogue of the deaf, like one overheard between intimate relations in which anguish makes it impossible to hear anything but inner voices. They continue to speak, in search of a meaning that eludes them— which it cannot fail to do because they can no longer distinguish between just and unjust, beautiful and ugly, or good and evil. The only sound that reaches them is a confused clamor that they have no way of organizing. Barbarous deeds are preceded by barbarity of spirit: the two mutually reinforce one another in an infinite hall of mirrors. The political result has become all too obvious. The idea that the actions of a few men can have consequences comparable to natural disasters or major epidemics is no longer understood as it was and as it should continue to be. And yet such men and such actions continue to define the greatness of politics; therefore, politics cannot be rehabilitated without a serious consideration of ethics. In the absence of a rehabilitated politics, moreover, we will have neither the strength to avert the ordeals the present century has in store for us, nor, more important, the courage to confront them if we have the misfortune of being unable to avoid them. That is the subject of this book.

In its capacity for horrors, history has never lacked imagination. And the perverse inventiveness displayed by recent events is so dark that it sorely tests our inner strength. Bringing politics closer to ethics is a duty not only to the living but also to the dead. Do we need to be reminded of that by a Chinese photographer who describes an execution that took place near Harbin in 1968?

On April 5, 1968, during the Qing Ming Festival, I photographed the execution of seven men and one woman. . . . The eight condemned people were made to climb two by two onto the backs of trucks and they were driven through the town and into the countryside northwest of Harbin. There they were lined up with their hands tied behind their backs inside the walls of the desolate cemetery of Huang Shan, and they were forced to kneel. They were all killed with a bullet to the back of the head. No one asked me to take close-ups of their bodies, but I did it on my own. . . . When I enlarged the photos of the people who had been executed, in the dim red light of the dark room, I spoke to them in a quiet voice. I said to them: 'If your souls are haunted, I beg you not to haunt me too. I am simply trying to help you. I took pictures of you because I wanted to immortalize History . . . I want people to know how you were scorned.'[25]

PART ONE

THE TELESCOPE

*We are living in the
aftermath of something.
Are we on the eve of
something else?*

—CHARLES MORICE, 1905

CHAPTER 1

POLITICAL RESPONSIBILITY

No age has ever held such great
power or borne such great responsibility.

—HANS JONAS

Schopenhauer, who wrote extensively about relations between politics and ethics, proposed an experiment for politicians in which they imagine themselves a few decades into the future looking back through a telescope to judge their present actions. The *retrospective* vision, he thought, should allow them to evaluate the long-term consequences of their acts and to recognize that political activity should be conducted not only for the benefit of the current generation—a demand that is already too great for many—but for coming generations.[1] To do justice to future generations, you have to be able to identify with them, not merely invoke them ritually. Putting yourself in their place with an imaginary telescope pointed at the past is the best way to feel toward them the sympathy you feel for your contemporaries.[2]

The difficulty of the exercise lies first in the tyranny of current events in politics, where the future is primarily for rhetorical purposes. Despite the speeches on climate change or underdevelopment,[3] we observe a declining interest in long-term political questions in favor of immediate economic and social issues. The difficulty also lies in the multiple potential consequences of any given decision in a future environment about which we know almost nothing. In the strict sense, there are neither *causes* nor *effects* in the development of history. Bertrand Russell provides a facetious

3

illustration of that in his critique of dialectical materialism, offering to demonstrate that the industrial revolution was a consequence of drought in Central Asia, or that the United States owes its independence to the marriage of Henry VIII to Anne Boleyn.[4] Historians speak of immediate or distant causes as approximations only to impose some order on historical chaos.

What was difficult in the recent past is even more so today. The set of variables governing human action that has been introduced by globalization has considerably complicated any efforts at prediction. Political phenomena now have nearly infinite interconnections. And if it is true that no period can be conceptually identified in its own time but only after the fact, and sometimes long after, the next period is even harder to define. That is not necessarily anything to complain about, since contingency, whose influence we tend always to underestimate, also means the reintroduction of freedom into history. But understanding of contemporary history suffers as a result.[5] When have we finally found the right angle, the right perspective, the proper distance? Pascal before us raised that essential question about the exercise of historical judgment.

The conditions for carrying out Schopenhauer's experiment seem problematic for another reason as well, a more directly ethical one, because *at its core* it concerns the sympathy we are supposed to feel for our contemporaries. For Schopenhauer, this is the root of ethics: we are moved by the suffering of our fellow humans. But is that really true? After believing it for a while during the Balkan tragedy, particularly in 1999 when the disasters of Kosovo led off every nightly news broadcast, we may once again question ourselves.[6] At that time, all the talk was of humanitarian intervention, and of limits on the sovereignty of governments—at least when, sweeping aside their most elementary duty, that of protecting their citizens, they began massacring some of them. That more engaged stance marked a reversal on the part of Western countries, driven by public opinion, quite different from the prevalent attitude of indifference and helplessness during the Cold War. The internal conflict in the United Nations Charter between the protection of human rights and the defense of national sovereignty, which protects actions taken by governments with respect to their people, provoked countless commentaries toward the end of the twentieth century. Reactions from Moscow and Beijing defending the status quo were intense: Where were we headed on this slippery slope? But the Western countries most attached to their sovereignty—France, for example—asked the same question. The debate led United Nations Secretary General Kofi Annan to adopt courageous positions supporting a duty to intervene—or a *responsibility to protect*[7]—which gained increasing legitimacy. That was just seven years ago. Since then, governments and people seem to have settled back into indifference,[8] except when confronted with major national disasters receiving heavy media coverage, such as the terrible tsunami of Christmas 2004 that caused more than 300,000 deaths. Jan Egeland,[9] who coordinated UN aid to Asia, has had to constantly remind us of "the twenty forgotten crises," from Uganda to North Korea.[10]

With good reason. The tragedies unfolding in the Darfur region of Sudan (where 2.5 million inhabitants have been driven from their villages, 300,000 of them dying of hunger and disease, with 200,000 civilians massacred by militias[11]); the genocide perpetrated with impunity by the Russian army in Chechnya since 1999;[12] Chinese citizens rotting in psychiatric hospitals for dissident acts; chemical experiments to which entire families have been subjected in special camps in North Korea[13]—all these provoke little compassion, and even less action. It is not information that is lacking, rather that the misfortunes of the world are so numerous that it seems, as Chamfort said, "that the heart must break or harden."[14] We only wonder whether that choice was really made, or whether indifference decided the matter. If the latter is the case, what good does it do to ask people who only glance distractedly at dramatic events unfolding in front of them to project themselves twenty years forward to discover some standard of prudent conduct to protect those who will come after them?[15]

Though one might wish them to be stronger, it is not *feelings* that are most cruelly lacking, and the foregoing is in no way a call for a politics of feeling. Feelings are ephemeral, unworthy guides for judgment, and frequently create nothing but disorder. "Bleeding hearts and bloody mess" was the apt title of a British article on the international chaos. It is political thinking—to recall the image of the telescope, political vision—that is necessary to prevent catastrophe. Political vision can foresee that a policy systematically favoring regimes over the peoples they govern will lead to violent outbreaks for which the price will one day have to be paid. Political vision would encourage firmness toward President Vladimir Putin in the name of the strategic relationship one wishes to establish with Russia. It could advise against the resumption of arms sales to China at a time when tensions among China, Japan, and Taiwan are on the increase.[16] Judgment and character have always been the most important qualities in politics, and they remain so. But feelings too must play a role in strategic judgments. The most enlightened minds and the most seasoned temperaments should not be allowed to forget the "brother humans that after us shall live," from whom François Villon hoped to receive forgiveness in the *Ballade des pendus*. Their inheritance will be our actions—and our mistakes—at a time when actions can have huge consequences. Unlike almost all the generations that have gone before us, we can now stage what Jung called the *end of the world*.

The history of the last century showed the ease with which historical transformations of unprecedented violence could follow without warning on the heels of the best of times. As in Greek tragedy, crime engendered crime in the house of Europe, which twice set the rest of the world ablaze. From the experience, lessons were drawn for the reconciliation of the European nations. But what is now at stake is Europe's capacity to assume international responsibilities in a deeply troubled world. And from that point of view, the *internal* lessons just mentioned are insufficient. The unprecedented historical eruption from which the entire twentieth century arose does not speak only for the madness of Europe and of national passions. It is evidence of a wider adventure concerning humanity as a whole: the sudden appearance of storms whose warning signs on the horizon we Europeans have too long pretended to ignore, storms no one can control once they have been unleashed. When such sudden acceleration of history occurs, it signals the defeat of political action, which can do nothing but run after events until it is swallowed up by them. If Europe has any message to transmit to the world, it is truly this one.

In 1905, with the Russo-Japanese War, the first Russian Revolution, and the Tangier crisis, many signals were starting to turn red, but only a few astute observers saw the storm coming. Nine years later, in 1914, tension had reached its peak, but history was not yet written. Major errors in more than one European capital were still necessary before the doomsday machine could be set in motion. Twenty-five years later, Hitler's military victories were heralded by six years of conquests carried off without firing a shot, while the democratic powers refused to see what was plain to anyone who cared to look. The war really began with the rearmament of 1933 and the fight against the principle of collective security. The withdrawal from the League of Nations and then from disarmament negotiations by the three Axis powers, Germany, Japan, and Italy, were important stages in a conflict that applied what Hitler himself called a broader strategy (*erweiterte Strategie*). Bombs came later. Before them, several battles were won without encountering any resistance. Those included the annexation of Austria and then of Czechoslovakia, followed by the pact with Stalin that nullified the East-West alliance of the First World War.

After the war, in a letter to Raymond Aron, Carl Schmitt quoted a sentence from Clausewitz with a commentary by Lenin. "The conqueror always loves peace," Clausewitz asserted. "He would happily enter our country quietly." And Lenin comments in the margin: "grandiose, aha!" This sequence is instructive for other parts of the contemporary world, especially East Asia, where the situation often calls to mind the European rivalries of the last century. There, too, the clouds gathering on the horizon are visible. China's legal and diplomatic offensives proliferate, while it claims to be pursuing a "peaceful rise to power." That has not prevented the Europeans from sending the worst possible signals to Beijing, whether it is a matter of multipolarity, arms sales, or craven warnings addressed to Taiwan rather than China.

Anxious minds at the beginning of this century bear little resemblance to those of a hundred years ago, whose carefree nature has often been noted. In a sense, they seem better prepared to confront hard times than their ancestors were. Yet they seem somehow *crushed* by the weight of the past, fearing any kind of change lest it bring on trouble. In 2005, even the campaign in France on the draft European Constitution showed, disturbingly, that the refusal to take risks overwhelmed any other feeling. While the supporters of a yes vote ensured that nothing was going to change, those against denounced all possible change. Seen with a forgiving eye, present-day anxiety proceeds as much from the weight of the past century as from the anticipation of new ordeals.[17] Jung claimed that the iron curtain, bristling with machine guns and barbed wire, ran through the soul of modern man, no matter which side of the frontier one lived on. Europe has finally been reunited, but its enlargement has not been experienced as a victory in most of the western part of the continent. The unity of the European consciousness has not yet been accomplished, as though it is evolving much more slowly than events. Above all, the unconscious ignores time, and bad memories are still lurking there. In circumstances in which control over the fate of nations and individuals seems increasingly uncertain, it is not surprising that feelings of vulnerability prevail, especially when it is no longer possible to ignore the savagery of which history is capable.

In the twentieth century, one of the principal causes of regression was the dynamics of *the egalitarian passion*, best analyzed by Tocqueville:

> Nations today cannot change the equality of conditions within them; but it is up to them whether equality leads to servitude or freedom, to enlightenment or barbarism, to prosperity or poverty.[18]

While the twentieth century conducted political and social experiments on a grand scale, it was often by following out "equality of conditions" to the most extreme consequences of modern tyranny. It was in the name of equality that some of the greatest crimes were committed in Russia, China, North Korea, and Cambodia. The speed with which liberty was sacrificed to equality, the magnitude of the human suffering allowed in equality's name, and the complicity of a portion of the "free world" have taken their place among the great human disasters. Historians produce book after book on modern tyranny but often succeed merely in deepening the mystery.[19] Only novelists have come close to capturing the radical strangeness of those crimes. It is impossible to read George Orwell's *1984* without a feeling of palpable horror that history books are powerless to communicate.

Except for small, absurd nations like North Korea that continue to cultivate the lunacies of totalitarianism at their people's expense, the question of equality of condition raised by Tocqueville has gained new momentum with globalization. The globalizing process has spread the egalitarian message around the world, while offering even less hope that its promises will be fulfilled either on a national or a local level. As it is, envy and resentment have no proper outlets in any society.[20] In a globalized world, those passions remain fierce and their expression is given more impetus, while the hope that they might be fulfilled appears increasingly utopian. The situation is intensified by the possibility of endless comparisons throughout the world. Successive industrial revolutions have created such large gaps between nations, regions, and peoples that even substantial investments, which are nowhere to be seen, in conjunction with strong literacy campaigns, which are not being undertaken, could hardly reduce them significantly. The egalitarian passion has assumed a worldwide scope, and information technology has helped sharpen it. Its strength can no longer be contained within any borders, and the contemporary world is therefore an unhappy world. Comparisons are perpetual, whereas progress toward equalizing conditions remains what it has always been: as limited in space as it is finite in time.[21]

That has licensed fertile minds to imagine more transformations than the history books can contain, especially in a hurried world where the youthful population of the most destitute countries has little tolerance for injustice. The clash of civilizations that has been so widely discussed is perhaps nothing more than a desire for universal equality that can never be fulfilled and that will therefore bring forth nothing but frustration and violence.[22] That frustration has been the breeding ground for the monster of *Western domination*, a chameleon present in every nook and cranny of modern history, and the myth of the American empire, which is of more recent origin but awakens equally powerful passions. America, however, has neither imperial institutions nor, above all, imperial ambitions, unlike the European powers of the last two centuries. To confirm this, one need merely read the many accounts of American reluctance to engage in conflict or to remain in territories where the United States has won military victories. But those realities do not alter the imperial image.

Power, especially when it appears in so impressive a form as the American version, inevitably has effects like those described in Balzac's *Comédie humaine*, whether we are looking at a particular society or the entire world: it creates envy, competitiveness, and resentment. Peace in the world would require the satisfaction of those collective passions, which is impossible. Hence the seeds of future great disorders are still to be found in the dynamics leading toward equality of conditions. This does not call for a lament about globalization, but rather for recognition that, while democratic passions have become universal, democratic regimes have not. Universalization is the bearer of revolutionary movements of a new kind, of which terrorism is only one manifestation.[23] In light of recent experience, it may be feared that those revolutions will be of the type—"disordered, furious, powerless revolutions that destroy everything and create nothing"—that Balzac presents in his novels.

A second phenomenon, which concerns governments as much as peoples, must be mentioned. Some countries believe that history never gave them what was rightfully theirs. The stability that European societies worship is not what such countries have in mind. To imagine that they will be satisfied with some sort of reform of the Security Council[24] or with speeches on the beauties of multipolarity is pure diplomatic romanticism. What they want is not official positions or speeches but a genuine redistribution of power. If Iran has acquired ballistic and cruise missiles with a range of two to three thousand kilometers and is attempting to develop nuclear weapons in spite of its international agreements and multilateral pressure, it is largely to secure regional hegemony. If New Delhi conducted nuclear tests in 1998, it was to gain greater heft in world affairs as much as to guarantee its defense. India is not lacking in intellectual, economic, or political resources for pursuing that aim, and it will not have to pay the price of extricating itself from communism like China. Of all the nations on earth, China is the most intent on transforming power relations in the twenty-first century for its benefit, and it will also have the fewest scruples about choosing the means to reach that goal. China has never forgotten how the European powers dismembered it, beginning with the Opium War of 1839–42. The revenge to be taken on history guides its foreign policy, as the preservation of power by the Communist Party guides its domestic policy. China's aim often seems to become the rival power to America and to outstrip it if possible. It already thinks of itself as the leading world power.

The questioning of the international status quo by new powers is natural in a time of historical transition like the one we have been passing through since the end of the Cold War. Those rising countries' calls for change have regularly brought the Security Council to consider—though to no effect thus far—enlarging its membership, so as to regain some degree of legitimacy. But, as already underlined, even a successful enlargement would not be enough. Correct handling of the situation would involve the great powers' first accepting the concept of change and not regarding it systematically as an enemy.

Thus what the telescope clearly shows is both the discontent of societies that get nothing from their governments and blame outside *evil influences*, the West foremost among them, and the appearance of new powers on the world stage. The ever-present memory of colonization and the humiliation it continues to generate are even more significant elements in the accusation because America, and Israel with it, are stand-ins for the colonizing power for a good part of the world. The two countries have replaced the real colonizers—the Europeans—in the popular imagination. That the

United States has no colonial past[25] gains it no credit, because Washington's support for Israel is experienced as support for an enterprise of a colonial character. That is why an America concerned with justice and development and a resumption of the peace process in the Middle East is a factor in world stability, both real and symbolic, even if the most radical enemies of the United States and Israel remain unmoved. That is also why the *dignity* of the Palestinian people has symbolic value in so many parts of the world.

The intention of some nations to take revenge on a West that from their point of view has imposed its law on the rest of the world for too long poses a question of a different nature. The desire for strategic rearrangements is strong. Nations delivering that message, whether India, China, or Iran, will make their voices heard. The problem is less containing their ambitions than framing them so that they do not disturb regional and world peace. In the twentieth century, that is precisely what we Europeans failed to do when faced with the rise of Germany. We know the consequences of that error. It is dangerous to ignore these two phenomena, the desire for revenge and the necessity for strategic rearrangement, or to pretend not to understand their implications.

Another cause for the return to barbarism in the twentieth century has been the growing gap between the progress of science and technology and the absence of comparable progress in the ethical realm. The instability of the contemporary world stems largely from the ever-increasing dependence of people on technology, while the human psyche remains as vulnerable as ever at a time when moral values have lost much of their solidity. The powers of human beings have expanded considerably, whereas the ends of action are more and more confused and psychological equilibrium is constantly threatened by too many stimuli. Jung wrote on the subject frequently, comparing his age to the early days of Christendom:

> As at the beginning of the Christian era, so again today we are faced with the problem of the general moral backwardness which has failed to keep pace with our scientific, technical, and social progress. So much is at stake and so much depends on the psychological constitution of modern man.[26]

The available material means of destruction combined with the psychic forces of destruction may justify anxiety in circles far broader than psychoanalytic ones. In the last century, the gap between the means available to humankind and humankind's intellectual and moral condition had already led to putting industrialization to work for destructive purposes. Industrial methods revolutionized war in 1914, and as early as 1918 they made possible the advent of the most monstrous forms for the organization of societies and camps.

A scholar of the concentration camp system, Anne Applebaum,[27] explains how the new prison industry was set up at the end of the First World War, with internment camps for prisoners proliferating across Europe.[28] Both Nazis and Soviets organized and managed their concentration camps along industrial lines; otherwise, such large numbers of prisoners could never have been taken in hand and, later, exterminated. All parties involved used the methods of industrial warfare perfected during the 1914–18 war. And beginning in 1937, Stalinism had at its disposal a deadly system modeled on the five-year plan: it was a simple matter of filling quotas. On July 30, 1937, Nikolai Yezhov, the head of the Soviet secret police, presented to the Politburo order no. 00447, which decreed that regions would be assigned quotas beginning in August for two categories of individuals: those to be killed and those to be sentenced to deportation. The initial suggestion was 72,950 people for category 1 and 259,450 people for category 2. The families of both categories were to be deported. The regions quickly filled the quotas, then asked Moscow for new authorizations. In the end, order no. 00447 led to 767,397 arrests and 386,798 executions. A month later, order no. 00485 mandated the liquidation of members of the Polish opposition and spies and legitimized 350,000 arrests, including 247,157 executions. The regions engaged in real competition to fulfill the quotas. The killing machine was even freer to operate because it had nothing to do with real crimes.[29] One of the great problems for Russia today—and an even greater one for China—is that, unlike Hitler's concentration camps, theirs were never liberated and no Nuremberg tribunal ever judged the crimes that had been committed.

The possibilities for political crime opened up by industrial methods were frequently denounced at the end of the Second World War. The bishop of Clermont-Ferrand, on being liberated from a Nazi concentration camp, had this to say:

> The criminal institutions of which we were witnesses and victims carry within themselves all the scourges of ancient barbarity and servitude, to which they

have added a new systematization and a new method able to magnify human suffering to the full extent made possible by modern science.[30]

The most accurate accounts of Nazi and Stalinist documents dealing with the bureaucracy of death are sometimes metaphorical, as in this passage from *The Last Days of Mankind* by Karl Kraus, in which the quick transformation of trees into a newspaper represents the efficient killing of people and disposal of their bodies in the death camps:

> Wishing to establish the precise amount of time it takes to transform a tree standing in a forest into a newspaper, the owner of a paper mill had the idea of undertaking a very interesting experiment. At 7:35, he had three trees cut down in the nearby forest and, after the bark was removed, had them transformed in the wood pulp factory. The transformation of the three tree trunks into liquid wood cellulose was so swift that by 9:39 the first roll of printing paper came out of the machine. This roll was taken immediately to a newspaper printing plant two and a half miles away, and by 11 in the morning the newspaper was being sold in the street.[31]

We are not protected against a return to the kind of abstract thought that treats people as things. The increasing influence of virtual reality on modern psychology has revealed new prospects for the negation of the individual and his transformation into a mere statistic.

It is difficult to believe that human misery can be deepened yet more by technology, but there are new fearsome applications available, particularly in the realm of biology. A few months after the Ukrainian presidential candidate Viktor Yushchenko was poisoned using a particularly toxic form of dioxin, a former member of the Soviet Main Intelligence Administration (GRU) revealed the existence of a KGB laboratory that specialized in the creation of biological agents capable of killing undetected.[32] The sequencing of the human genome has also opened up possibilities for behavior modification and interference with the immune system unknown to the last century. As Karl Kraus remarked, every age has the epidemic it deserves; ours could be literal rather than symbolic. Finally, the globalization of violence has palpably changed the situation:[33] International terrorism has pursued a privatization of violence that has put into the hands of small groups or even individuals destructive capacities that were formerly the preserve of states. In this sense, September 11 expressed the brutality of our age and the negation of the value of human life. It belongs to the entire world as much as to America.

If we consider the causes of violence, we cannot fail to see them as the expression of an imbalance that has to do with the gap between techno-logical, social, and political developments. One of the great constants in German histories of the nineteenth and twentieth centuries that attempt to explain the Third Reich has been their highlighting of the speed with which industrialization was carried out in a country that was in no way prepared for it. Rapid industrialization, in that view, was an even more negative force in society because it took place at a time when Germany possessed neither the political balance nor the cultural unity of the other countries of Western Europe. This encounter of modern technology with political and social backwardness—frequently noted by Karl Marx—bru-tally transformed the life of the German people.

The judges of the Nuremberg tribunal referred in 1945 to that destruc-tive social transformation as they sought the roots of the new political ideology that had suddenly appeared in Germany:

> The communitarian racial mystique came out of the spiritual and moral crisis that Germany went through in the nineteenth century, with the abrupt change of its economic and social structure brought about by particularly rapid indus-trialization ... While inner spiritual life grew weaker, cruel uncertainty afflicted men's minds, an uncertainty admirably defined by the term *Ratslosigkeit*, an untranslatable word meaning roughly not knowing which way to turn, a cruel state of mind of the nineteenth century that many Germans have described with tragic eloquence. A gaping void opened within souls unhinged by the search for new values.[34]

The contemporary world provides many illustrations of the same phenom-enon, and an important part of present-day violence can be explained in similar ways.

In any account of the regression that took place in the last century, we must therefore consider another major factor. Franz Kafka meticulously described it in his work: a view of the world suddenly deserted by the idea of the divine, revealing unsuspected depths in man. The end of religion and the death of the Father for the majority of Europeans left an enormous void in Western civilization, of which all thinkers and artists of the nine-teenth and twentieth centuries were aware. George Steiner has gone so far as to say that the entire political and philosophical history of the last 150 years in the West can be understood as a series of efforts to fill the central void left by the erosion of theology. We continue to build the Great Wall of a China whose emperor has disappeared. We continue to produce laws although we have no legislator any longer. The replacements for religion that have sprouted from this soil have quickly proved more destructive to mankind and civilization than the faiths themselves ever were.[35] Religions, at least, had been restrained by the idea of a superior power, by belief in the corruption of mankind, and by the need for close monitoring of one's actions and impulses. With the end of those beliefs, which constituted so many barriers to action, there appeared tyrannies without limits, capable of any crime.

In the wake of the collapse of so many utopian political experiments, "the unlimited promise of the future" that André Gide trumpeted has ceased to exercise its charm. But the desire to find simple explanations for complicated problems remains. It continues to produce aberrations, one variant of which is Islamic fundamentalism. Scholars of Islam have pointed out how monstrous a deviation this is from Islamic faith.[36] But every soci-ety and every religion has its share of follies. The followers they attract are secure in their complacency because the "terrible simplifiers" of the day are legion and credulity is one of the most troubling characteristics of the information age.

After the collapse of comprehensive explanations, the establishment of the kingdom of justice still captivates the human mind, but the means to attain it seem more than ever out of reach. Greater justice would require both genuine sacrifice by rich countries and unparalleled political courage on the part of the elites of poor countries. Declarations about worldwide taxation of the products of globalization are rhetoric that deceives no one. That tax has the huge political virtue of being paid by no voter. Donor countries have proved incapable of fulfilling their promise to devote 0.7 percent of GDP to development aid (France gives only 0.5 percent). In addition, development aid as it has been conducted for fifty years, whereby sub-Saharan Africa received more than one trillion dollars while growing more impoverished, is often, like debt forgiveness, an encouragement to bad management and corruption.

The key to development remains education and the capacity for innovation. Neither one is encouraged in countries whose authoritarian regimes understand all too well the risks of a better-educated population. To choose this path would be finally to choose the interest of the people against the interest of governments, instead of prolonging a Faustian pact with regimes that often are detested and have never seriously been required to reform. Africa was a priority of the G8 meetings in Genoa in 2001, Kananaskis in 2002, Evian in 2003, and Sea Island in 2004, and was one of the two principal themes of the Edinburgh meeting of 2005. Conferences on the global problem of poverty, which have tended to become an industry, will produce no results without a lowering of tariff barriers, the development of enlightened local elites, the improvement of the health and education systems, and finally, above all, relentless struggle against corruption and the flouting of law.

CHAPTER 2

The Pleasure Principle

Anyone desiring a quiet life has done badly to be born in the twentieth century.

—Leon Trotsky

And does the same hold true of the twenty-first century? Worry and anxiety have rarely been as visible, perhaps illustrating Freud's conviction that *neurosis* had replaced evil in the contemporary world. Writers bear witness to the unease, as do the consumption of tranquilizers and the consultation of psychiatrists in Western countries. Yet the peaceful life of Europeans seems to have been endowed with a grant of perpetuity. The disturbances of the twentieth century, most of which touched Europe deeply, have receded in the minds of the young into the distant past, so that they no longer have any existential meaning, despite all the "commemorative ceremonies" and speeches that evoke the ordeals of the dead. The youth of Europe have even fewer images of more distant periods, when their ancestors wondered every year whether their crops would be ravaged by soldiers and looters and whether their children would be massacred before they could reach adulthood. Such images would help them understand the lives of many of their contemporaries: they describe daily life in a large part of Africa, as well as in other places. But they might also serve as reminders that the prosperity, hedonism, and tranquility of the European peninsula could again come to a violent end.

The denial of reality is a psychological mechanism whose benefits have always been appreciated, but today virtual reality plays an unprecedented role in the relationship of consciousness to the world, and it seems to have nearly unlimited possibilities. With the expansion of leisure activities and the possibilities opened up by new technologies in every domain, Western societies have happily taken refuge in the realm of the virtual, which makes possible the denial of the most threatening aspects of reality. By enhancing the virtual, a large number of innovations have simultaneously devalued the real. Immersion in virtual experience is also a good preparation for the most violent activities. A recent work with the brutal title *Generation Kill* shows how the young men who fought in Iraq sometimes viewed the battlefield the way they would a video game scenario; they thought it was "cool." This intrusion, not of simulation, which is part of all modern military training, but of *play* into a war situation, where questions of life and death may arise at any moment, ought to trouble the people in charge of the conduct of war and the officers who command individuals who have been shaped—or have ended up misshapen—by virtual reality. It might also concern anyone interested in the evolution of moral conscience to discover that life and death have to some degree lost their reality.[1]

Reality, when pushed aside, always takes its revenge, and its reappearance is often catastrophic. One thinks of George Orwell's description of his return to England in 1938, after serving in the Spanish Civil War:

> Down here it was still the England I had known in my childhood: the railway-cuttings smothered in wild flowers, the deep meadows where the great shining horses browse and meditate, the slow-moving streams bordered by willows, the green bosoms of the elms, the larkspurs in the cottage gardens; and then the huge peaceful wilderness of outer London, the barges on the miry river, the posters telling of cricket matches and Royal weddings, the men in bowler hats, the pigeons in Trafalgar Square, the red buses, the blue policemen—all sleeping the deep, deep sleep of England, from which I sometimes fear that we shall never wake till we are jerked out of it by the roar of bombs.[2]

A few years later, that is exactly what happened. The denial of imminent disaster has a long tradition in the Western world. The West saw nothing coming: not the Russian Revolution, the Chinese Revolution, the two world wars, the extermination of the Jews, the Chinese Cultural Revolution, the Cambodian tragedy, or the World Trade Center towers falling.[3] If it were up to the West, the troubles roiling the planet would be relegated to the periphery, even though we realize that the distinction between internal and external no longer makes much sense. That is especially true on the *front line*. Those who find themselves at the front are usually the ones who kick most against acknowledging the danger. That was true, for example, in Germany during the Cold War, where the risk that Warsaw Pact forces would use nuclear or chemical weapons was undoubtedly greatest: after Soviet troops left, maps were found on which German cities were surrounded by two circles, the first indicating the range of the effects of chemical weapons, the second that of nuclear weapons. The terrifying nature of the Soviet threat against Germany explains why denial of its existence was nowhere so passionate and imaginative as among Germans on German soil. That was also the case for Europe as a whole: Isaiah Berlin, who spent most of his life in England, claimed that the events of 1918 "haunted" American minds whereas Europeans after the Great War soon went from exaltation to complacency. Twenty years later the tragedy began again. The best analyst of the phenomenon of forgetting in our literature is probably Honoré de Balzac, who described, in the post-revolutionary period, how the social fabric is rewoven after catastrophes: "the bloody saturnalia of the Terror" were soon obliterated. Thus those on the front lines cope with the constant sense of danger by denying it. For instance, the expression and the concept "war on terrorism" has encountered fierce resistance in Europe. That opposition is often justified by a simple and apparently irrefutable argument: since terrorism is a form of action, rather than an actor, how can war be declared on it? If that were the true reason for the resistance, however, I am willing to bet that people would not be so passionate about it. Another, more serious, argument is that, as in any war, one should avoid giving the enemy any more importance by acknowledging that he might win. But we do not always choose our enemies. This one has declared ruthless war against the West, a war that shows no sign of ending anytime soon. It may indeed inflict serious setbacks on our societies and destabilize a world already beset by other imbalances. At the core of the problem is the use of the word *war*, which both requires that we recognize that war has returned to our world, which is disagreeable, and implies that we must take action that goes beyond police operations like those mounted in the 1970s against Action Directe, the Rote Armee Fraktion, and the Red Brigades. Military action has indeed been undertaken, and France was one of the few countries that responded to the 9/11 attacks by participating in the American bombing of Afghanistan in the spring of 2002; currently, apart from its participation in the international stabilization force (ISAF), France still has 200 special forces troops engaged in operations on the border between Afghanistan and Pakistan. Finally, there is another significant difference to recognize: in the entire history of terrorism before September 2001, there were no Security Council resolutions adopted under Chapter VII of the UN Charter asserting the victim's right to self-defense. Now, in Resolution 1368 of September 12, 2001, the world has recognized and at least begun to deal with a kind of war—war taking countless forms, as Clausewitz always maintained.

Psychological factors account for the resistance of many Europeans in the face of the new conflict. Historically, war has weighed much more on Europeans than Americans, for the Europeans have experienced a major conflict in every generation since the seventeenth century. Moreover, the desire for peace is one of the noblest human sentiments—provided, however, that it is not a desire for peace at any price, also known as cowardice, and that war is not in every case presented as "the worst thing." Making war against Hitler in 1936 would not have been such a bad idea: it would probably have prevented fifty million deaths. As Karl Kraus, who cannot be suspected of a passion for militarism, said: "Greater than the shame of war is the shame of men who no longer want to know anything about it."[4] What, then, is the source of the inane romanticism that wants history suddenly to adopt a peaceful course? How can we not think that such strong resistance to the idea of conflict springs from the conviction that the times to come will be hard, *especially perhaps in Europe*, which will have to face domestic problems of integration that are much more serious than those of the United States, at a time when continued immigration has become an economic necessity?[5] Fear that European societies will disintegrate plays a major role in the denial of the reality of terrorism.

In fact, in recent years, troubling events have taken place on European soil. The assassination of the filmmaker Theo van Gogh in Amsterdam in November 2004 indicates that European societies will have difficulty maintaining—or rather, instituting—a social pact with the immigrants who have arrived in their countries and intend to stay. In one of the calmest cities in Europe, van Gogh was stabbed, then finished off with a revolver, and had his throat cut from ear to ear for good measure. In a crowning gesture, a threatening message was impaled on his corpse with a knife. Coming after the March 11, 2004, train bombings in Madrid, the filmmaker's murder once again brutally challenged European societies' ideal of nonviolence in one of the nations where it is strongest. The assassin, a 26-year-old Moroccan, had attended the Al-Tawhid mosque, a fundamentalist center like many others in Europe. More than 300,000 Moroccan immigrants live in the Netherlands,[6] and the anti-Islamic reprisals that took place in early November 2004—the bombing of an Islamic school, the desecration of a mosque, and attempted arson—were clear signs of a dangerous break between the immigrant and the native Dutch communities. At the same time, the Council of Moroccan Immigrants, which works for the integration of Moroccans into Dutch society, received threats from Muslim fundamentalists. The trauma suffered by the country and its difficulty understanding what had happened were expressed pathetically in the persistent assertion of the Dutch spirit of tolerance, as though this tolerance had nothing at all to do with the *motive* for the crime.

A few months after van Gogh's assassination, in March 2005, France was the site of a declaration against "anti-White racism" launched by figures representing a wide range of political views (although mostly on the left), after demonstrations by secondary school students during which "anti-French racist attacks" had occurred. Among immigrant youth, whose propensity for violence tends to increase in proportion to the difficulty they have expressing themselves, hatred of the French and of the Jews came together in a single ball of rage. Comparable events took place in the United States in the 1970s. But Europe has had a different historical experience; thus fears about fragmented societies on the path to tribalization began to spread beyond the circles of political scientists and sociologists who had been watching the situation for years. The question that should be asked is: How could young people who hate France be integrated into a France that does not love itself?[7]

Throughout Europe, except in countries to which there has been little immigration, such as Finland, the same agonizing question has arisen, and public policies designed to answer it are nowhere in sight. The four suicide attacks in the London Tube in July 2005, carried out by young British citizens of Pakistani origin, gave this question special intensity. In November 2006, Prime Minister Tony Blair said that the threat from homegrown Islamic terrorism would last "a generation." The communitarian model is in an open state of crisis. But is the same not true of the republican model?

Whether dealing with foreign or domestic threats—often difficult to tell apart—we must stop sacrificing the reality principle. If we would bequeath our descendants a *possible* world in which political decisions will not be empty of meaning because disorder has grown to such proportions that nothing can stop events, as happened in 1914 and in 1937, we must see the pleasure principle for what it really is: a gambit to replace a painful state with a pleasant one, with its ultimate objective, guided by entropy, complete stability. Freud concluded that the pleasure principle is in the service of the death instinct.[8] Pathological fear of political or social innovation, along with the rejection of any changes in strategy, ought to be seen in this light. Countries with welfare states that fight only to defend conservative positions will in the end be swept away. Contemporary historical reality, more unstable than it has been for decades and giving indications of great changes to come, is so deeply out of phase with developed societies' desire for peace that those societies' grasp of events is likely to grow increasingly precarious. If you persist in wanting to be fooled, you will eventually succeed. The taste for virtual reality, which bears a troubling likeness to schizophrenia, risks bringing about a profound alteration in our sense of reality and will block any understanding of the forces actually operating in the world.

The sense of reality cannot be recovered without an effort of memory, if only to help avoid inadvertently committing the same fatal errors that were committed in the past: waiting for crises to seriously deteriorate before intervening; paying insufficient attention to multiple warning signs; condemning the UN to helplessness, like the League of Nations before it, for fear of taking the required collective action; meekly observing the restoration of a regime in Moscow that is rehabilitating Stalin. Memory alone is not, of course, sufficient for making the necessary decisions: as a Chinese proverb has it, experience is a lantern one carries at one's back. But memory does impose a reality check, and makes it possible to combat the fictions that populate the imaginary worlds of politics and strategy. It reminds us in particular that peace and freedom are fragile conquests whose endurance can never be guaranteed. It is no doubt absurd to try to ward off the reprise of historical events, because strictly speaking history does not repeat itself, but preventing the return of storms of *identical magnitude* is a reason-

able aim. One of the most lucid thinkers of the last century issued a warning on this point: "If the overall lesson of the twentieth century does not
serve as a vaccine, the huge hurricane might well recur in its entirety."[9]
Contempt for the past dooms us to repeat it and carries with it the seeds
of intolerance and despotism.

The ultimate consequence of modern experience—the annihilation of
tens of millions of human beings in wars and revolutions—has *already* happened. The discovery of the means for the moral and physical annihilation
of the human race has *already* been made. It was not possible to bury the
weapons that were developed or the moral barbarity that was explored in
a desert where they could be concealed from the experience and consciousness of future generations. On the contrary, those extreme experiences have been globalized, often on our initiative, and weapons have proliferated along with the spread of knowledge and technology.[10] The French
monarchy in the eighteenth century helped distribute the instruments of
power that would bring about its own destruction, and Western societies
tirelessly spread around the world technological capabilities that they
alone possessed a few decades ago. As for the moral barbarity that European history has revealed, it plays a major role in the refusal of societies
that know neither peace nor prosperity nor, above all, the freedom to take
Europe as a model. While our reason and our speech may decline to recognize that fact, we cannot deny it in our hearts. We cannot be unaware
that profound changes are occurring and that Europe could well pay the
price for them. We have only to observe the mood of our contemporaries,
who sense that *something* is not quite finished and that that something is
threatening. Terrorism concentrates those fears and helps explain the
denial that it has provoked, in Europe more than in the United States,
where the burden of memory is lighter.

There is another justification for an effort of memory, the one mentioned by the Chinese photographer in the Prologue: to preserve the history of the dead who have been "mocked." Memory is a protection against
the risk of abstraction and political experimentation. It is also what enables
successive generations to share the harshest aspects of the human condition. The photographer's father-in-law was a renowned doctor. During the
Cultural Revolution, he was denounced as a "reactionary university authority" and died as a result: "One night, the rebels set him in front of a coal
stove until he was pouring with sweat, then they forced him to strip to his

underwear, and sent him out into the snow until he was almost frozen. The next day, he hanged himself." His story was salvaged and preserved in memory. During the worst years of the Stalinist terror, when women stood in line for hours outside prisons waiting for news of their sons and husbands, one of them one day asked Anna Akhmatova if she would be able to describe what they were enduring. The poet, understanding what was at stake, took on the task. For those who disappeared into the prison cells and the camps, often one of the worst tortures was the feeling that they were already dead, that their existence had already been annihilated, and that their suffering would remain forever futile and unknown. Akhmatova preserved the knowledge of such suffering

We offer a final reason for looking again at the past century, one that is never brought up: the end of the play begun in 1914 has perhaps been set a little prematurely at the time of the collapse of the Soviet Union. It is not that Russia may still have surprises in store for anyone who advocates strategic partnership with Moscow; its surprises are now disastrous mainly for the Russians themselves, because of the Kremlin's reactionary policies and the corruption of elites. But the stage for that play was the world, not Europe, and the dénouement has not yet come in Asia. The world we are familiar with is a more or less reduced portion of the real world: we retain only the Western history of the two world wars, then comes the beginning of the Cold War in 1947,[11] the division of Europe, Stalin's death, the Cuban missile crisis, the fall of the Berlin Wall, and there you have it.

In another part of the planet, another story prevails, with the Japanese occupation, the advance of Soviet troops in East Asia, the Chinese Revolution, the retreat of the Kuomintang to Taiwan, and then the Korean War. In that vast region, the dénouement of the great tragedy that began in the last century is not yet known. All the talk of the *short century*, an elegant but inaccurate expression that sets the limits of the twentieth century as 1914 and 1989, makes it impossible for us to understand the most important strategic challenges of our time, which are no longer in Europe. The question of whether the Cold War was a substitute for war or a preparation for total war was for certain observers the most important strategic question. Has it become obsolete with the end of the Soviet Union? We now see only interethnic or transnational conflicts, as though the events of the last decade had opened an entirely new period in the study of war.[12] Historians know, however, that major wars, using all the weapons available in the various arsenals, are a permanent possibility, as long as there are states and balances of power, and that world government is a utopia, attractive but absurd. The Third World War—an alternative to the Cold War—never happened. But who can assert that it *never will happen?* Asia in the twenty-first century will be what Europe was in the twentieth: the epicenter of strategic affairs, not just of business. As a Singapore official pointed out in a private conversation, there will always be people willing to invest, but war and peace are too serious to be left to chance.

That it is necessary to recall this shows how "provincial" Europe has become. The provinces have their charm, but they are disconnected from the news of the world. European provincialism is the result both of the loss of Europe's colonial empires, which narrowed its view of the planet, and of its inability to guarantee its own security for a period of fifty years. Added to the mix was a sturdy egocentrism and a desire to cultivate our own garden. As early as the middle of the nineteenth century, Marx understood that the industrial activities of England and France could destroy the livelihoods of whole communities in India and China. Did that realization lead to a new sense of moral responsibility toward far-off contemporaries? A century later, we are just beginning to take steps so as not to penalize cotton-producing countries too heavily. In general, we speak of sharing more than we actually share. The vision of the world that European bourgeois societies are fond of is so conservative that they find it almost impossible to discern what is foreign to them. They believe in a world without surprises, in the victory of the past over the future, of the near over the distant, and of the known over the unknown.

In 1905, as the first Russian Revolution was rocking the czar's empire, France, forgetting its own revolutionary experience, calmly renewed its loan to Moscow. That financial contribution enabled so strong an economic and industrial recovery in Russia over the following decade that in 1914 the German general staff, especially Helmuth von Moltke, had reached the conclusion that an attack against the czar was necessary to prevent Russian domination over Europe as a whole and Germany in particular. According to documents on the period discovered in the 1990s, Sarajevo served as a pretext. In that interpretation, the Kaiser, who wanted to stop the war machine, was outflanked by his own army.[13] Nearly a century later, a German chancellor demonstrated almost unimaginable blindness in East Asia. In 2004, when Taiwan was one of the few strategic problems that could provoke a world war as certainly as Alsace-Lorraine had at the beginning of the last century, Gerhard Schröder declared in Beijing that China could do what it pleased with regard to Taipei. Before then, no foreign leader had been so complacent. In March 2005, while German public opinion and his own party were opposed to lifting the arms embargo on China, Schröder persevered. His concerns in Asia were not, of course, primarily security matters: this chancellor, whose nickname in China was "Mister Automobile,"[14] was thinking chiefly of the German economy (just as, after leaving office, he seems to be focused on his own financial well-being, serving as chairman of the supervisory committee of the North European Gas Pipeline Company, whose majority shareholder is Gazprom). Even from that limited perspective, however, how was it possible to fail to understand in 2005, with regional tensions being reported on the front pages of newspapers, that trade relations could not survive a conflict in the region—that they might well be the first casualty? The world of business is no more immune to the pleasure principle than any other part of the world.

CHAPTER 3

Ensavagement

Monsters—No longer extant.

—FLAUBERT, *Dictionnaire des idées reçues*

The most significant regression of the twentieth century was savage indifference to human beings. Four years in the trenches of the Great War produced men who were "weary, broken, burnt out, rootless, and without hope."[1] In some cases, soldiers revealed their dehumanization in frightening ways, as in Erich Maria Remarque's account of a German fighter who is so afraid of leaving his trench that he "crouches back against the wall, and shows his teeth like a dog"[2] when instructed to join an assault. The Second World War subsequently permitted the transgression of all the barriers painstakingly constructed by centuries of civilization.[3] As early as 1933, Nazi writings stated that "the distance between the lowest human being still called by that name and our superior races is greater than the distance between the lowest man and the highest ape."[4]

The crimes committed on this doctrinal basis, if they can be so characterized, were known early in the war and denounced by Winston Churchill in October 1941. "The atrocities committed in Poland, Yugoslavia, Norway, Holland, Belgium, and especially behind the German front lines in Russia, go beyond anything we have seen since the darkest and most bestial ages of humanity," said the British prime minister. He looked ahead to the trials of Nazi perpetrators at Nuremberg: "The punishment of these crimes must count among the primary aims of the war."

Such ethical collapses also occurred in the Soviet Union and China, but neither of those countries ever had to pay the price, as Germany did as a defeated power in 1945.[5] The memory of the camps, of totalitarianism, and of the Cultural Revolution ought to be preserved. The responsibility rests not only with citizens of the countries where crimes against humanity occurred but with the international community as a whole.

In some cases, as in China, examination of the past remains taboo.[6] How much attention, for example, has been given to the scenes of cannibalism that took place in the midst of the Cultural Revolution in Guanxi in 1968? A terrifying account of them, barely repeatable stories of horrors, can be found in *Stèles rouges* by Zheng Yi.[7] We learn that students sometimes ate their teachers, not in the course of a famine like the one that ravaged Ukraine and the rest of the Soviet Union in the early 1930s, but because years of daily brutality had brought about the resurgence of cannibalism as an act of supreme cruelty. The author of the book barely believed the rumors circulating about the villages where instances of cannibalism had occurred. But after collecting many accounts of practices even more terrible than those that had been reported to him—in paroxysmic scenes, some victims were eaten alive—Zheng reached a despairing conclusion: "A people that has incited its children to eat human flesh like savages had no hope for the future!" Worse, the collective madness was not completely devoid of "rationality." Many bureaucrats climbed the ladder of power by means of such demonstrations of revolutionary faith:

> In the modern period, when progressive Chinese men of letters inveighed against of the misdeeds of cruel officials who built their careers on assassinations, they often used this expression: "he does not hesitate to stain the feather in his cap with human blood." But this expression is not suitable in the case of Wang Wenliu and other cadres in Wuxuan. In fact, to guarantee their success, they were not satisfied with merely killing human beings, they also ate them.[8]

None of those acts would have been possible had it not been for the years of public confessions and public executions in China that twisted moral sense and the concept of justice. Nor would these acts have been possible in the absence of terrible mass pressure, which tolerates no resistance whatsoever. The dominance of a distorted collective soon leads to the absolute negation of any individual feeling. Moving testimony to that dehumanized state and the despair to which it gives rise comes from the director of the Wuxuan secondary school, where a teacher had been murdered:

After witnessing and personally enduring much violence, he suddenly had the feeling that his life no longer had any meaning. He sneaked out of the school and walked to the river bank. He climbed up on a dike, took off his shoes and carefully set them down, and then, as he was about to jump into the turbulent river, an old shepherd passed by leading his flock. The old man, whose eyesight was weak but who had a shrewd mind, quickly understood the situation: "It will pass! It will soon pass!" These simple words full of wisdom made Wu Hongtai give up the temptation of dying. He put his shoes back on and returned to this crime-filled world. However, his misfortunes did not soon pass....

and Wu was forced to participate in the execution of another teacher and a subsequent act of cannibalism. After such excesses and such exploration of evil, it is not likely that the spectacular economic development of the country can ever make up for the torments of Chinese society and of the Chinese soul.

It may be said, all that is in the past and everyone knows all about it. In fact, few people and almost no Westerners have heard about the crimes in question. Moreover, recent, readily available accounts from the North Korean work camps show that they bear a chilling resemblance to their Chinese predecessors. More than 250,000 prisoners on starvation rations and subject to daily torture work 72 hours a week in what are, in effect, death camps: "All the camps are characterized by high levels of mortality because of particularly harsh forced labor joined with deliberate famine." The aim is to extract the maximum production from prisoners before they die. The report *Hidden Gulag*, published by Human Rights Watch in 2003, contains interviews with former prisoners who had been interned in 36 different camps. Some of the camps are for people serving life sentences for political crimes while others are detention centers set up to punish people who sought political refuge in China.[9] In the latter, sentences are short, but the extreme conditions result in very high mortality among the prisoners. Getting out of certain kinds of labor alive is quite a feat. An Hyuk, a student who was repatriated by force in 1987, was sent to camp number 15. His first job was gathering stones in a frigid river, up to his waist in water: "It was a literally murderous task. Many prisoners died on the spot and even more of them lost their fingers and toes." Kim Tae Jin, prisoner in a camp called Yodok during the same period, said that "to stay alive, he ate plants, grass, rats, snakes, and frogs."

At the same time those accounts were appearing, survivors implicated in the selection of prisoners as subjects in chemical experiments revealed what they had witnessed, and those reports were confirmed by former guards who had taken refuge in South Korea. The horrifying practices they recounted were denounced in a BBC film screened in London in the fall of 2003. According to Kwon Hyok, former head of camp 22, the dehumanization of prisoners was exactly like that under the Nazis: "The prisoners were like pigs or dogs. You could kill them, their lives and deaths were of no interest." The historical model for North Korean leader Kim Jong Il, and his father and predecessor Kim Il Sung seems to have been Hitler rather than Stalin—the latter was the favorite of another dictator, Saddam Hussein. Following the revelations of 2003, the United Nations in March 2004 asked North Korea to authorize an investigation on the spot. Pyongyang's refusal surprised no one. The authorities there fear that disclosure of government atrocities will tarnish their reputation abroad and threaten their continued rule. The denial of access to the camps also enabled South Korea—which is afraid of having its policy of rapprochement toward the North questioned—declare that evidence of Pyongyang's criminality was insufficient. While this is technically not incorrect, given the small number of accounts, Seoul did not attempt to collect more data. Even more frightening, the intelligence services in Seoul know that the purpose of the North Korean experiments is to calculate the quantity of poison that would be needed to exterminate the population of the South Korean capital in the event of conflict.

The experiments did not begin yesterday. Documents in the Soviet archives show that chemical and biological experiments were conducted on human beings in North Korea as early as the 1950s.[10] With the advanced satellites available today—even in the commercial realm—the daily life of these wretched of the earth can be followed in great detail. Nongovernmental organizations have gathered testimony. Have the authorities in Western nations consulted those documents? Have they procured those pictures? If our governments have taken the trouble to do so, continuation of diplomatic relations with a regime that deals with its own citizens as if they were pigs or dogs should certainly be challenged.

Even someone without humanistic inclinations can well imagine that the foreign and defense policy of a regime that mistreats its citizens to that extent inspires little confidence. Would Pyongyang hesitate to violate an agreement that did not suit it? Would the regime hesitate to use all the weapons at its command if it thought it necessary? And what can *judgment* about a strategic situation possibly mean to a regime of this kind? These questions are legitimate and necessary, as is the question of continued diplomatic relations with North Korea.

Two experiences in the last century imposed serious ethical reflections—the atrocities of the Second World War and the advent of atomic weapons—but only the second made it possible to establish, in the form of deterrence, an effective system of restraint on the destructive instincts of the human race convincingly illustrated in the two global conflagrations. The Second World War, indeed, raising as it did radical questions about civilization, led in 1948 to the introduction into international law of limits on the activity of states in time of war, both within and outside their borders, and to a questioning of the classic distinction between these two aspects—domestic and foreign policy—of political life. A few short years later, lack of action by the democracies in the face of continuing large-scale massacres clearly showed the limits of the innovations introduced in 1948.[11]

Denunciation of the various gulags has consistently given rise to vigorous debate, sometimes even to legal proceedings, in the free world. In 1949, for example, it was a lawsuit brought by the magazine *Les Lettres françaises* against David Rousset that opened the door to exposure of the Russian gulag. Twenty-five years later, Solzhenitsyn, visiting Paris, appeared on French television and heard Jean Daniel express regret at the absence of Communists among the program's participants; then, although he had come to speak about his own work and experience, Solzhenitsyn was asked to make pronouncements about Vietnam and Portugal.[12]

As for the Chinese Cultural Revolution, its admirers abroad always outnumbered its detractors, and in Europe in particular only a few rare individuals raised their voices in opposition. Concerning the incidents of cannibalism, they were revealed only to a narrow public in the early 1990s. At about the same time deeply moving films like *Farewell, My Concubine* gave a wider audience a clearer picture of that period of collective madness. As we witness the beginning of a new cycle of extreme violence, one that can again place humanity in grave danger, a reminder of the worst excesses of the twentieth century is necessary. There is no need to find all sorts of exotic explanations for new forms of terrorism. It has familiar roots: unlimited violence, systematic self-destruction, and the absolute negation of the Other.

The second experience often characterized as "extreme" was the advent of atomic weapons. To grasp how shattering their appearance was, we must reread the article Robert Oppenheimer published in *Foreign Affairs* in July 1953, which began with this extraordinary sentence: "It is possible that in the bright light of history, if there is any history, the atomic bomb will not seem very different than in the dazzling light of the first atomic explosion." The end of history did not mean for Oppenheimer the universalization of the doctrines of freedom in which some have wanted to believe after the end of the East-West confrontation.[13] What he had in mind was the possibility, pure and simple, that history would be interrupted. That vision came to him in the aftershock of the first test at the Alamogordo proving grounds in Nevada in 1945, before the bomb was used. Such was the *progress* achieved in a mere one hundred years—what the deepest pessimism could not conceive of in 1848, at the time of Schopenhauer, had become an element of political realism in 1953.

Oppenheimer's radical anxiety does not spring solely from the dropping of the atomic bombs on Japan at the close of the Second World War. Two other events with incalculable consequences intervened between 1945 and 1953: the appearance of a second nuclear power, the Soviet Union, which gave the East-West confrontation a scale hitherto unknown in international relations, and the development of thermonuclear weapons much more powerful than the A-bomb. At the time, deterrence was already in place—its origins have been traced to 1949—but no one knew if it would stand up to a genuine test. That came in 1962 with the Cuban missile crisis, from which deterrence emerged as an established fact.

If we judge by the results, the lesson of the telescope worked better for atomic weapons than for the defense of values. Fear of physical annihilation is infinitely stronger than fear of the rise of moral savagery. By introducing into relations between states an unequaled capacity to destroy people and their environment, nuclear weapons forced the countries that possessed them to think of foreign policy in terms of restraint, whatever their violence or madness in other areas.[14] We can hardly go so far as to say that there was an ethical dimension to such thinking, because what was involved was one camp's avoiding destruction by taking the civilian population of the other camp hostage. But it contained at least a recognition of the necessity to care for one's survival by limiting the exercise of violence. The question now is how seriously that wisdom is threatened by the possible misunderstanding of new actors whose strategic thinking remains obscure. To make matters worse, the memory of authoritarian regimes and what they are capable of is being lost with alarming speed.

Does anyone still remember Raymond Aron's statement: "We should not discuss deterrence in the abstract, but know who is deterring whom, from what, by what threats, and in what circumstances?"[15] With the end of the Cold War, the caution that surrounded the treatment of nuclear weapons has declined, as has the quality of thinking that those weapons once imposed. John Lewis Gaddis came up with the suggestive expression the "long peace" to describe the Cold War and the role of nuclear weapons in it. But that long peace, and the resolution of the East-West confrontation that came at the end, have led to a considerable weakening of strategic thinking, evident when one compares works written between 1950 and 1980 with those from today.[16]

With regard to the other question related to values, however, the news is even less favorable. In recent years, Diderot's remark that it is much easier for an enlightened people to return to barbarism than for a barbarian people to advance one step toward civilization has been illustrated in tragic fashion. The protection of human life and of the humanity of mankind has suffered spectacular reverses, in large part because history has been seen by many intellectuals as a process without a subject in which the individual has no value and can therefore always be replaced. Stalin, Mao, Pol Pot, and Saddam Hussein were able to exterminate their citizens—and some of their neighbors—rather serenely, sometimes even with our help. Lying prospered with the active cooperation of the free world.

When Boris Souvarine wanted to reveal what was happening in the 1930s in his prophetic book about Stalin, just before the beginning of the Great Terror, André Malraux rejected the manuscript at Gallimard. It was not that Malraux doubted the author's statements, but the intellectual climate at the time was not propitious for such revelations. Thirty years later, during the Cultural Revolution, the *Little Red Book* found so many readers in Paris (not to mention New York and London) that the most merciless detractor of Western worshipers of Mao, Simon Leys, left for Australia. In 1973, before the Khmer Rouge exterminated one third of the Cambodian population, their arrival in Phnom Penh was hailed by Patrice de Beer, a reporter at *Le Monde*, as the entry of liberators (the Paris daily published an editorial apologizing on April 17, 2005).

Altogether, in the Soviet Union, China, Cambodia, and Vietnam, 100 million people may have been killed for political reasons since 1945. We should add to that figure forgotten tragedies like the million dead Afghans after the Soviet withdrawal from 1981 on. But those are only statistics, like the ones cited since the end of the Cold War: 150,000 dead in Algeria, 180,000 dead and 20,000 missing in Bosnia, 200,000 dead in Chechnya, 1 million dead in Rwanda, as many in Congo, more than 300,000 dead in Darfur. Statistics do not speak to the imagination. They are even dangerous for our conscience in that they inure us to large numbers and countless victims. We catch ourselves one day thinking, *only* 50,000 dead?

Tragedy is made palpable only by individual stories. They represent the victory of contingency over history. Many people deserve a hearing, especially the people who find themselves in North Korean camps. Among present-day martyrs, they are the most difficult to give voice to and the least often thought about. Former camp guards recount that, when they arrived at the camps, they were impressed by the short stature, the thinness, the premature aging, and the physical deformities of the prisoners, many of whom had suffered amputations due to work accidents or frostbite. Guards compared prisoners to "dwarves, skeletons, cripples." And yet, are they not the same as us?[17]

CHAPTER 4

THE CORRUPTION OF PRINCIPLES

To shoot down a European is to kill two birds with one stone, to destroy an oppressor and the man he oppresses at the same time: there remains a dead man and a free man.

—JEAN-PAUL SARTRE

We may well wonder where the intellectual confusion of the twentieth century could have come from. Then we reread certain passages from great European intellectuals, and we ask another question: How could they have written such absurdities? After a while, the two questions end up being linked. Corruption of governments always begins, now as in the time of Montesquieu, by the corruption of their principles, but the corruption of principles must be transmitted by elites in order to attain any kind of legitimacy.[1] For this, there is nothing like a historical lie. Lying about history was one of the major pillars of the mass Machiavellianism of the last century.

George Orwell, one of the few who grasped the essence of totalitarianism, saw history's falsification as one of the most terrifying forms of violence: "If the Leader says of such and such an event, 'It never happened'—well, it never happened. If he says that two and two are five—well, two and two are five. This prospect frightens me much more than bombs."[2] The idea that lying is one of the worst forms of the destruction of our humanity is not held by many today, for a simple reason: there are too many *collaborators*, and everyone has something to be ashamed of. In totalitarian systems, the torturers' lies were necessary because they were looking not for truth but for an indictment, and the victims' lies were inevitable because the interrogations induced the disintegration of personality.[3] But one wonders what could justify the lies of those who, risking absolutely nothing, nevertheless help the killing—from a distance.

For example, the French poet Louis Aragon, hardly known for his knowledge of agronomy, wrote an article in defense of the Soviet pseudo-scientist Trofim Lysenko that would be comical if the battles fought in the name of that crank had not involved so many crimes.[4] Lysenko, once an obscure agricultural technician, had gained enormous influence in many areas of Soviet science. His preposterous biological theories, put into practice in the 1930s, caused a famine in which millions of people perished, along with three decades of stagnation in Soviet agriculture. Aragon, writing in the periodical *Europe*, dispensed this authoritative judgment on "Lysenkoism" in 1948:

> It is in fact the bourgeois character of science that has prevented the creation of a pure, scientific biology, that is preventing the scientists of the bourgeoisie from making certain discoveries whose underlying principle they cannot accept for sociological reasons. In the USSR, the bitter struggle conducted by the Mendelians against the Michurinians could not possibly be considered . . . as a biological, scientific struggle within the species of biologists; but it is naturally seen as a sociological struggle on the part of scientists who are under the sociological influence of the bourgeoisie (even if only through the intermediary of bourgeois science, full of sociological metaphors), as the effect of the traces of the bourgeoisie still present in the USSR. This is why . . . the victory of Lyssenko [sic] is indeed a scientific victory, the most striking rejection of the politicization of the chromosome.

In the Soviet Union, Western genetic theories were deemed "Hitlero-Trotskyite," and followers of Mendel found themselves labeled "enemies of the Soviet people." Genetics, it was held, could not be true, since it was incompatible with dialectical materialism! This provided justification for the millions of deaths in the famine created in Ukraine, the breadbasket of the Soviet Union. In villages where only corpses remained, visitors to these strange cemeteries found heart-rending messages: "God bless those who come under this roof. May they never know the suffering that we have endured."[5] Villagers' last letters to absent children have also been recovered: "Is it too much to ask to get a letter from you, where you say that you've said Kaddish for your mother, at least once, and that you'll do the same for me? That would help me so much to die." Some parents, made desperate by hunger, ate their children.[6] Lysenko was also responsible for the death sentences passed on many geneticists, particularly the great Nikolai Vavilov, who died in the Saratov camp in 1943.

For decades afterward, Soviet officials declared that the government had not known at the time about the famine in the countryside. But the opening of the archives covering the period during the Gorbachev regime revealed documents that proved that claim untrue. These documents were put on display at the Library of Congress in 1992. Here is an official account written by a certain Comrade Feigin, dated April 9, 1932, and addressed to Georgy Ordzhonikidze:

> People move like ghosts, without speaking. I see four very small children, as pale as wax, drinking from the same bowl, filling a spoon with hot water tinged with a revolting white liquid. To get it, the sick mother has just sold her last skirt.

The same day, in a letter to the same recipient, a doctor reports his visit to the Borodin family:

> The father is sitting on a bench. He is smoking without stopping cigarettes made of disgusting tobacco, crying like a baby, and he asks that all his frightfully thin children be killed . . . He begs: "at least give me a kilo of potatoes, I have been working all my life" . . . Sometimes Borodin looks at his children and grumbles: "Those devils don't want to die, how I would love not to see them any more". . . . I assure you that this man is sinking into a hunger psychosis and that it can bring him to eat his own children.

These scenes should be recalled by anyone who takes up his pen to justify unjustifiable regimes. What is striking today about Aragon's article is not merely the intellectual perversion manifest in its catalogue of idiocies but its participation—involuntary, but real—in a crime of enormous proportions. At the time, any sense of *intellectual ethics* was often lost. Orwell was quite right to be more frightened by that than by bombs. Twenty years later, examples were still legion, as apologies for Maoism became fashionable in Western capitals. In the midst of the Cultural Revolution, Simone de Beauvoir wrote these incongruous lines:

> These masses are educating themselves, they are deepening their bonds, they are simultaneously elevating the level of production and the level of friendship. This is the main impression I take back from China: friendship is the other side of an economic necessity, it is the engine of production.

Teachers thrown out of windows or killed with a bullet to the back of the head would no doubt have appreciated the Parisian subtlety of these remarks.

After the collapse of ideologies, the human mind might have found some realm of freedom, but binary thinking is part of our heritage, and the information age has accentuated the tendency toward it. The proliferation of data has brought about further simplification. One of the most difficult feats for humans is to think in ways that are not dichotomous. Certain excesses—Sartre's "An anticommunist is a dog," for instance—have disappeared from Western writing (similar statements now appear in the writings of Osama bin Laden and Kim Jong Il). But humankind's violent split into two camps, which held for decades, has cast lasting suspicion on moderation. As for subtlety and a sense of nuance, elements of all refined civilizations, recapturing them will take a long time. Intellectual ethics and our sense of balance are further threatened by terrorist and anti-terrorist rhetoric, which has relaunched the binary impulse with a new theme, in which fear is crucial.

An important portion of political life and international relations—to say nothing of individual intellectual work—depends on the improvement of intellectual training and of logical thinking. In a 2003 UN report on the Arab world,[7] the authors, all economists from the Middle East, indicated that the principal problem they had identified was the decline of education and training in advanced thought. Authoritarianism and the suppression of investigation, exploration, and initiative have had devastating economic, social, and political effects in the Arab world. This is one of the breeding grounds for violence, terrorism, and political radicalism that have made substantial gains in this part of the world. But at the same time, one cannot fail to be struck by the fact that Europe, too, suffers from intellectual degradation; of which the invective, the absence of debate, and intellectual confusion on the continent provide troubling illustrations. It would be well to worry about problems close to home before complaining about those elsewhere.

Thought arose from the need to give order to the world. But order can be found, as Plato said more eloquently than anyone, only if the changing, various world in which we live, subject to degradation, is seen in the light of some principles that do not change. Otherwise, no intelligible world is possible. Those principles are lacking today. It would, however, be naïve to think that the "chaotic" or "fragmentary" ideas that characterize the contemporary world have no force. They have brought together those for whom rejection without reason or principle has become the rule. That is one of the lessons of terrorism, of the success of the theories that feed it, and, more generally, of the attraction of negation. The problem lies in the lack of an intellectual and moral response to this phenomenon, which has produced a deep discouragement among the young. Karl Kraus diagnosed a similar situation between the two world wars: "How understandable is the disenchantment of an age that remains steadfast in the face of its own collapse, one that feels as little remorse as it does the effects of action." Except for a narrow elite without real influence on society, the decline of general and historical knowledge has reached such depths that it is not unusual to find students with master's degrees in modern history who do not know the date of the fall of the Berlin Wall, or students of the Middle Ages who cannot remember the year that Charlemagne was crowned Holy Roman Emperor. That is one of the results of education's tendency to focus on very recent events, thereby strengthening an already powerful cultural development that gives pride of place to the immediate present. In such circumstances, how can one grasp the meaning of the words *collapse, remorse,* or even *effects of action?* The values that are trumpeted in speeches seem good for absolutely everything, except for action because they have become too weak. Europe today is going through a phase that is not only troubled but deeply incoherent. And this at a time when the world has so much need of what long characterized Europe's historical role, even more than its adventures on the seven seas: organizing of the world of ideas and values.

The mechanism set up after World War Two by the founding fathers of Europe, with its steady and unspectacular progress, is in its final moments. The younger generations of Europeans no longer believe in the slow, gradual nature of European Union (EU) reforms. They want greater upheavals, and perhaps most of all, greater ambitions. And they are right. Like the youth of the French Restoration, the youth of the early twenty-first century could complain that it received as the legacy of the Cold War only "cheerless mores," with no room for enthusiasm or plans for the future.[8] Now that the unity of Europe has been established, the machine seems literally worn out, to the point where the magnitude of the task accomplished is no longer admired or even recognized.

Despite the achievements of a uniting Europe, the essential question remains to be answered: What role do we now want to grant Europe in the world? It cannot be satisfied with working against AIDS and global warming, even if those are noble causes of strategic importance. It must recognize that more arduous tasks await it than the foreign operations it boasts of today in Afghanistan and the Balkans. The hope of escaping from the world's unrest and finding shelter within a stabilized zone is a vain one. The stabilization is of course a historic accomplishment in light of the centuries that the European nations devoted to their mutual destruction. But the stabilization of the European continent—leaving aside that it is now threatened by the pause in the enlargement process—is a unifying factor only for the generations that went through the wars. It is not enough for the rising generations. And it by itself is no longer an adequate response to the responsibilities of Europe in the world, especially when the "stabilized zone" demonstrates such obvious lack of judgment on its eastern border as to encourage the dangerous regression of Russia.

The United States, by its very nature turned more toward the future, more dynamic and mobile than Europe, and now persuaded of its own vulnerability, has retained the conviction that human will has a role to play in history. As of 2005, the results of its activities of the last few years were not as bad as they had often been accused of being, but 2006 brought a number of serious setbacks that showed the fragility of previous successes. Afghanistan had been taken back from the Taliban and Iraq from Saddam Hussein; Colonel Muammar al-Gaddafi gave up unconventional weapons; Washington re-engaged in the Israeli-Palestinian question after the death of Yasser Arafat; and Lebanon was at least partially liberated from Syria. 2006 showed that many of those advances were not irreversible: Afghanistan has again become a very dangerous place, Iraq is more violent than ever, and the war between Israel and Lebanon was at best inconclusive and at worst a victory for Iran, Syria, and Hizbollah, the forces most opposed to the peace process. All this at a time when the dossier on Iran's nuclear development was standing before the Security Council with no effect. These events do not mean, however, that the American analysis was wrong: continuing a Western policy in which regional "stability" depended on contempt for the will of the people was increasingly dangerous. As international terrorism has shown in both America and in Europe, that policy did not have any positive effect on the security of the West; stability purchased at the price of oppression is an illusion. But it certainly means that major mistakes were made and should now be corrected.

On the other side, although Europeans often like to believe that postponing decisions or protecting the status quo can lead to good results, this is seldom true. History has little mercy for sleepwalkers. As in Hermann Broch's novel, passivity in the face of rising violence is often even more troubling than the violence itself, because it makes the victory of violence possible. Violence tends to benefit from the failure to oppose it. From this viewpoint, the crisis is moral as much as political and has to do with a deficiency of the will. Nietzsche spoke in those terms more than a century ago, but political thinkers never feel at ease in that domain. The best of them maintain that political choice is not a choice between good and evil but between "the preferable and the dreadful."[9] That is a judgment that has the virtue of moderation. It also makes it possible to draw a helpful distinction between public and private spheres of action. But because that is still speaking in moral categories, the real difficulty remains.

To have a real debate about the "preferable" and the "dreadful," we would have to bring into the open what was possible during the Cold War for the "other Europe" and the victims of the Soviet regime in the Soviet Union. We would have to consider that it was criminal to support the Chinese Cultural Revolution, and reassess the nature of European, French, and UN responsibilities in Rwanda,[10] as well as French policy in Algeria during the civil war of the 1990s[11] or the silence that has greeted the tragedy of Chechnya. All those stories unfortunately seem to belong to the second—dreadful—moral category. The twentieth century is still with us. It was the century that called into question the autonomy of politics established since the Renaissance, particularly with regard to ethics. It is precisely because mass Machiavellianism has triumphed that the ethical question has resurfaced with such force.

It has often been said, particularly since the September 11 attacks, that it is no longer possible to separate foreign and domestic politics, a distinction that was long key for experts in international relations. The reason for this seems simple: domestic and foreign threats are now connected in hitherto unknown ways. Yet one often has the feeling that Europe and America draw very different conclusions from that principle. The former remains thoroughly turned in on itself and seems to be slowly absorbing its enlarging territory like a boa constrictor. The latter has an increasingly pronounced tendency to project its forces and its ideas outward, somewhat like a cobra.

That contrast between a Europe concerned primarily with making a twenty-five-member Union function without losing its bearings and an America that is omnipresent throughout the world, is, however, a bit exaggerated. The Europeans have about 60,000 troops deployed in various foreign operations, and they provide extensive financing for development aid. For its part, America intervened in world affairs in the twentieth century only to attempt to put an end to the insane violence the Europeans had introduced into international affairs. Before complaining about America's stature or action, we should remember that America's natural impulse is not projection but protection of the American dream and territory. But it sees more clearly than Europe that its security interests have to be defended far from its borders, and it has extensive security commitments abroad. We are thus witnessing a role reversal at the beginning of the twenty-first century, with a Europe tired of prolonged involvement around the world, not very concerned with assuming international responsibilities, and an America that has made foreign and defense policy a major political issue. In a world in which instability is ubiquitous, however, we cannot forget that Europe and America are the only parts of that world that are simultaneously peaceful, prosperous, and powerful. Do they have any choice but to work together to contain the principal dangers threatening international security, even if they are not in agreement on every subject?

The difference between the two sides of the Atlantic does not stop there. For reasons that are difficult to understand, Europe seems to have more trouble than America in remembering the dangers that authoritarian regimes and dictatorships pose to peace. It often speaks and acts as though it could adapt to any existing situation. And yet it was Europe that had the *internal* experience of the most terrifying abuses of political power. Why did that not leave in its wake a code of conduct toward dictators for democracies to adopt? Not only did Europe not find a way of condemning Iraq in the 1980s for its large-scale use of chemical weapons against Iranian troops and its Kurdish civilian population,[12] but according to the memoirs of the French ambassador to the United Nations at the time, Pierre-Louis Blanc, Jacques Chirac, then prime minister, intervened to block Security Council condemnation of those monstrous acts. In the 1990s, massacres carried out by Yugoslav President Slobodan Milosevic and his allies were slow in awakening the conscience of European states, even though they were happening on their doorstep. It is true that a state does not have a conscience—it is the grandeur of individuals to have one. But nations are also responsible when well documented atrocities last for years without any serious attempt to stop them. For instance, the militias that have been carrying out genocide in Darfur for many years are still active and unpunished. If anything, the situation has worsened in 2006. Is it tolerable that China veto the deployment of UN troops because of its oil deals with Khartoum?

The weakness of the classic distinction between domestic and foreign is not merely the consequence of the growing risks that cannot be clearly attributed to one realm or the other while in the past they were more separable and distinct. Nor is it tied solely to the fact that our security can be threatened very far from our territory—after all, that has been a banality ever since ballistic missiles came on the scene. It is also connected to the fact that contemporary versions of "everything is permitted"—wherever they may arise—can no longer be dismissed by governments as disagreeable phenomena in an era when information systems and the precision of military and commercial satellites make it impossible for anyone to remain ignorant of what is happening. Political tolerance for the most extreme doctrines and ambitions fosters political monsters. That was true in the 1930s, and still is today. One of the principal moral questions confronting our time—one that confronted the last century as well—is how to respond to that situation, which makes one wonder whether the slightest progress has been made in this domain.

Europe's problem is not so much its modest investment in defense, or the difficulty twenty-five members have in reaching decisions or expressing a common will.[13] Nor is it the rejection by the citizens of major countries of the proposed Constitution that was supposed to guarantee the progress of the Union. Europe's principal problem, after having invested enormously in historic action, is to be tempted by an exit from history, which presupposes a *formidable effort of forgetfulness* of its recent and more distant past. If it succumbs to that temptation, it will find it all the more difficult to return to the historical stage because it will have lost any urgent desire to do so. Europe's problem, after having been the great provider of ideas in the world, is to recognize that ideas no longer arise in Europe, and that the ones that remain are no longer strong enough to persuade even its own inhabitants. So how could they influence anyone else? In the name of what could they foster the integration of immigrant populations crowding into the EU's territory? How could they establish a will for external action? In strategy as in politics, European thought is primarily reactive. Europe has nothing to say. As Alain Frachon and Daniel Vernet point out in their book on the neoconservatives, Europe behaves "as though problems existed only when the United States raises them."

The year 2004 provided a barometer for the state of Europe. The long-awaited reunification of the European continent produced no demonstration commensurate with the event. A few timid ceremonies greeted the new arrivals from the other Europe from which we had been separated since 1945, thereby reminding them more of our frequently expressed hesitations about enlargement than demonstrating our joy at European unity restored. A few months later, the sixtieth anniversary of the Warsaw uprising, one of the most heroic episodes of the Second World War, was attended by not a single French official. Vladimir Putin was even allowed to take advantage of the event, although in 1944 Russian troops had waited impassively for the Nazi massacre to end before they crossed the Vistula River. Finally, in the year of enlargement and the adoption of the Constitutional Treaty, there was a record level of abstentions in the European elections, better evidence than any opinion poll of the pervasive lethargy of European citizens. This was confirmed in 2005 by the mediocrity of the debates during the referendum campaign in France, one of the key countries in the construction of Europe, as well as by the disastrous results it inevitably produced.

While Europeans sleep, others become aware of the power of ideas. But the ideas that are spreading most widely are very much contrary to European values. Contempt for human life, the refusal to distinguish civilians from combatants, assassination presented as a duty—these are direct challenges to the values that our societies are supposed to defend. What price are we ready to pay to do that? Considering the EU's reaction to the appalling massacre in Beslan, South Ossetia, in September 2004, we may conclude that that price must not be very high.[14] Apart from the Netherlands, not a single Western government dared question Putin about his incompetent and ambiguous handling of the tragedy. It seems, however, that more than one question would be relevant, since information about the attack was available beforehand and not provided to South Ossetia; since the explosives and the weapons came from the Russian Interior Ministry; and since at least one of the hostage takers belonged to the Moscow police internal affairs service.[15]

Europe is at once turned too much toward the past to be a major actor in the twenty-first century and too cut off from that past to find its inspiration there. Like the other Western societies, it lives in the moment, and that prevents it from adapting its present to its past and from imagining a future for itself. The reason it does not have a politics based on its thought is because that thought has ceased to be vital. Its democracy has become abstract, like its values, unable to exercise the kind of influence in the world that the world needs. In a period of great international stability, this might have no consequences. In an era of profound transformations and exasperated passions, this exhaustion is charged with danger. It is time for Europeans to interrupt the subterranean ruminations about history and start thinking about the future. Otherwise, others will do it for us.

Modern physics has tried to explain irregular events in nature. It is more difficult to find explanations for historical chaos once it has taken hold, because it entails a general loss of control and of meaning. As in nature, however, imbalances that appear in history tend to engender other events in a chain reaction. The theory in physics known as "catastrophe theory" has a kind of correspondence with the course of human affairs. Are we then *on the eve of something?* This is what Charles Morice, a Symbolist poet and art critic, asked exactly a century ago. In that he was echoed by a great writer, Léon Bloy, who evoked the "prologue to an unprecedented drama." Before turning the telescope toward the future, we should focus it on 1905, a year that was to be decisive from its opening days. The first Russian Revolution broke out on January 23, 1905.

PART TWO

1905

We are in the prologue of an unprecedented drama, of a kind that has not been seen for several centuries

—LÉON BLOY, 1905

CHAPTER 5

PORTENTS

Ah, children, if you only knew how cold
and dark it will be in the days to come!

—ALEXANDER BLOK

The year 1905 was one of the most dramatic of the early twentieth century. It saw a wildly varied series of events that was to transform world affairs. By 1905, it was already difficult to remain satisfied with dreams of the Belle Époque. Everywhere, from Europe to Asia to the Americas, in Russia and in China, one could sense the approach of what would later be called the century of wars and revolutions. It was the year of the first defeat of a Western nation by an Asian power in a modern war. That, along with the first Russian Revolution, was a solemn warning for the government in Saint Petersburg. The year also saw the first Moroccan crisis between France and Germany—which the Algeciras conference barely prevented from turning into an armed conflict, nine years before the outbreak of the war that was to decide the fate of the entire century. Finally, 1905 saw a considerable widening of the international stage, the increasing interconnection of worlds, and the opening of new horizons. Two major actors, the United States and China, made their appearance, in strongly contrasting roles. Washington played its first major diplomatic hand in Portsmouth, as a mediator between Russia and Japan in negotiations for a peace treaty. It was now beginning to replace Britain on the world stage. As for China, it was in this year that Sun Yat-sen, the most important thinker of the Chinese revolution, published his fundamental work, the declaration of the nationalist movement. The twentieth century had begun in earnest.

Of all those events, the one most fraught with consequences was the Russo-Japanese War, which, after the Russian defeat, encouraged Russia's tilt toward the Balkans, one of the root causes of the chain of events leading to the First World War. The defeat precipitated the 1905 revolution in Russia, which can be seen as a rehearsal for the 1917 revolution. Tokyo's victory also encouraged Japan's imperialist ambitions, the consequences of which appeared in the 1930s and 1940s.

The evidence that the Russians were responsible for the defeat inflicted on them in a few short months is overwhelming. Czar Nicholas II, who had little natural inclination for war and only a foggy idea of affairs of state, allowed himself to be persuaded by a dilettante that he could seize Manchuria and Korea without difficulty. He decided on war without taking into account the rising military power of Japan, even though it had shown what it was capable of in China ten years earlier in the Sino-Japanese war. Saint Petersburg went into the war with an insane lack of intellectual and material preparation. After a series of Russian missteps, Tokyo launched a surprise naval attack on Port Arthur one night in January 1904 and carried the fighting into Manchuria. From then on, instead of the promised easy victory, humiliating Russian defeats quickly followed one another on both land and sea and the fleet was practically destroyed.

This was a modern war, full of lessons that European military commanders might well have considered had they been less obsessed by familiar problems: new methods were used, the fighting lasted much longer than anticipated, and serious international complications arose at several junctures. The psychological effects in Russia were devastating, and they were still felt at the time of the Japanese surrender in 1945, when Joseph Stalin recalled the defeat of 1905 to emphasize the revenge Russia had taken in the Second World War:

> Our people always believed that a day would come—and it has been waiting for that day—when Japan would be defeated and the stain removed. We have waited for that day for forty years, we of the older generation.

What Stalin neglected to say was that Russia had played no role in Japan's defeat, which was due entirely to the United States, and, especially, that the Russian revolutionary movements had been the primary beneficiaries of the 1905 defeat and the ferocious repression that ensued.[1]

Once the Russo-Japanese War was over, the fragility of the old world immediately became apparent. Imperial power was discredited, like the army, and for the same reasons.[2] The monarchy was able to resist the forces aiming at its destruction only through repression, which doomed rather than protected it. In January 1905, a year after the beginning of the war, the czar's police brutally repressed a huge peaceful demonstration, inflicting countless casualties. That was the beginning of the revolutionary conflagration. Peasant revolts in the countryside—a certain Koba (Stalin) helping to organize one in the region of Kartli in Georgia—soon assumed bloody forms. The first general strike was declared. During the next two years several thousand people were executed.

The revolution failed, but it had launched a movement that would end only with the total defeat of the imperial order. Leon Trotsky, with his characteristic strategic intelligence, was one of the first to understand this: he never stopped reflecting on the events of 1905 and deriving lessons from them, as though the real revolution were not the 1917 one, but the first one, despite its failure. The uprising convinced him in particular of the *stupidity* of the peasants, who revolted locally and later fired on the workers in the cities. In a country still essentially made up of peasants, Trotsky's remarks illustrate his deep contempt for the Russian people. He spoke of the "political ineptitude of the muzhik," of his "moral cretinism," and of the "historic curse of rural movements." Is it surprising that later the unfortunate souls who had already suffered so much under serfdom were systematically deported by Stalin after the revolution, or exterminated by him by means of a famine that caused 7 million deaths in the early 1930s?[3]

Russian literature also hailed the conflagration of 1905. Andrei Bely devoted his most remarkable novel, *Petersburg*,[4] to the 1905 revolution. In it one can see hatred for anything that represents state authority, the activities of terrorist networks with close ties to the police forces,[5] and a disintegration of the sense of society the likes of which only Jean Renoir's *La Règle du jeu*, filmed in 1939 on the eve of another catastrophe, can give some idea.

The First World War completed the process that had thus been set in motion. In 1917 Russia was the first state that collapsed as a result of the war, to the surprise of the Germans, who had anticipated fighting the principal battle on that front. The Russian soldiers' support for the insurrection had nothing to do with freedom, land, or revolutionary ideas of any sort: they simply did not understand why they had to fight. Two million deserters left the battlefield in tremendous disorder. Four days of a popular uprising—to the surprise of the Bolsheviks this time—were enough to bring down the regime. Lenin had called for transforming "imperialist war into civil war," and that is exactly what finally happened. War had indeed engendered revolution. But none of the principal Bolshevik leaders had participated in the war, and they would never have anything but an abstract image of the massacre and of the disaster it represented for all Europe. Stalin, on the other hand, remembered that war could bring about radical political changes. That is perhaps one of the explanations for his frightened retreat at the beginning of the Second World War, and for his refusal to recognize the numerous German preparations for the invasion of the Soviet Union.

In Paris, the 1905 revolution remained an abstraction. The Republic had staked a good deal on the alliance with Saint Petersburg, counting on its support in what had become a French obsession, revenge on Germany. Lack of political judgment among leaders and of recognition of the reality of Russia kept France from understanding the tragedy that was being played out in Russia. Thus the events of 1905 were minimized and France continued to shower Saint Petersburg with credits, including a loan that enabled Russia to get back on its feet.[6] In 1917, the French were again surprised, despite the national experience of revolution and the warning of 1905. The Third Republic, although it had maintained close relations with Nicholas II, cast a distracted glance Russia's way. But as Isaiah Berlin has remarked, an attentive observer, concerned with the future of liberty in Europe, could have borne in mind as early as 1905 the pronouncements made at the conference of the Russian Social Democratic Party held only two years earlier that were charged with meaning:

> During the discussion of what seemed at first a purely technical question—how far centralization and hierarchical discipline should govern the behaviour of the Party—a delegate named Posadovsky inquired whether the emphasis laid by the "hard" Socialists—Lenin and his friends—upon the need for the exercise of absolute authority by the revolutionary nucleus of the Party might not prove incompatible with those fundamental liberties to whose realization Socialism, no less than liberalism, was officially dedicated. He asked whether the basic, minimum civil liberties—"the inviolability of the person"—should not be

infringed and even violated if the party leaders so decided. He was answered by Plekhanov, one of the founders of Russian Marxism, and its most venerated figure . . . Plekhanov, speaking solemnly, and with a splendid disregard for grammar, pronounced the words, *Salus revolutiae suprema lex*. Certainly, if the revolution demanded it, everything—democracy, liberty, the rights of the individual—must be sacrificed to it.[7]

The Russian earthquake attendant on the Russo-Japanese War and the 1905 revolution sent powerful shock waves through a world that had already had its equilibrium shaken. The idea that one could change established situations was beginning to make its way into men's minds. The peoples of Asia were as dumbfounded by the Japanese victory as the Russians or the West. Particularly in China, they drew a conclusion that would have major consequences for the future: Europeans were not as invincible as they seemed to be. They could even be beaten.

The Russo-Japanese treaty of August 1905 confirmed the defeat of the Russian army, which had been considerably weakened, and partially emptied the military alliance with France of its content. It ratified Japan's rise to power in the Far East and gave Japanese militarism, already well established after a successful expedition against China, grounds for pride as substantial as Russian humiliation was deep. The Westernization begun in the late nineteenth century had borne fruit. This first recognition of the Japanese imperial idea in the Far East would have repercussions throughout the first half of the twentieth century. Japan's rights in Korea were recognized, and Tokyo occupied the peninsula that same year, encountering not the slightest international protest, and then annexed it in 1910. In 1917, Japan intervened in what at the beginning had been a purely European war by seizing German positions in the Far East and the Western Pacific. Even though it was in the camp of the victors in 1918, Japan did not appear to be satisfied: in 1931 it invaded Manchuria without any reaction from the League of Nations; then in 1937 the Japanese army attacked China, committing the classic mistake, after repeated victories, of believing in a blitzkrieg. The Second World War provided Japan with an opportunity to establish its empire in East Asia.

As for Russia, once its dreams of expansion in the Far East were destroyed, it turned to the Balkans. Some saw in this a gain for the alliance with France, because Saint Petersburg was no longer distracted by its

Eastern escapades. But Russia was a weakened and embittered ally for the French. The 1908 crisis in Bosnia-Herzegovina brought Russian exasperation to a peak, as it was not in a position to intervene to support its Serbian allies when Austria-Hungary annexed Bosnia-Herzegovina. Inside Russia, the Russo-Japanese War also gave rise to a series of pogroms against the Jewish population. That was the origin of one of the great waves of emigration to the United States.[8] Unlike the emigration during the last two decades of the nineteenth century, which had a peasant and lower-class component, this group was often cultivated, and was a mix of secular and religious. It included both rabbis and members of the Bund. The Jewish intelligentsia understood that it was time to leave Russia, where a new time of troubles was dawning. Departures were epidemic between 1900 and 1914: each year, sixteen of every thousand Jews living in the Russian Empire emigrated to America. One would have to go back to the Irish emigration of the mid-nineteenth century to find similar rates. The fact was that life was becoming increasingly difficult for Russian Jews. Before 1914, pogroms struck Bialystok, Gomel, Siedlce, Kishinev, and, most important, Odessa. Then the pace accelerated: immediately after the First World War, tens of thousands of Jews were killed in Ukraine. In the town of Proskurov alone, the number of victims was greater than in forty years of pogroms in all of czarist Russia. The sizable Jewish community in the United States well before the rise of Nazism was thus the direct result of persecution in Europe.

Another dramatic episode was taking shape in the western part of Europe in March 1905. The first Moroccan crisis between France and Germany broke out at Tangier and there was a risk that it could lead to a decisive confrontation. A second, even more serious crisis broke out in 1911. In themselves, the events were minor. Emperor Wilhelm II delivered a speech in Tangier in which he declared himself prepared to protect the independence of Morocco, the last independent country in North Africa at the time.[9] France, which had decided five years earlier to establish a protectorate in Morocco, saw this as a provocation. The crisis would not have had much impact had the two countries not allowed the development of an atmosphere in which the slightest disagreement became dangerous, especially after the accession of the new emperor, Wilhelm II. In March 1905, any compromise between France and Germany, on any subject, seemed impossible. War threatened, but it was delayed for a few years by the Algeciras conference. When it came, as Hannah Arendt remarked, it meant the end of a world:

> The days before the First World War and the days after it are separated not like the end of an old era and the beginning of a new one, but like the day before and the day after an explosion.

The countries involved in the war did not foresee these enormous repercussions. In the early years of the century, advocates of a solution through law rather than arms were in the minority. Elementary school teachers, for example, who were beginning to unionize, became aware of the risks posed by the idea of revenge in all school textbooks. It was in fact in 1905 that new textbooks were published that were less traditional and less bent on revenge than their predecessors, no longer presenting Germany as the hereditary enemy, and leaving open the possibility of achieving peace through law. But the "crisis of patriotism in the schools" was denounced by all who were obsessed with Alsatian villages with geraniums in every window; few seemed to grasp that revenge in Europe was suicidal.[10] It was a moment when one might have wished for a more harmonious dialogue between humanity and history. But it seemed as though both were already *carried away*.

In Europe, only Switzerland, Spain, the Netherlands, and the Scandinavian countries managed to stay out of the conflict. The network of alliances made it clear that this war would not be confined to Europe. Even though the fiercest battles were waged from Belgium to the Alps, on the Russo-German front, in Austria-Hungary, and in the Balkans, war also broke out in Asia, Africa, the Middle East, and the Pacific islands. Soldiers came from around the world, from the French and British empires, Australia, New Zealand, Canada, and the United States. Who at the time foresaw that the war would determine the course of the rest of the century? No one, it seems.

And yet, as early as the mid-1890s, Ivan Bloch, a Polish engineer, had sensed that a war would deeply change European societies and penned a long report to the czar on the subject:

> Most military writers consider the technical aspects of war and treat future conflicts in so objective a manner that they altogether leave out of account

psychological and sociological questions. In short, they neglect the whole human side of this great question. Research on the conditions of the future of war cannot be limited to the comparative effectiveness of various states. Armies are the products of societies. Peoples, as Taine has already observed, judge with their brains but also with their hearts. Hence, it is in the feelings of the general population that we must seek indications of the state of mind with which armies will join battle and of the effects that early victories or defeats will have on them. One remarkable characteristic of our time is the speed with which changes are occurring in material and intellectual spheres. Greater social upheavals have taken place in a few years than during the past several centuries. This great movement of life has come from the spread of education, the activities of parliaments, associations, and the press, and from the growth of means of communication. Under the influence of these new conditions, minds find themselves in constant movement. Another characteristic of our age is the link between the movement pushing our century forward and the instinct inspiring the masses. It is a very remarkable fact that people move as a mass. What degree of patience can be expected from modern armies in a prolonged war? What will be the effect of bad news from the front on the civilian population? Will civilians themselves become a front line? What convulsions will ensue on the cessation of hostilities when millions of soldiers return to their devastated countries?[11]

Bloch also understood that the balance of forces between the combatants posed the risk of an interminable war in which no decisive battle could be fought. The principal combatants might also have sensed the same thing. Marshal Joseph Joffre himself recognized that each of the adversaries believed in "a vigorous offensive," and that each of them had "an unshakable determination."

The eminent military historian Michael Howard correctly notes that Ivan Bloch was mistaken on a number of points.[12] But Bloch the engineer, who devoted his long years of retirement to understanding the changes that technological developments would cause in warfare, strikingly illuminated some of the most significant aspects of the wars of the twentieth century: the lunatic scale of the number of deaths, the large number of civilian victims, the growing role of the economy in the preparation for and conduct of the war, the difficulty of controlling the immense changes in progress, the role of the masses in the twentieth century, and the inability of the military to grasp in time the consequences of technological transformations. The unpreparedness of the generals, especially in the Russian army, many of whose officers had never seen a battlefield in 1914, was one of his major areas of concern. In fact, as Solzhenitsyn describes it in *August 1914*, those officers often led their men to their deaths through a series of tragic errors.[13] The real weakness of Ivan Bloch, who had devoted the quiet hours of his retirement to the composition of a work on the madness of modern warfare, was to base his argument on the hypotheses that utopia could not be a powerful engine of human activity and that suicide was an impossible choice.

Another revolution had begun in Asia, led by an outstanding figure who would, had he succeeded, have steered the history of modern China on a totally different course from that taken by Mao Zedong. In April 1905, Sun Yat-sen, leader of the Chinese Nationalist movement, published a solemn declaration of the three principles of his movement: nationalism, democracy, and the development of the Chinese people.[14] Nationalism was an affirmation of Chinese identity in opposition to the Manchu dynasty and represented a desire for independence, sovereignty, and unity. The intent was to enable China to take its place in the family of nations on an equal footing, at a time when it was experiencing humiliation and division. Democracy was the recognition of the power of the Chinese people and of the responsibility of the government to the people. Sun Yat-sen always advocated gradual, moderate, and peaceful political evolution. In none of his writings can we find a defense of violence to achieve political change. The third principle, development, concerned industrialization, reconstruction, and the establishment of a modern economic system in China.

The historical importance of Sun Yat-sen, systematically underestimated in most Western studies, was respectfully acknowledged by his two principal successors, who recognized him as their master. Simon Leys pays this homage to him:

> The personality, thought, and action of Sun provide a fundamental key to the understanding of modern China and its revolution. This obvious fact is universally accepted in China. Sun is the only Chinese political figure in the twentieth century who has succeeded in earning the unanimous respect of posterity, and the historical impact that he had on the Chinese people as a whole is so substantial that even the adventurers who later came to power, from Chiang to Mao,

always felt obliged to legitimate their authority by claiming to be his spiritual heirs. In contrast, the determination that Westerners have always shown to ignore, minimize, or ridicule Sun's role is all the more striking.[15]

For Sun Yat-sen, the real Chinese revolution was the accession of the Chinese to democracy—even if he had a rather authoritarian picture of the democracy that would be possible in China. If his ideas had triumphed, China would have avoided the tens of millions of deaths caused by the Great Leap Forward and the Cultural Revolution.[16] Sun argued that the tragedy of China was that the Chinese had always fought to conquer the imperial throne while Western countries were fighting for their freedom: "For thousands of years in China there has been a constant struggle over the single question of becoming emperor." His aim was not simply to overthrow the Manchu dynasty but to establish a republic. Is this the reason he is treated with contempt in the West? Because there is something suspect in praising "western inventions"? That is what Simon Leys thinks, and here is his response: "The Chinese did not invent the steam engine or the internal combustion engine. Should we therefore conclude that transportation and communication systems in China are forever confined to wheelbarrows and mules?"

In China as in Russia, the West has always favored the leaders over the people. Whenever a new potentate crushed the people, he was hailed by governments and intellectuals:

> Thus in the middle of the nineteenth century, the West chose to back the crumbling Manchu dynasty against the Taiping Rebellion. At the dawn of the twentieth century, it demonstrated hostility and contempt toward the first revolutionary architects of the republican movement, once again choosing to bet on the fossilized empire. It never considered Sun Yat-sen as anything but a sort of picturesque clown, half dangerous, half stupid, but was prepared to take a Yuan Shih-kai seriously.[17]

After his death, battles raged between the Kuomintang and the Communists, and Sun's principles sank into oblivion.

The year 1905 showed the world not only Japan's rise to power but also the first significant appearance of the United States on the world diplomatic stage. Theodore Roosevelt played a conciliatory role in Algeciras, which—temporarily—ended the Moroccan crisis, but it was his role as United States mediator between Russia and Japan that captured the world's attention. The Russian emissary was Sergei Witte, who had been opposed to the 1904–1905 war. He set as conditions not giving up the Russian Pacific fleet and not ceding territory. In fact, Russia lost its spheres of influence in China and Korea but ceded only the southern part of Sakhalin Island, still a subject of dispute between Russia and Japan. The peace treaty signed in Portsmouth on August 23, 1905, earned a Nobel Prize for the American president.[18] Before then, Washington had had only a slight presence outside its region, despite the victorious war against Spain in 1898 that had given it Guam, Puerto Rico, and the Philippines.[19] The irony of history was that the United States itself was to be the victim, almost forty years later, of a surprise attack similar to the one on Port Arthur that determined the outcome of the Russo-Japanese War. In 1941, American seaplanes patrolled during the day, not at night. The Japanese therefore moved their aircraft carriers forward at full speed under cover of darkness. Their planes took off before dawn and reached Pearl Harbor in two hours. When Asian matters are in question, we must never forget strategic surprise and strategic imagination.

At the beginning of the twentieth century, the United States was in the process of finding a political space matching its capacities, and in 1902, the first book on the Americanization of the world was published. The suicidal actions of Europe would offer it much more in 1918 and again in 1945. Washington intervened in world affairs more to reduce the excessive power of other nations than to exercise its own. In 1914, no observer foresaw that powerful Russia would collapse so quickly or that the United States would play a major role. President Woodrow Wilson was at the center of the 1919 Peace Conference, and the United States was present around the world in 1945: it fought in the European and Asian theaters and achieved victory in both. Stalin was one of the few statesmen who immediately understood the lesson. The only thing that reassured him was that he found it much easier to deceive the Americans than the British. In Potsdam, while Churchill asked what the word "Germany" now meant, Truman merely asked, with a naïveté that is still staggering: "How does the Russian delegation understand that question?" The Russian delegation indeed had an opinion: Germany should no longer be anything but a geographical concept. It did not need to be asked twice: "To answer the question, we merely have to define the borders of Poland."

To conclude, in December 1905 a document was produced that the historian John Keegan considers "the most important official document written in the first decade of the twentieth century and perhaps even in the last hundred years." This was the Schlieffen Plan, named after its architect, a German officer who had devoted a large part of his life to refashioning the plan of attack of the German army, which was carried out in 1914. The plan did not precipitate the war. Nor did it foresee what would happen when it was executed: it was a plan for quick victory in a short war. But in the mistakes it contained one can find all the premises for turning the conflict into a quagmire. In Schlieffen's plan, almost all the German forces would execute a crushing offensive against France; the failure of such an offensive was not even considered.[20] The violation of Belgian neutrality, guaranteed by three countries (Britain, France, and Prussia) since 1839, was bluntly recommended, with no qualms of conscience.

It seems that the great inspiration for Schlieffen, whose sole occupation until his death in 1912 was to improve his plan in its smallest details, was Hannibal's overwhelming victory at Cannae in 216 B.C. That gives one pause. The man was interested neither in politics nor in international relations and had an exclusively military view of history.[21] But his plan was followed, and the terrible years in the trenches vividly described by Erich Maria Remarque were its direct result. John Keegan emphasizes the importance of the Schlieffen Plan for strategic reasons. But when daily slaughter destroys psychological defenses in the face of death, it is difficult to distinguish strategy from morality. After the war, observers recorded lasting insensitivity to the international and social violence that ran through the entire century. We are its unhappy heirs.

The Schlieffen Plan was concerned only with victory in the west, whereas the key aim of the German general staff was not to crush France but to put Russia out of action before it became too powerful: industrialization had been very rapid, and railroad building was transforming the transport of troops and matériel. Russia was considered an existential threat—which it in fact became—but later, thanks to the war. Fear of the Russian menace was reflected in the curious exchange between Wilhelm II and his general staff when he learned that war had become inevitable. He exclaimed: "So our men are leaving for Russia?" and received this answer: "No, sire, for France." The idea was to avoid fighting on two fronts, which the Franco-Russian alliance had made unavoidable and to carry off a lightning victory in the west before a more difficult war in the east. The opposite happened in 1914, but the original prediction was fulfilled twenty-five years later. In 1940, the repetition of a known plan surprised the French, who were not at all prepared to counterattack. The lessons of 1914 had been forgotten.[22] On the German side, Hitler never agreed with Schlieffen's view that a coalition between *Latins* and *Slavs* was inevitable because of the central position of Germany. He therefore prepared for war with intense political and diplomatic activity, leading to a series of offensive actions followed by a division of the two camps thanks to the pact with Stalin.

In Europe, there were very few who understood the extent to which the events of 1905 followed one another like warnings of the great tragedies to come. We ought therefore to pay homage to those who had a sense of history sufficiently keen and wide-ranging to discern symptoms that were even more troubling because they occurred in very diverse spots on the planet. In France, Paul Valéry was one of those who best understood the global nature of the events at the turn of the century:

> I do not know why the attacks of Japan against China and the United States against Spain, which followed one another rather closely, made a particular impression on me at the time. They were only very restricted conflicts involving forces of no great size; and as for me, I had no motive for taking an interest in those distant things, to which nothing in my affairs or my ordinary concerns inclined me to be sensitive. I nevertheless experienced those distinct events not as accidents or limited phenomena but as symptoms or harbingers, as significant facts whose significance went well beyond their intrinsic importance and apparent impact.[23]

If we compare this passage to the nearly universal lack of understanding with which the strategic questions raised by East Asia are greeted in Europe today, questions about which we are much more informed than Valéry could have been, we are reduced to silence. The exceptional loss of European influence in world affairs in the space of only one century is remarkable.

CHAPTER 6

The Birth of Modernity

*Do you have the sense that art
today is tending in new directions?*

—QUESTIONNAIRE PUBLISHED IN
Mercure de France, 1905

Isaiah Berlin claims that chronological milestones rarely coincide with turning points in the history of ideas. That may be untrue of 1905. Intellectual and artistic life experienced profound transformations, as though the twelve months of that year were destined to play a very specific role in the history of human consciousness. In science and art, 1905 is known for three events. In physics, the publication in Switzerland of Albert Einstein's paper presenting the theory of special relativity and of three other papers by him would spark a revolution comparable to Newton's three centuries earlier. In the history of painting, the year saw the first exhibition of the "Fauves" in the Salon d'automne in Paris, a show art historians point to as the beginning of twentieth-century art. Finally, 1905 witnessed the publication of one of the most important and certainly the most provocative of the works of Sigmund Freud, whose thought was to dominate the century to such an extent that it is not an exaggeration to speak of the *century of the unconscious*. A century later, everyone knows that 1905 was the miracle year for Einstein, who, isolated from the scientific community, had for some time been attempting to solve the problems that the mathematician Henri Poincaré considered the most important ones remaining unsolved. In that year the publication of Einstein's "On the Electrodynamics of Moving Bodies" and three other papers—on light, on Brownian movement, and on the equivalence of mass and energy—revolutionized modern physics.[1] Thanks to this work, the difficulty of relating the laws of motion to Maxwell's law within a unified theory was resolved.[2] Einstein's work, which was completed in 1916 by the theory of general relativity,[3] opened a century shaped by physics—as the twenty-first will probably be shaped by biology. The new physics had both civilian and military applications, with the latter playing a substantial role in combat. The most revolutionary of them for international relations was nuclear weapons, which would endow mankind with an unprecedented power of destruction.

Einstein was well aware of the dangerous ramifications of the new physics. He wrote a letter on the subject to the president of the United States in 1939, in which he explained that the work of Enrico Fermi and Leo Szilard on uranium might make possible the development of a weapon of unparalleled power. He mentioned the fear that Germany might develop an atomic weapon, pointing out that Berlin had taken over the Czech uranium mines. Although his letter was not a major factor in the decision to undertake the Manhattan Project, which began only in December 1941, Einstein bitterly regretted having played even a minor role in the development of nuclear weapons. When he learned that Germany had never gone beyond preliminary work on a plutonium reactor, he said of his letter: "If I had known that the fear was not justified, I would not have helped to open Pandora's box." July 1955 saw the issuance of the Russell-Einstein Manifesto, in which scientists warned governments of the dangers of modern warfare. It began:

> In the tragic situation which confronts humanity, we feel that scientists should assemble in conference to appraise the perils that have arisen as a result of the development of weapons of mass destruction ... We are speaking on this occasion, not as members of this or that nation, continent, or creed, but as human beings, members of the species Man, whose continued existence is in doubt.

Following that manifesto, an international conference of scientists met at Pugwash, Nova Scotia, in July 1957. It was the first step in the formation of an international organization that now includes representatives from fifty countries. There is still nothing comparable in the community of biologists, who represent the science of the twenty-first century.

Einstein is said to have attributed the enormous fame of his theory, even among people who did not understand it in the slightest, to the concept of relativity, which resonated with the consciousness of the age. He was not referring to the way in which the relativity of time changed the theory of universal gravitation, or of possible digressions around the fact that the flow of time depended on the systems of reference considered—a very contemporary theme. He was thinking of much more general propositions that he himself sometimes ridiculed. He is supposed to have often repeated: "Relative, relative, everything is relative, that's the secret of my success." Where scientists saw a renewal of theoretical thought unprecedented since Newton, others saw only the scientific expression of a much larger intellectual movement: historical relativism. The connections between the two, however, were not clear—the roots of historical relativism lie in the nineteenth century with Herder, but the spread and persistence of this school of thought have been astonishing. A hundred years later, we are still living in an atmosphere imbued by it, in a world in which nothing seems stable or solid, even though science has called into question the principles of Einstein's physical theory.

Nineteen hundred and five was also the year in which an awareness developed that a new form of art had arrived with the new century. The notion was solidified by the paintings exhibited at the recently established Salon d'automne, and had been prepared for by two articles in the *Mercure de France* in August and September presenting the results of a survey on modern art by the poet and critic Charles Morice. That spring, Morice had sent a number of painters five questions, the first of which dealt with the future of painting: "Do you have the feeling that art today is taking new directions?" Answers from sixty artists showed that in artistic circles at the time, the feeling was that art had reached a turning point. Further, painters felt they were living in a time of great change: "the possibility of novelty in art . . . has strangely stamped and colored the present time." As if to illustrate that belief, the 1905 Salon d'automne showed for the first time works of the painters that soon became known as the Fauves, or "wild beasts." The name originated in a remark by the critic Louis Vauxcelles on the "savagery" of the paintings by Matisse, Derain, and their circle, with their vivid colors, spontaneous, violent brushstrokes, and drawing that broke with academic norms.

Writing on these artists, Vauxcelles said: "They have shown a kind of rage in presenting works that demanded from the spectator the broadest understanding of painting and in declining to accommodate themselves to the multitude's habitual way of seeing." In fact, the art that was coming into existence did much more: it expressed the destruction of existing aesthetic notions and prepared the public for an authentic transformation of the relationship between consciousness and the world. Another critic, Michel Puy, wrote of the Fauves: "Their harmonies no longer sing, they roar; they do not caress you, they grab you by the throat." Theirs were inner landscapes, an art that gave more weight to feeling than to the description of the world. A brutal and troubled subjectivity appeared on the canvases. The Fauves were soon followed by other artistic movements, each proclaiming the intrinsic value of a new kind of subjectivity. Cubists, for example, painted their quasi-abstractions with a kind of scientific objectivity, asserting that they were seeking superior truths. An obscure mixture of descriptive and structural forms took the place of the traditional artistic image.

A few years after the Fauves burst on the scene, the Futurist movement arose in Italy, containing clearly apocalyptic elements and openly declaring itself in favor of a major war, which alone, the Futurists believed, could bring about the hoped-for renewal of art and culture more generally: "We want to sing of the love of danger . . . we want to exalt aggressive movement, somersaults, slaps in the face, and blows of the fist." In a terrible irony of history, the movement's greatest artist, Umberto Boccioni, died at the front in 1916, in a manner that could not have been more "archaic": falling from his horse. Hermann Bahr later saw in the art of the century the perfect expression of an existential anguish: "Art, too, is crying in a profound darkness; it is calling for help."

Finally, 1905 was the year in which Freud published *Three Essays on the Theory of Sexuality*, a little book that transformed research on the human psyche. Some consider it, along with *The Interpretation of Dreams*, published in 1900, the most memorable and original contribution of the father of psychoanalysis. True or not, it is the work that Freud revised most often for new editions. It is also the one that created the greatest scandal. Fewer than ten thousand copies sold between 1905 and 1920, but countless commentaries on the little-read work left its author extremely unpopular. In *Three Essays*, Freud described the child as "polymorphously perverse," and assigned to sexuality purposes much more diverse than mere procreation. Childhood took on an entirely new dimension in the work.

If relativity and quantum theory were the scientific theories of the twentieth century, neurosis was its psychic reality. The capacity to embody utopias gave political thought exceptional power. Doctrines of arbitrary authority, contempt for freedom, belief in the necessity of violence and the morality of war captured the imagination of the masses. Above all, the crimes of the twentieth century were largely crimes of the unconscious. That is why they have remained deeply enigmatic.

Freud, whose final book was on Moses, wanted to be a *Gesetzgeber*, a giver of laws, like the great man of the Bible. In a sense, that is what he became for the twentieth century through his discoveries of the most hidden aspects of human relations and his gradual taking on of all the mental content of existence. His vision of fragile reason as the mediator between an id and a superego in perpetual conflict was much more pessimistic than the view held by thinkers of the nineteenth and even the twentieth century. In his view, reason would never be truly emancipated. The modern science of the mind thus echoed religious pessimism and shared its views on the inevitability of corruption. Its influence was not really felt until after the First World War, which destroyed confidence in morality and in civilization. The pressure of the unconscious continued to increase after 1918, and psychoanalysis made it possible to enter the forbidden territories of the soul. But every attempt to explain human beings made them yet more incomprehensible, revealing mankind's contradictions in all their starkness. Good and evil came from the same source, and inhumanity was part and parcel of human nature. Thus, one day, when the physicist Viktor von Weizaecker reluctantly admitted to Freud, "There is something we do not know," Freud immediately replied, "There I think I beat you hands down."

CHAPTER 7

An Unforeseeable Actor

A frightening mystery.

—Hugh R. Trevor-Roper

What might a perceptive observer in 1905 have seen in the future? Perhaps he would have anticipated the collapse of the Russian Empire, the rise of Japanese militarism, an absurd war between France and Germany touched off by nationalist passions, the realization of Tocqueville's prediction about the role of the United States in world affairs.[1] He might also have foreseen trench warfare and the inability to fight a decisive battle because of the balance between the opposing forces. He might have dreaded the carnage produced by modern weapons and the way terrible wars would end up being inevitable to resolve the tensions within societies. He might have noticed the increasingly crushing weight of the state. He might even have imagined Stalin, as Osip Mandelstam suggested in his troubling reading of the Russian past:

> Looking back at the entire nineteenth century of Russian culture—shattered, finished, unrepeatable, which no one must repeat, which no one dares repeat— I wish to hail the century, as one would hail settled weather, and I see in it the unity lent it by the measureless cold which welded decades together into one day, one night, one profound winter, within which the terrible State glowed, like a stove, with ice.[2]

Stalin might have been understood as the monstrous continuation of a specific national experience in which the state ends up devouring its subjects because of its use of an individual whose psychology is entirely focused on political power.

All that could have been imagined. But no one could have imagined Hitler, for at least three reasons. Unlike Stalin, who had roots in the Russian tradition of tyranny, Hitler had hardly any in German history. No precursor can be found for him. This was one of the most noted questions of François de Menthon, the French chief prosecutor at the Nuremberg trial: "How can we accept that Germany . . . could come to this astonishing return of primitive barbarism?" Some have asserted that the triumph of Nazism was the culmination of all German history and of the difficult experience of democracy in that country, but most believe that only exceptionally traumatizing circumstances made it possible. In the second place, at a time when European expansion was taking place *outside* Europe, with colonization, it was difficult to imagine a German will to expansion *in* Europe. On that point, French and British responsibility is considerable: leaders of both countries, who understood very well the importance of colonial expansion for their own states, did not deem the lack of similar possibilities for Germany a real problem. One of their most serious mistakes was their failure to control the development of German ambitions in Europe and to find a solution to what is generally called the "German question."

Finally, who could have foreseen not only the appearance of Hitler, like a devil popping out of a box, but the *success* of that cruel and incoherent individual, who "wanted everything, immediately," in Albert Speer's words, and whose pathology seems obvious to anyone listening to his speeches today? How could anyone predict that unfettered madness would hold sway in Europe or that a psychopath would triumph in Germany? One of the best judgments on Hitler's case was the comment about historical figures by Joseph Stalin, an expert in the matter: "History is full of abnormal people."[3] Hitler was abnormal in many senses of the term.

More than six decades after his death, Hitler remains "a frightening mystery"[4] who does not fit into the line of perpetrators of massacres preceding or following him, the engineer of "the most monstrous enterprise of domination and barbarity of all time."[5] Some even see him as an eruption of radical evil in history.[6] If that is indeed the case, which most historians hesitate to say, with their characteristic reluctance to speak openly of the problem of evil,[7] then he defies explanation. Historians, however, have endlessly reconstructed his ascent to power. They have noted that his rather slow rise made use of the technique of gradual "entryism," no stage of which was taken seriously by either Germans or neighboring countries. But what remains surprising was that once he came to power through direct election he was able to stay there and to systematically implement the plans set out in *Mein Kampf.* His hypnotic power over crowds, at a time when the masses played a more important role than ever before, shows the psychological disturbance of his listeners as well as his own and irresistibly brings to mind the films of F. W. Murnau.

The most prophetic words about this period of German history are those of the poet Heinrich Heine. He predicted the advent in his country of a revolution of unprecedented savagery, next to which the French Revolution would seem "an innocent idyll" and in which one would see "Kantians mercilessly destroying with hatchet and sword the very ground of our European existence in order to eradicate the remaining roots of its past."[8]

Whether the appearance of Adolf Hitler in history is a matter for theology or whether he was the plaything of historical and psychological forces, he was possible only in an environment marked by what Fritz Stern has called "cultural despair."[9] In either case, Hitler represented a perversion of political authority that exceeded all limits. Only Nietzsche had considered that phenomenon in its ethical aspect, seeing it as one of the unavoidable consequences of what he considered the major fact of the nineteenth century: the death of God and the unlimited nature of political power that would ensue. Hitler would not have been possible without the explosive force of the German people's resentment, or had the state, that "cold monster," not been able to exercise absolute power. Finally, he could not have existed had not all moral law suddenly disappeared. Those were the major themes of the philosopher who saw in the coming two centuries the spectacle of the destruction of morality. Nietzsche died in 1900, and the twentieth century proved him right beyond anything he might have feared. But he was speaking of two centuries, not one, and the second has barely begun.

Hitler has retained a portion of his power after death because he shows that crimes unthinkable before him are *possible*. Humanity cannot rid itself of that experience. The indestructible reality of his massacres is still with us. By that fact alone, he advanced the "brutalization" of Europeans a giant step beyond what the First World War had begun. Moreover, he demonstrated the fearsome psychological effectiveness of propaganda by frightening the ruling class with the idea of revolution while simultaneously propagating the spirit of revolt by denouncing the plutocrats and the Jews. He himself identified his principal weapons as "mental confusion, contradictory feelings, indecision, and panic." The war of nerves lasted without interruption from 1933 to 1939, but as military preparations constantly alternated with diplomatic initiatives, the storm was greeted with some surprise when it finally broke. Finally, this relentless critic of Western culture accurately pointed out real flaws in that culture and in European political life. Like other great projects for reform or revolution, Nazism arose from the recognition that a gaping void lay at the core of modernity, in which utopias could take up residence and from which they could draw a terrible force.

CHAPTER 8

Against the Grain

"I am sick at heart."
—*Macbeth*, V, 3

If one had to define the twentieth century with a single word, *Herzelend*, the German for "sick at heart," would be the most accurate. It designates a form of melancholy and a debilitation of the emotional side of human nature. Twentieth-century man finds a natural companion in the most universal of tragic heroes, Prince Hamlet, whose paralysis of will he shares. The century's tragedies all arrived without having been willed, just as Hamlet never *willed* the death of anyone, except for Claudius. The detour down which the human species began to travel early in the last century resembles a storm whose causes and ultimate consequences it remains ignorant of. Those consequences are still washing up on our shores, like the belated waves of a great catastrophe of which we have not heard the last. Elsinore thus possesses exceptional symbolic power for the Europe of the twentieth century.

By chance, the two world wars were the occasion for many studies of Shakespeare's play: like the Elizabethan hero, cultivated Europeans found themselves engulfed in barbarism with no time to understand what was happening to them. In a sense, the mystery of Hamlet's character held up a mirror to them: the more he was examined, the more there was to elucidate. Death is the theme of the play, as it was of the century.[1] As Stalin said: "Death resolves all problems. No men, no problems." The cataclysm inaugurating the century in 1914 even has a counterpart in the appearance of the ghost at the beginning of the play. From 1914 on, destruction spread progressively around the globe, as it spreads through Shakespeare's kingdom of Denmark. And though the ghost calls for only one victim to secure his revenge, we find the bodies of Polonius, Ophelia, Laertes, Rosencrantz and Guildenstern, and Gertrude laid out beside that of Claudius. Similarly, the war might have touched only Serbia, and it did not have to extend beyond Europe, but the interplay of alliances and the dynamism of violence carried it throughout the world. Finally, if the secret of Elsinore, protected in the play by Hamlet's oath, was a family affair, so was the secret of the 1914 war, which put an end to the concert of European nations. Nothing was able to contain either one.

If Sigmund Freud's genius lay in discovering a treatment for family histories, diminishing the pathological effects of childhood on the mental health of adults, there was no psychoanalytic cure for the community. Political pathologies were resolved only in historic tragedy. But childhood, which plays such an important role in psychoanalysis, was not absent from the drama. The twentieth century shared with childhood the rejection of authority and the absolute submission to authority. José Ortega y Gasset wrote in 1925: "Europe has entered on a period of puerility." A few decades earlier, one of the greatest psychologists, Fyodor Dostoevsky, had had the same feeling. In *The Brothers Karamazov*, the central figure of the father, Fyodor Pavlovich Karamazov, is a representative of the new world and its pathetic infantilism. This unworthy father, incapable of fulfilling his role of making his children respect him or of passing values on to them, is at the source of the violence to come. He is the cause of his own death, his murder by his bastard son, while his other sons, Dmitri and Ivan, are prepared to accuse themselves of the crime because they know in their hearts that they too could have committed it. The twentieth century's dictators would follow such incapable fathers, with their ideas about values, memory, and the role of violence.[2]

Despite its success at the beginning of the twentieth century, Europe was experiencing intense frustration. And yet the successes were striking. Scientific, technological, and industrial advances were impressive. European wealth and power had no equivalent in the world. And finally, Europe largely controlled that world: Great Britain, France, Austria-Hungary, Germany, Russia, Italy, Holland, Portugal, and Spain dominated Africa and Asia. Economic interdependence in Europe was so extensive that a war was absurd. But an armaments race among Europeans began early in the century, accompanied by a change in ways of thinking that fostered belief in the regenerative virtue of violence and destruction. That belief spread through a world that seemed in no way inclined toward resentment, but a deep sense of resentment was in fact present. Anarchism was an eloquent political expression of it, and Futurism was its most developed artistic expression. Futurism's apology for violence and war was presented as a return to the heroic virtues that had been stifled by materialism. The intellectual and spiritual crisis of the early years of the century made war probable, as much as the succession of international crises, the networks of alliances, and the growth of arsenals. Strange remarks began to appear, such as this one in *Pages françaises* by Paul Déroulède: "Forward! Too bad for those who fall. Death is nothing. Long live the tomb!"

Will the twentieth century remain inscribed in humankind's memory as the century of great human catastrophes? To know the answer, we would have to know what the future has in store. Seventy years of practically uninterrupted violence—including eight wars and revolutions—will in any event make that century one of the darkest in history. When Napoleon declared that tragedy had ceased to be individual and that generals and statesmen would take the place of dramatists, could he have imagined the zeal that would be displayed in proving him right? Napoleon's campaigns were still far from foreshadowing Verdun, where mud and men became indistinguishable, the siege of Leningrad, where the living no longer had the strength to bury the dead, or the battle of Kursk, where combatants could no longer tell day from night. As for the great French Revolution, it was only a pale precursor of the revolutions to come. The historian Edgar Quinet understood this when in 1865 he compared the death of victims of the Terror, executed in broad daylight in the squares of Paris, to that of the convicts of the future, such as those who would be sent to the frozen deserts of Siberia: "What terror needs is hidden and muffled torture; distant exile to certainly homicidal climates, prisons from which no one gets out alive . . . These are the punishments appropriate by nature to a regime of terror . . . Death in the shadows, far from the living, unknown, forgotten, with no echo, that is the true terror." But he lacked the imagination to think of the campaign of cannibalism that ravaged the Chinese province of Guanxi in 1968, at the height of the Cultural Revolution, in a monstrous collective regression in which the enemies of the people had to be eaten.

The First World War produced, like the second act of an unfinished play, the war of 1939–45 and everything that followed.[3] It tore apart the concert of nations, with no hope of restoration. And as Hannah Arendt said, "the slightest event took on the inevitability of a last judgment, a judgment that was the work neither of God nor of the devil, but rather resembled the expression of an irremediable fatality." The two wars took place on the same battlefields, in the vicinity of the Meuse River and Arras in the west and the Bzura River in the east, and often involved—in different posts—the same personalities: Pétain, Churchill, the French general Gamelin, and Hitler. Only twenty years separated the end of the First World War and the beginning of the second. In 1945, the end of the Japanese occupation of Asia in turn opened the way to the Chinese Revolution and thirty years of violence. Is the play over, or does it have a third act? In light of the differences that in 2005 divided the countries commemorating the sixtieth anniversary of the end of the Second World War, one wonders. On the other side of the globe from Europe, hostility and hatred are still palpable.

Neither the intellectual and spiritual void of the contemporary world nor its ubiquitous violence encourages optimism. We seem to be prisoners of both. The most eloquent witness of the Russian camps, Varlam Shalamov, spoke of a freezing of the soul in which we might recognize ourselves: "Frost, the same frost that changed spit in flight into ice, reached the human soul. If bones could freeze, the brain could go numb, and so could the soul."[4]

PART THREE

THE WORLD IN 2025

*Thought precedes
action just as lightning
precedes thunder.*

—HEINRICH HEINE

FORESIGHT AND MEMORY

*The past, whether in the form of fantasy
or organized after the fact, has just as powerful
an impact on the future as the present itself.*

—PAUL VALÉRY

Among the ancients, one of the most valued skills was the ability to cast some light on the future, particularly when important decisions were to be made. But that skill depended on the ability to remember. The past was the source of light, and man's relationship to temporality was characterized by a constant contemplation of the past, the great font of wisdom. In that state of fullness, the past was an open book and the ancestors provided protection. When Christianity triumphed and endowed time with direction and meaning, the world adopted a different system of representation: while facing the darkness of the future, that darkness held an expectation, a promise that human freedom was to help bring to fruition. The procession of generations was supposed to make it possible for humanity to accomplish its destiny.

What of today, when humanity can no longer count on the wisdom of the ancients, of which it is ignorant, or on the promise of the future, in which it does not believe? Trapped between the burden of history and fear of the future, humanity is being crushed, rather than liberated, by time.

One thing links Greek wisdom to Christian faith: with both, knowledge of history is open only to those who have preserved the memory of those things that do not change. Nothing is more alien to the modern era, which has fundamentally modified the representation of time. It has rather deliberately turned its back on the past, frequently quarreling with it, seldom receiving any enlightenment from it, and believing even less in omens visible in the present.[1] After the twentieth century, which swept away ideals, destroyed illusions, and made the concept of historical progress dubious, great programs and ideologies provoke more suspicion than enthusiasm.

Modern democratic societies wish to live in an ordered world whose laws can be understood. But order presupposes repetition and, to some degree, a recognition of the authority of the past, two elements largely foreign to modernity. That is why, like Peter Pan, members of these societies find it so hard to become adults: their memories are short, they do not like to hear about the lessons of the past, but at the same time they hardly recognize their responsibility for the present and the future. They prefer to think that events merely happen, without noticing the abdication that way of thinking implies.

Reintroducing the idea of freedom in history is more difficult in the twenty-first century than it was when Gibbon, for example, imagined what would have happened if Charles Martel had not been victorious over the Saracens in 732:

> A victorious line of march had been prolonged above a thousand miles from the rock of Gibraltar to the banks of the Loire; the repetition of an equal space would have carried the Saracens to the confines of Poland and the Highlands of Scotland: the Rhine is not more impassable than the Nile or Euphrates, and the Arabian fleet might have sailed without a naval combat into the mouth of the Thames. Perhaps the interpretation of the Koran would now be taught in the schools of Oxford, and her pulpits might demonstrate to a circumcised people the sanctity and truth of the revelation of Mahomet.[2]

The great historian of Rome thereby reminds us that students of history must be extraordinarily sensitive to events and contingencies—in other words to freedom—just as they must resist the idea of historical necessity. Humanity, like individuals, always confronts choices, and all its acts have consequences. The difficulty, when we consider the future, is to discern the major lines of force in present events and not be blinded by the events themselves.

Writers have produced clashing readings of the future, some of which would be enough to discourage readers from any consideration of the subject. That is the case with Simone de Beauvoir, writing to Jacques-Laurent Bost on August 28, 1939:

> I think no one believes war will come; Sartre doesn't believe it will either. Of course, we're a little impatient and nervous today waiting for Hitler's answer; but as a whole he is in no position to start a war . . . What can be said is that Germany is on the wrong footing for a war and if one were to break out it would not be in very good shape and it probably wouldn't last long . . . Sartre is as calm as anything.[3]

We also find visionaries like Léon Bloy and Nikolay Berdyayev, who saw the violence of the twentieth century approaching well before 1914. Other predictions are all the more remarkable because they were based on reasoning more than intuition. Tocqueville provides the best example, after completing his study of the Ancien Régime and the Revolution, in a celebrated passage:

> Amidst the darkness of the future, we can already discern three very clear truths. The first is that all men of our time are driven by an unknown force that they hope to be able to regulate and slow down but not to conquer, which sometimes pushes them gently and sometimes precipitates them toward the destruction of the aristocracy. The second is that, of all the societies in the world, the ones that will always have the greatest difficulty avoiding absolute government will be precisely those societies in which there is no aristocracy and one is no longer possible. The third, finally, is that despotism can produce no more pernicious effects than in those societies, because, more than any other form of government, it fosters all the vices to which those societies are particularly subject and thereby drives them in the direction in which they were already heading out of natural inclination.[4]

The boldness of that judgment on the despotic deviations of democracy has excited a good deal of envy among experts in political science in the twentieth century.

Today, it is true that the speed and scope of the repercussions of anything that happens have considerably complicated any reflection on the future and have made predictions ever more uncertain. The interactions of causal chains seem almost unlimited. It is therefore true, as Paul Valéry suggested, that

> As we go on, effects will grow less simple, less predictable, and political operations and even armed intervention, in short, obvious and direct action, will not turn out as anticipated . . . It is not that there will no longer be any events or *monumental moments* in the passage of time; there will be huge ones! But those whose function is to anticipate, prepare for, or ward off those events will perforce increasingly learn to be wary of their consequences. It will no longer be enough to combine desire and power to undertake an enterprise.[5]

This passage, written after the First World War, is applicable to the war begun in Iraq in March 2003.

The end of the Cold War gave rise to a flowering of studies on the new world, the new international order, the universalization of liberalism, or the clash of civilizations. The planes that flew into the towers in New York out of a clear blue sky on a beautiful September morning cast doubt on all those exercises. With the ability the United States has to shift suddenly from euphoria to panic, the strategic debate now is all about surprise attacks and preparation for unprecedented events. To be sure, *surprise attack* was one of the main notions of the Cold War, and the greatest fear of military commands, but by September 11, 2001, no one any longer anticipated it. At present, few would risk betting on the situation that will prevail at the end of 2007, or even less 2008, in the Middle East, South Asia, or East Asia. And about the world that will exist two decades from now, we think we know next to nothing. But that, as we shall see, is perhaps an exaggeration.

CHAPTER 10

Three Bets for the Future

Man will never give up true
suffering, that is, destruction and chaos.

—Dostoevsky

It would be a mistake to claim that nothing enables us to imagine the future: we usually go in the direction our thinking takes us. Martin Rees, professor of cosmology and astrophysics at Cambridge, believes he expresses the thoughts of his contemporaries in a book titled *Our Final Hour*.[1] The ideas he expounds are based on known facts. He claims that the future is seriously threatened by the development of new technologies that are inadequately controlled or may be used for terrorist purposes. He specifically emphasizes the risks posed by biotechnology, a booming sector of science, and the new capacity of human beings to alter themselves through genetic manipulation, targeted medicines, and the implantation of microcomputers in brains. He points out the growing vulnerability of an ever more connected world, in which breakdowns of subsystems can have repercussions on the whole of the global system. He does not even exclude the possibility of a new world conflict, one likely to be less well managed than the Cold War. Finally, he reminds us that in an arms race, defensive forces do not always succeed in keeping up, and, further, that offensive forces usually have the advantage. For his pessimistic scenarios, Rees has been dubbed the prophet of the Apocalypse, but what is striking about this book is the rigor of his presentation and the cool British tone of a scholar who, drawing on the scientific experience at his disposal, has merely presented his thoughts.

Fortunately, one might retort, history seldom follows rigorous patterns: chance has a large role to play.

Reasoning from the present, one can make three general bets: that terrorism will persist, that weapons of mass destruction will continue to proliferate, and that China's role in world affairs will be central to international security. First, the chances are good that the world will still have to fight international terrorism in 2025, whether against networks directly linked to Al Qaeda or others who have emulated it or will use it as a model in the future. The battle such networks are waging against the West and against modernity is long term in nature, and both sides are aware of that. In a television interview before the Republican National Convention in New York in August 2004, President Bush admitted for the first time that victory in the classic sense of the word was doubtful: "I don't think you can win it. But I think you can create conditions so that the—those who use terror as a tool are—less acceptable in parts of the world." The United States has compared the war on terror to the Cold War because of its ideological component and the time it will take to bring to an end. While avoiding such dramatic analogies, other Western countries—Britain and France for instance—have emphasized the duration of the conflict and the importance of the battle of ideas. On the terrorists' side, the situation is even clearer. Their patience has become legendary: their training takes years, their targets are examined down to the minutest detail before being struck, and they are certain that this relationship to time, along with the strength of their convictions, is one of their major assets in the face of their enemies.

In the minds of the terrorists, that patience stands in contrast to Westerners' inconstancy, our desire to move quickly, and our eagerness to finish things off. The long-term struggle is indeed a war, even a war to the death, in the minds of those conducting it. Statements of terrorist leaders leave no doubt on the subject. That is one of the great differences between them and their predecessors, whose ambitions were more limited, national, and "realistic." Today's terrorists are not seeking partial or merely tactical victories; what they want is a transformation of the organization of the world as it is now. They are authentic revolutionaries, like nineteenth-century anarchists or Russian Bolsheviks. That they are promoting utopias does not lessen their influence—on the contrary, for utopias had some remarkable ideological successes in the last century. They appeal to the imagination and the passions in a way that politicians in power are no longer capable of. Twenty years is thus a very short period in this war, and neither Washington nor any European capital expects to be able to eliminate the terrorist scourge in so short a time.

Moreover, terrorist networks have an exceptional ability to adapt and rebuild and to influence the younger generations of the Muslim world. After hundreds of arrests in Europe, the United States, and Asia, after thousands of deaths in Afghanistan (nearly 5,000, so far as we know), their ability to recruit does not seem to have been affected. Arrests and disappearances, which took out of action key elements of the command structure, highlighted the importance of recruitment for the networks. A comparable result was observed in the fight against the major drug cartels. Between 1989 and 1996, police succeeded in decimating the Medellin and Cali cartels, arresting the principal leaders and seizing ever larger quantities of drugs along with millions of dollars, while watching the trade flourish more than ever.[2] That is no reason to be discouraged, because arrests and seizures of money and documents do affect the activities of terrorist networks—and sometimes even enable the prevention of attacks. But we must recognize that terrorism will still be with us twenty years from now if the stream of recruits remains as large as it is today.

There is also a gap between the progress made by terrorist groups and that made by their opponents. Changes by Western countries since 2001 in intelligence, law, and policing have been significant. Cooperation between Europe and the United States is also much more active than citizens of European countries may suspect, and the same is true of cooperation within Europe. European legal and police integration has undeniably accelerated since 2001, and the attacks in Madrid in March 2004 and in London in July 2005 further strengthened the process. Unfortunately, opponents' adaptation and inventiveness may have outpaced it. Efforts in the last four years against those who finance terrorism have yielded pitiful results because of micro-financing, informal transfers of funds, and the criminal activities of terrorist cells. Networks are so fluid and individual movements from one cell to another so frequent that it is extremely difficult to keep track. With respect to communication, the use of mobile phones or multiple telephone cards has been largely replaced by written messages, undetectable through phone taps; one of the surprises of the Madrid and London attacks was the silence preceding them. The principal weakness of the Western camp, however, is in the battle of ideas. The battle has never been launched on our side, while it has never stopped progressing on the side of the Islamists. Sites of teaching and ideological recruitment in Muslim and European countries have proliferated. The Islamists have cleverly learned to convert the frustrations of young men into political energy. The challenges posed by activities taking place on European soil have resulted only in timid responses, and even those measures frequently come up against our principle of freedom of expression. Until very recently, it was impossible in Great Britain and the Netherlands to prevent many terrorists from speaking publicly. In France, there has been no response save for something called "city and integration policy," which one would have difficulty describing with any exactitude. In fact, the question of integrating the 20 million Muslims of Europe *into what* is never asked, nor whether successful integration can take place in societies that have no internal cohesion. We Westerners do not believe strongly enough in our values to teach them, much less to defend them;[3] this is the root of the problem, and the terrorists are well aware of it. It is one of the main reasons for their conviction that they will win in the end.

Experience shows that it is very difficult to implement integration policies when dealing with mass immigration within a short period of time, as is now the case in Europe. Integration of immigrants has been more successful in the United States, but then, America had certain historical and geographical advantages. Legal restrictions introduced in 1924 made it possible to regulate the flow of immigrants into America, and the oceans that had to be crossed were a significant natural barrier for those contemplating coming from overseas. More recently, the huge numbers of Mexican and Latin American immigrants crossing its borders have sparked in the United States a debate comparable to the one in France on assimilation and non-assimilation. Samuel Huntington, for example, wrote in 2004 that "the flood of Hispanic immigrants threatened to divide the United States into two peoples, two cultures, and two languages. Unlike earlier immigrants, Mexicans and other Latinos have not assimilated, establishing their own political and linguistic enclaves— from Los Angeles to Miami—and rejecting the Anglo-Saxon values that have made America." Huntington's, however, is a minority view in the United States, and integration of Latinos there, in any event, is being accomplished with enormously greater success than that of North Africans in Europe, particularly in France.

There are several reasons for the differences between Europe and the United States when it comes to integrating immigrants. First, the United States is a country of immigrants, mainly populated and built by waves of immigrants from many different lands. Americans have always accepted the idea that immigrants are coming to the United States to become citizens—as seen in many American books and celebrated movies such as *West Side Story* and Elia Kazan's *America, America*. A central element in U.S. political life has been the continual adaptation of the political system to successive waves of new arrivals. And each wave changed the country. In Europe, on the other hand, immigrants were received as temporary workers and stayed without being welcomed. In some cases, attempts were even made to repatriate them by force. But that unwelcoming policy did not work to limit immigration. In France, where there were only 100,000 North Africans in 1945 and 600,000 in 1962, people of North African descent now number about 6 million, making up ten percent of the population. That growth has sounded many alarms, in the national education system in particular,[4] but no defined policy has emerged. Added to the fundamental difference in approach to immigration, there have been specific mistakes. For instance, sometimes France agreed to let Algeria and Morocco keep a degree of control over their communities on French soil. That has become a matter for bitter dispute between Paris and the two other capitals.

Considering the terrorist networks' ability to rebuild and to find new havens, the influence of radical doctrines on the young of many countries, the difficulty of encouraging economic and political reform in the Arab and Muslim world, the demographic explosion of developing countries, the very modest performance of those countries in the areas of education and employment, and our own inadequacies in the West, there is every reason to think that terrorism is indeed a long-term threat. The belief that international terrorism will still exist in twenty years may acquire a very different meaning if one of the following events occurs: an Islamist seizure of power in Pakistan, Saudi Arabia, or one of the North African countries; terrorists' use of a weapon of mass destruction; or a major attack in Europe even more devastating than the ones in Madrid and London. A seizure of power by Islamists in Pakistan would bring up in radically new terms the issue of that country's possession of nuclear weapons. In Saudi Arabia, control of Saudi oil by Islamists would lead to international instability. If a North African country went Islamist, the countries of Southern Europe would confront mass immigration that would have to be absorbed under conditions made all the more difficult because integration of Muslims already there has not taken place. Another major attack in Europe, which many think is inevitable in the next twenty years, would put European societies' cohesion and their ability to resist to the test and might have unforeseeable consequences for political life.[5] Use of unconventional weapons in an attack, which has been on everyone's mind since 2001, would catapult humanity into a new and terrifying world.

That brings us to our second bet for the future, the proliferation of weapons of mass destruction. Forecasts were optimistic in 1995, four years after the demise of the USSR, but that is no longer the case. After decisive successes in the first half of the 1990s, nonproliferation has suffered repeated setbacks since 1996, when negotiations on the Comprehensive Test Ban Treaty (CTBT) ended. In May and June 1998, tests in India and Pakistan demonstrated the interest of new parts of the world in nuclear weapons. One now wonders whether those tests did not primarily benefit Pakistan, whose instability is as troubling as the nuclear trafficking of the A. Q. Khan network, in which about twenty nations participated, as revealed by the inquiry into the December 2003 revelations by Libya.[6] North Korea, for its part, announced its withdrawal from the Non-Proliferation Treaty in January 2003 without any response whatever from the Security Council, not even a presidential statement. How much plutonium has North Korea reprocessed? What stage has its enrichment program reached? Does it really have several nuclear weapons, as it claims? Nobody can provide precise answers to those questions, even after the October 2006 nuclear test. What is certain is that Pyongyang is trying to blackmail the rest of the world and that the multilateral discussions in Beijing with Russia, the United States, Japan, and the two Koreas have produced no substantial progress so far.

As for Iranian nuclear development, after concealing for nearly twenty years an enrichment program begun in 1985, in the midst of the war with Iraq, Iran was obliged to acknowledge numerous clandestine activities whose military purpose can hardly be doubted. By 2006, European intervention, greeted with praise when it started in 2003, seemed essentially to have allowed Tehran to gain time rather than putting the program on hold for good. Iran refuses to stop its enrichment and reprocessing activities in return for the provision of nuclear fuel by foreign suppliers. Russia, which is building the only nuclear power plant on Iranian soil, has guaranteed the fuel supply for the next ten years, but still Tehran wants to maintain its own enrichment capacity. Iran acquiesced to a suspension of nuclear-related activities in a November 2004 agreement, but even before the election of an ultraconservative to the Iranian presidency in June 2005, the Europeans knew there was a serious risk that Tehran would start up again. That indeed happened in August 2005 and submission of the case to the Security Council took place in February 2006. The important question now is whether proceedings in Vienna and New York will move more rapidly than Iran's nuclear program, and whether known—and possible unknown—installations will finally be able to build a bomb. Europe, along with the rest of the world, has every interest in seeing the Security Council succeed, but such success is increasingly doubtful.

One of the new elements in the last twenty years has been the increasing sophistication of proliferating countries' strategies in their acquisition networks, as well as their skill at concealment.[7] After overestimating Iraqi capacities, the international community runs the risk of underestimating developments in Iran, North Korea, and even Syria and Egypt.[8]

The principal problems that will likely have to be confronted twenty years from now are clear: Will North Korea and Iran have nuclear weapons and delivery systems? How will Israel and the Arab countries react? What will Japan and Taiwan do in East Asia? Will the reunification of the Korean peninsula confirm the new situation that this will create? How will China use this card in its relations with Washington? The answers to these questions may mean the difference between war and peace. The appeal of nuclear weapons has increased rather than diminished. After seeing nuclear weapons withdraw from center stage after the end of the Cold War, we have since the mid-1990s witnessed their return to prominence. In 2025, both the Middle East and East Asia may be heavily nuclearized regions. In both cases, deterrence might be problematic because the number and the diversity of participants will considerably complicate its operations. International treaties do not function as they should, because enforcement mechanisms are too weak and the Security Council does not play its role in cases of noncompliance. The permanent members still hold different positions, have different interests, and pursue different strategies, despite growing dangers. Sensitive materials and technology circulate more easily around the world thanks to globalization and to corruption, as demonstrated by

A. Q. Khan's clandestine network. Last but not least, delivery systems are not subject to adequate controls, and manufacturers of cruise missiles refuse to accept the restrictions that should be imposed on them.

However, the situation in 2025 will be very different if the Nuclear Non-Proliferation Treaty has imploded after further withdrawals; if a nuclear, chemical, or biological weapon has been used in a conflict; or if open hostilities have been declared between two major powers who are permanent members of the Security Council.

Along with terrorism and proliferation, the likely third bet for international security in 2025 concerns the evolution of Chinese-American relations. In the next twenty years China may experience a peaceful transition to democracy, a military coup d'état, or a war with Taiwan. It may also sink into chaos. All these possibilities exist in theory, and the question is which one the Western countries want to favor. To answer, we would first have to be persuaded of the importance of the stakes, a conviction absent from Europe today, whereas the United States is beginning to understand that China is the true strategic issue of the twenty-first century. China needs twenty years to modernize its army. After that, Chinese regional ambitions can come out in the open and it will be too late to block them. By then, Beijing may have won its bet that it could achieve the status of a great power, and we will have a less romantic view of multipolarity. China is interested in Europe only as a supplier of advanced technology or as a political alternative to the United States, a role in which France excels. And Beijing, unlike Moscow, does not even trouble to express superficial admiration for the European model.[9]

Unlike today's Europe, China will not be satisfied with a regional role. It has been preparing for years to replace the Soviet Union in the role of superpower confronting the United States, and it has devoted a great deal of determination and intelligence to the enterprise. If in 2025 the world is looking at an authoritarian China that is prosperous and enjoys the benefits of thirty years of ten percent annual military budget increases—economic growth having enabled the financing of the army's modernization—it will be impossible to exercise any influence over the country. The problems that it then poses will not be limited to Taiwan and Japan—which would have been enough to cause disquiet. China is building bases all along the route connecting it to the Middle East and has the ambition of developing a navy worthy of the name in the Pacific Ocean. It would then find itself facing the American Seventh Fleet, the most powerful naval force in the world today. But the technological superiority of the United States, which may still hold twenty years from now, will in no way guarantee a systematic advantage in the face of a well prepared and extremely determined opponent that has studied in great detail the wars the United States has waged since 1991. One of the problems that will have to be faced in the Pacific is the future of the island of Guam, lying very close to China, whose potential use in case of a conflict with Taiwan cannot have escaped Beijing. Even with the most favorable outcome, there is thus the risk in twenty years of a Cold War situation between the two countries, with regular incidents—especially dangerous in a general climate of tension—like that in the spring of 2001, when an American Navy EP-3 surveillance aircraft was forced to land in China, although it had been patrolling in international airspace.

If Europeans want to prevent the most dangerous episodes, we must begin by identifying possible developments and thus cultivating an awareness of what is at stake. That is the only way to ensure that the Chinese question finally will be taken seriously in European capitals, and the only thing that will make it possible to define a strategy to counter Beijing and prevent unpleasant strategic surprises in the region and widespread negative effects beyond it. We may dream of the gradual birth of a pluralistic China that has undertaken political reforms and will take into account its regional and global responsibilities instead of thinking solely about the growth of its own power. But that is not the reading suggested by the year 2005, and realism leads us instead to acknowledge the strength in China of nationalism, the only force holding its people together and the only authorized public passion. Europe knows this passion from experience and probably cannot do much to control it, but is not obliged to encourage it, or worse, to supply the military means for its expression. China is today, and will be for many years to come, an importer of advanced technology. That is a lever that ought to be used.

In Europe, war was an undertaking that still had some nobility until the First World War. That conflict delegitimized it. The Second World War continued and strengthened that trend, as did the fear of nuclear annihilation during the Cold War. That was, however, a three-stage crisis whose lessons are specific to the West. International studies, as a distinct intellectual discipline, came out of that experience and is generally aimed at preventing a reprise of the catastrophes of the past. This is why modern political science devotes so much effort to conflict prevention. But such reflections are at best uncertain in a large part of Asia. And as Clausewitz reminds us, "you can do everything with bayonets, except sit on them for any length of time." The impressive modernization of the Chinese army reminds us of that more forcefully every year.

CHAPTER 11

Open Questions

History is an ever-living, ever-working
Chaos of Being, wherein shape after shape
bodies itself forth from innumerable elements.

—Thomas Carlyle

Mastery of Technology Development

The fear that technological developments could escape from human control goes back to the early nineteenth century. With dependence on technology constantly growing, however, and with the number of technologies increasing at a pace no one can keep up with, the twenty-first century is particularly vulnerable. From this point of view, the century began in 1986 with the explosion of reactor number 4 at Chernobyl. Moscow's first concern was to attribute the accident to human error and to protect Russian reactor technology, in line with the Soviet tradition that gave machines primacy over men. But the flaws in RBMK reactors, particularly the lack of a containment shell, were quickly recognized. The accident, due to the conjunction of a series of human errors and a very dangerous technology, served as a warning well beyond the borders of what was then still the Soviet Union, and has lingered in people's minds. It cropped up again in 2005 with the recurrence of the debate about the French government's clumsy handling of the information at the time.

The most recent fears concern the dangers of biotechnology, a field that often seems to be populated by sorcerers' apprentices. As an example, an Australian team conducting research on smallpox managed in 2003 to accidentally destroy the immune systems of all the mice involved in an experiment. One may imagine the consequences if the manipulation were applied to human beings. Among the difficulties one comes up against in biotechnology is the inability of governments and officials to follow current developments, which are too numerous and too complex. It is thus up to representatives from industry and science to establish codes of conduct that create conditions for research and testing secure enough to prevent serious accidents.

Another field that raises the specter of ungovernable technology is the weaponization of space, which many say is inevitable in the twenty-first century. During the Cold War, space was a transit zone for ballistic missiles, or an area for observation and surveillance to ensure compliance with arms limitation treaties. In the 1990s—as the first Gulf War showed—it was transformed into a force multiplier for military operations. Since then, in a few short years, space has become necessary for the functioning of the American armed forces and a catalyst for military strategy of the future. Hence the strong temptation to perfect weapons that could destroy the satellites with remarkable civilian and military uses that the other side has in store. The way in which the proliferating objects in space, which is already crowded, could be disrupted by anti-satellite weapons, or even by the positioning in space of weapons designed for attack on earth, has not been sufficiently evaluated. But considering the dependence of contemporary societies on space for many civilian functions, such as telecommunications, any development, especially any deployment of space weapons, would create both security problems and the threat of social disorganization in case of a conflict. In any event, there is no doubt that in 2025 biotechnology and space technology could cause major disturbances if their development is not mastered.

Non-Conventional Terrorism

The chances of a non-conventional terrorist attack in the next twenty years are real, for three reasons. First, attempts have already been made, and some have even succeeded in killing people (the March 1995 sarin gas attack in Tokyo, and the October and November 2001 anthrax attacks in the United States). Second, the interest of new groups or networks in acquiring non-conventional weapons is established—Osama bin Laden has gone so far as to speak of a *duty* to acquire and use them. Finally, the technical barriers preventing the production of weapons usable by non-state groups are diminishing. And the presence in laboratories of agents working for terrorist networks is a problem difficult to counter. Even in a country like Switzerland, where one would not expect non-conventional terrorism, customs inspectors in 2004 found in the trunk of a car stopped at the border for routine inspection detonators and a GPS device containing the coordinates of a nuclear research reactor. One may well imagine that this stoked the anxieties of those in the Swiss capital who were already afraid the country would become a target because of the weakness of national and cantonal anti-terrorist measures. Several European countries, including Great Britain and France, have conducted exercises simulating this kind of WMD attack and practicing responses to it, showing that political authorities are not unaware of the probability that one may occur.

What is at issue is not a reprise of the Aum Shinrikyo sect's attack in Tokyo, which caused eleven deaths in 1995, or of the attacks with letters containing anthrax that caused five deaths in the United States in 2001, but a non-conventional attack of great magnitude in which the deaths might be counted in the hundreds or the thousands. For this order of magnitude, chemical weapons have little credibility. But biological or nuclear terrorism, in "good" conditions, could create countless victims. Biosecurity, efficient detectors, keeping laboratories and scientists informed, and the creation of antidotes and new vaccines have thus become indispensable components of defense policy. The United States spends millions of dollars on the Bioshield program, and the European Union is encouraging research teams to consider scenarios and countermeasures. Martin Rees, one of the first astrophysicists to postulate that the energy of quasars comes from giant black holes located at the core of distant galaxies, has bet one thousand dollars that between now and 2020 a bio-error or bio-terror will kill a million people. The possibilities are countless. Apart from deliberate biological terrorist attacks, a laboratory might commit a disastrous mistake in handling and allow viruses or bacteria to escape into the atmosphere (as happened in Sverdlovsk in the USSR in 1979). The current fashion for spreading computer viruses might also be transformed tomorrow to produce very real viruses.

In the nuclear realm, a 2004 exercise simulating a terrorist nuclear attack on NATO headquarters in Mons, Belgium, provoked little comment. Yet unlike other scenarios, that one did not involve a radiological weapon combining nuclear material with conventional explosives but a true nuclear weapon causing a million deaths on the very first day of the attack. The mere fact that such scenarios are now considered gives us an idea, if not of the impending threats for the next few decades, at least of the ones that are already present in people's minds.

The Consequences of the Disintegration of Africa

In the 1990s, there was much talk of the rebirth of Africa. No longer. Today's scenarios are either somber or totally despairing. There was no increase in per capita income in sub-Saharan Africa between 1975 and 2000. Thirty million Africans have AIDS, and many among the urban elite have been infected and are HIV-positive. More than 6 million Africans have died in the wars that have ravaged the continent in recent years and are still going on. Between 1970 and 1989, 72 percent of the continent's rulers were driven from power in violent circumstances. Apart from South Africa (although criminality there is at a record level), all the model countries have collapsed, one by one. Events in Côte d'Ivoire in 2004 may have marked a psychological watershed in West Africa and possibly throughout the continent. The head of the Institute of Global Cultural Studies at New York University predicts very significant changes in the region in the twenty-first century: "The French sphere of influence will be taken over by Nigeria—a more natural hegemonic power . . . Nigeria's borders will probably be expanded to incorporate Niger, Benin, and perhaps Cameroon." Should such a role fall to Nigeria, it would have little other than its size to back it up.

That judgment may be extreme, but it has the virtue of stimulating thought about a possible redrawing of the African map to reflect the ambitions of some and the weaknesses of others. Africa as a whole has an enormous need for targeted investments subject to oversight and for educational and health infrastructure. It also needs competent peacekeeping forces, as demonstrated by the inability of the African Union to play its proclaimed role in Sudan. The industrialized countries in the Group of Eight (G8) plan to train 75,000 men for operations on the continent. In countries like Mozambique and Namibia, only the presence of peacekeeping forces has made possible a return to normal conditions. Thanks to them, the massacres perpetrated in Liberia[1] and Sierra Leone were halted, but troops must remain in place to guarantee a fragile and still entirely relative stability. In cases like Somalia, the situation has deteriorated to the point that the country no longer has a government. The UN still has around

50,000 troops in Africa, and they are unable to deal with the proliferation and the increasing complexity of the operations they are called on to perform.

Political developments in the unhappy continent have had disastrous consequences for the people there. The risk of Africa's collapse under the weight of poverty, corruption, disease, and the ineptitude of most existing governments is only too well known. It is difficult, too, to see as a purely internal problem: aside from the humanitarian aspect and the *duty to protect* invoked in reports and speeches, the almost inevitable exploitation in crisis situations of poverty-stricken populations and the general chaos could have repercussions that cross borders and reach all the way to Europe. Rather than congratulating the victor in rigged elections in Togo, as Paris did in May 2005, when pictures were available of army troops carrying off ballot boxes, it would be wise to set up a program for oversight of methods of government and for the exercise of power in a continent in which Europeans have so many responsibilities to assume and security interests to defend. A new set of difficulties is now arising with China's burgeoning influence in Africa and the way Beijing is legitimizing and encouraging Africa's most repressive regimes. A telling example is provided by Sudan. But Angola is also an interesting case. In 2005, IMF officials believed they had got a landmark financing agreement with Luanda, according to which IMF loans would be linked to intense monitoring. But the Angolan government announced instead it would receive loans and credits for oil reconstruction from China, with none of the IMF's conditions.

A Proliferation of Nuclear Powers in the Middle East

A Middle East with four or five nuclear powers in 2025 is a real possibility, not a mere unpleasant fiction. In November 2006, a statement by a senior official of the IAEA indicated that six Arab states have shown interest in developing nuclear power. While energy may be the primary motivation for such renewed interest, building up a nuclear infrastructure can also serve as part of a hedging strategy. Far from fostering deterrence and helping to maintain the status quo, nuclear proliferation in the region would relaunch a cycle of suspicion, passion, and competition whose implications are difficult to gauge. There is every likelihood that the relations of the regional powers would deteriorate; nuclear deterrence in this context would be at best extremely unstable; American forces in the region would become more vulnerable; and even the security of European nations would be disrupted in light of the range of the ballistic missiles and aircraft available in the region; finally, the proliferation of nuclear powers in the Middle East would sooner or later lead to an existential risk for Israel. Taking into account the concentration of its population on a very narrow strip of coastline, Israel would be very vulnerable to any nuclear strike. As former Iranian president Hashemi Rafsanjani famously remarked: "The use of even one nuclear bomb inside Israel will destroy everything."

The most pressing suspicions of a military nuclear program have fallen precisely on Iran, and are based on eighteen years of concealment, multiple purchases or attempted purchases that cannot be explained by a civilian program, and an absurd gap between the Iranian nuclear-powered electricity program, which is supplied with Russian fuel, and significant indigenous ambitions in the area of enrichment. On top of all that came the belated acknowledgement, in March 2004, that Iran had acquired the design of a high-performing type of centrifuge, the so-called P2, from the A. Q. Khan network. Finally, a Pakistani offer made to Iran in 1987 and only discovered in 2005 might have included a weapon design. Right now, Iran may lack only fissile materials necessary to acquire a nuclear weapon. In such circumstances, the probable existence of clandestine sites with undeclared equipment—or even nuclear material—that has not been identified by intelligence services makes it difficult to evaluate the real progress that has been made by the Iranian nuclear military program. The Iranians have already demonstrated the ability to conceal large nuclear facilities for a long time. Tehran is trying to play a clever game to continue to gain time, but it might fall victim to its own devices, since its activities have become a matter of concern for the Europeans, the Americans, and the many countries of the region.

The last group, particularly the Gulf States and Egypt, where fear of Iranian hegemony is real, would be as disturbed as Israel to see an Iranian bomb, particularly in a regional context in which Shiism is advancing and a new generation of ultraconservatives has come to power in Teheran. The only difference is that Tel Aviv says so openly, whereas Riyadh and Cairo speak in more veiled terms. Iranian missiles can already hit targets anywhere in the Middle East, giving leaders food for thought in more than one capital. Relations between Pakistan and Saudi Arabia, which are close and likely to endure, suggest the possibility of cooperation with Islamabad, possibly leading to Saudi acquisition of nuclear weapons. As for Cairo, its claim not to have known of Libyan activities for twenty years is hardly credible, and the nuclear ambitions of the Nasser era might also resurface. In those circumstances, what would Turkey do, particularly in a context in which Turkish nationalism is growing? A Middle East evolving in that direction would soon escape the reach of any possibility of prediction or control. The efforts under way to stop the Iranian nuclear program have therefore profound strategic implications: nuclear weapons would enable the Iranian regime to act in a still more reckless fashion than it does now. And more generally, one can make the argument that Iran embodies the strategic realities of the post–Cold War world. The Middle East is one of the areas for which the telescope should indeed be pointed toward the future. Nor must we leave out of the picture the relations of many Middle Eastern countries with North Korea or the possible future alliance between Iran and China, two countries that maintain close ties in areas not limited to oil.

Israel and Palestine

In 2005, one could have contemplated the resumption of negotiations after the Israeli withdrawal from Gaza and four settlements in the northern West Bank. A viable Palestinian state—in terms of both borders and institutions—also could have been envisioned within the next years. The death of the Palestinian leader Yasser Arafat made resumption of the peace process possible, with a cease-fire in February 2005 and almost immediate reinvestment on the part of Washington, which again declared support for the Road Map adopted by the Quartet (the United States, Russia, the EU, and the UN). But nothing guaranteed that violence in Gaza would be controlled after the Israeli withdrawal, and it was not. Nor was there any assurance that the Israeli government intended to pursue the process after that difficult step. To be sure, the January 2005 elections enabled Palestinians for the first time to freely choose their president,[2] and Mahmoud Abbas set a new regional dynamic in motion by resuming dialogue with Israeli Prime Minister Ariel Sharon, taking clear positions on an end to violence, and involving the Jordanians and Egyptians. But the new president's authority was weak, radical elements have not been brought under control, and Sharon disappeared from the political scene at a crucial moment.

The real test took place after the disengagement from Gaza, welcomed by the Security Council in August 2005. Violence in Gaza and a large-scale operation in Lebanon in July 2006 introduced a new linkage between the Palestinian question, Iran, and the fate of the radical Lebanese Shiite organization Hizbollah, with its leader, Hassan Nasrallah, becoming increasingly popular in the Palestinian territories and in the Muslim world. On the Israeli side, neutralizing Syrian and Iranian bilateral ties and their involvement in Lebanon became a major objective, but difficult to reach. Many observers agree that the 2006 conflict might be a turning point—but in which direction, exactly? The regional strategic scene, already troubled and troubling, is becoming more complex, with an ever wider range of actors, both governments and non-state actors. The chance of seeing two states side by side in the coming years still exists, and should remain a goal for all concerned. In the absence of that goal, it is difficult to imagine a situation in which violence and terrorism would not continue to assume troubling proportions for which the two parties pay the price. Recent events, however, are anything but encouraging, and past experience also justifies caution, because the unresolved questions—Jerusalem, refugees, settlements—are essentially the same as in 1948.

There were two main new factors in 2006. First, the different regional issues are becoming increasingly interconnected and are clearly beginning to play off each other, making it ever more difficult to control events or prevent bad surprises. Second, for the very first time since 1948—with the possible exception of 1973—Israel did not emerge from a conflict unques-tionably victorious. On the contrary, Hizbollah, Syria, and Iran have all claimed to have won the 2006 fighting in Lebanon. The propaganda dimension notwithstanding, Israel's deterrence has been weakened and the conflict in Lebanon may well be the first act of a more serious confronta-tion in the years to come, especially if Hizbollah succeeds in overthrowing the Siniora government and increasing its own power in the country.

Turkey and Europe

In twenty years, the negotiations with Turkey that began in the fall of 2005 should be completed and the ratification process will determine the country's entry into the European Union. The worst outcome would be that after such lengthy negotiations—assuming they are successful—popu-lar referendums or parliamentary ratification votes end in rejection. Such a

rejection could potentially result in extremely violent anti-Western demonstrations in Turkey, of which we already had a taste in 2005. But rejection is not an unrealistic prospect, and even seems implicit since neither
the people of the EU member states, nor the European Parliament that is
supposed to represent them, has never been consulted on the commitments that the EU has made to Ankara over the past forty years. Because
the questions that Turkey raises for Europe concern its identity and its
borders, they can hardly be treated lightly. On one hand, the promise
about EU membership made to Turkey dates back to 1962. The country
has been part of the Western Alliance for fifty years, and it would have
been catastrophic if it had fallen on the Soviet side during the Cold War.
These circumstances created a debt that many have forgotten. Ankara's
most important reforms—a new constitution and a new penal code—have
been undertaken in anticipation of recognition by Europe. Future reforms
will be made with the same hope. When making them, the Turks must
finally give solid guarantees for the rights of their minorities. The acknowledgment of Jalal Talabani, the Kurdish president of Iraq, that he does not
aim for an independent Kurdistan, is likely to encourage the Turkish government to recognize the rights of Kurds in Turkey. Finally, a moderate,
secular, pro-Western, dynamic Turkey would also be an important symbol
for the Muslim world.

Those are weighty arguments. But even Europeans in favor of Turkish
entry into Europe recognize that since Brussels approved the start of negotiations in December 2004, Ankara's efforts in the direction desired by
Europe have some disturbing weaknesses. In March 2005 police in Istan-
bul harshly repressed a march for women's rights and hard-line official
statements on the Cyprus question were made. More recently, the head of
the Turkish human rights presidential advisory board and five other board
members resigned, criticizing the government. Finally, to our consterna-
tion, we learned that one of the best-selling books in Turkey in 2005 was
Mein Kampf. On the European side, two elements seem hardly open to
challenge. First, the "Turkish question" shows that we Europeans hardly
know any longer what we have become: are we a territory defined by history and geography or an area of democratic peace that applies criteria
established in Copenhagen for accession to the EU? Second, it is dangerous to undertake bilateral negotiations that might eventually end in a
rejection by national parliaments or, even worse, by referendums.[3] The

Turks will feel betrayed and angry at the Europeans for refusing to accept the political responsibilities the situation requires. With this blind rush forward on a path that has been deliberately chosen, we are laying the groundwork for a major crisis in twenty years. Here, the constructive ambiguity of the EU may well show its limitations. As of December 2006, negotiations are partially suspended between the EU and Turkey (on eight of thirty-five policy chapters), because no agreement has been reached on Cyprus.

The End of Pakistan?

The nature of the strategic problem posed by Pakistan has changed since Islamabad conducted nuclear tests in 1998 and the importance of radical Islamism in the country has come to light, this at a time of renewed Pakistani support to militancy and new waves of infiltration into Kashmir. In addition, in 2004 the Pakistani authorities were obliged to acknowledge the existence of a vast clandestine nuclear network led by the so-called "father" of the Pakistani bomb, A. Q. Khan. Under these troubling conditions, questions have been raised about the potential disintegration of the country in the next two decades and the consequences that event might have for the security of the region—and beyond. Most experts now believe that power is still firmly in the hands of the army, that the so-called "Islamist peril" remains a myth, and that in the worst-case scenario, the assassination of President Pervez Musharraf, a successor would be found within the military. The possibility, however, cannot be ruled out that, with the constant progression of radicals in the provinces, one day the Faustian pact that Musharraf's government—and his predecessors—made with the Islamists will backfire. That will be more likely if Islamabad continues disruptive interference in the provinces, particularly in Balochistan,[4] where the autonomist leader Akbar Bugti was killed by the Pakistani army in August, 2006, and proves unable to settle the Kashmir question, over which relations with India remain what they have always been, a mixture of tension and abortive dialogue. In Balochistan, attacks by Pakistani forces have been constant since 2004, and the port of Gwadar, under construction by China to ensure its navy's access to the Persian Gulf, is a subject of deep discontent because the local population in no way benefits from the project. On the question of Kashmir, the peace process between India and Pakistan is fragile and no major breakthrough has been achieved so far.

Some observers predict that it will be at best a cold peace between the status quo power, India, and the revisionist one, Pakistan. For that reason, violent Islamist demonstrations may break out in the coming years in the large Pakistani cities of Lahore, Karachi, and Rawalpindi, and the government may have to confront a division in the army between loyalist forces and forces won over by the Islamists. It is hard to imagine that India would not seek to contain a crisis of that magnitude to prevent trouble in its own territory, notably in Punjab. The disintegration of Pakistan is far from certain and remains improbable, but if it happens, it could lead to a major conflict.

A War between China and Taiwan

The wars in the Balkans, Afghanistan, and Iraq give no idea of how a confrontation between China and the United States over Taiwan might look. By 2025, hostilities may already have broken out, to the surprise of the Europeans, who do not even want to consider the possibility. In their opinion, economic relations between China and Taiwan make such a conflict improbable, as though the economic interdependence of European countries had succeeded in preventing the two world wars of the twentieth century. The question of the involvement of Europe in East Asia over Taiwan is not new. Five years after the end of the Korean War in 1958, there was a serious dispute between Communist China and Taiwan over the offshore islands of Quemoy and Matsu. Churchill warned Eisenhower that "an open war to enable Chiang to keep the islands might not find support" in Great Britain. There was fear of an American intervention in Asia, which would again plunge the world into war. This episode played a role in the British decision to acquire the H-bomb, which was intended to increase London's influence over Washington and dissuade it from embarking on dangerous adventures.

But circumstances have changed a good deal. The legitimacy of Taiwan has made progress—even if diplomatic recognition is very limited—and the Taiwanese are not in favor of reunification for both economic and political reasons. Per capita income in Taiwan is four times that in continental China, while China's population is seventy times that of Taiwan, and democracy has become well established on the island. Economic disparity and political opposition are serious obstacles to unification. That prospect is unacceptable for Beijing and the risk of conflict remains very real. Since the 1990s the policies of the three major players (Taiwan, China, and the United States) have become unstable in many ways. The possibility of a miscalculation by any participant with respect to the two others is quite high. China thinks that Washington will not sacrifice Los Angeles for Taiwan, the United States that Beijing will not sacrifice twenty or thirty years of development for Taipei, and Taiwan that it can confront Beijing with a fait accompli and not suffer the consequences. Those are three dangerous mistakes. If a conflict occurs over Taiwan, what the United States' allies, particularly in Europe, will do is a profound mystery. On the other hand, the position of regional players is in the process of being clarified. Japan tightened its security links with the United States after the spring 1996 crisis in the Strait of Taiwan, and openly declared in February 2005 that it would not be inactive in the event of a conflict between China and Taiwan. It began to pay the price for that as early as April, when violent anti-Japanese demonstrations broke out in China. Russia would seek to remain neutral, even if a victory by Beijing might be the source of later problems for Moscow in eastern Siberia.

Europe cannot remain neutral—not only because the United States is an ally, but also because European economic interests and the security of the sea lanes between the Middle East and East Asia would be immediately affected by the conflict. One cannot exclude the possibility of confronting in 2025 a very heavily nuclearized region, with Japan, the two Koreas (or a reunified Korea), Indonesia, and Malaysia all possessing nuclear weapons. A conflict in that part of the world would therefore quickly take on an extremely dangerous cast, and Europeans would at the very least have to help prevent a Chinese victory and a regional conflagration. For that reason, plans of action should be worked out now with the United States, Japan, and even India. The region demonstrated its potential to become very disruptive in 1996 (Taiwan Strait crisis) and again in 1998 (Taepodong test) and again in 2005 (violent anti-Japanese demonstrations in China). If a conflict breaks out, there will be no time to improvise.

Blitzkriegs

Finishing things off quickly has always been a military ambition in view of the human and financial costs of conflict, and uncertainty about the outcome, which grows as time passes. That constant, however, has undergone important development with the introduction of advanced technology and the possibility it offers of paralyzing the enemy's nerve centers even before the enemy can seriously engage in battle. The Gulf War illustrated the revolution in military affairs: after the initial B-52 attacks in the very first minutes of the conflict on January 17, 1991, Iraq had practically no communications infrastructure left. The idea that warfare was moving toward brief conflicts soon won thanks to the control over the battlefield that the new technology made possible, developed until the second Iraq war in 2003. That contest was settled in record time, eliciting the admiration of general staffs the world over. But the reality that everyone now grasps is the difficulty of stabilizing a country in which one has defeated the army, occupied the capital within a month, overthrown the government, and imprisoned almost all its dignitaries including the president. The articles on "shock and awe" that appeared at the beginning of the war had a short shelf life. Consequently, the United States has had to set up an organization in the Pentagon to deal with the complex operations of nation building and reconstruction.

In the twenty-first century, the notion of blitzkrieg must be considered in the context of East Asia. In a conflict with Taiwan, China would find it necessary to win very quickly in order to face the rest of the world with a fait accompli, rather than having to fight Taiwan, the United States, and Japan at one time. The only war against Taiwan that Beijing can be certain of winning is a blitzkrieg. That is one reason China has devoted much more attention than the Europeans to the revolution in military affairs that has been carried out in the United States. China is in fact the only country besides Israel to have taken it so seriously. The two colonels in the People's Liberation Army who wrote *War without Limits* after the Gulf War present an original version of the revolution, and although it does not reflect official Chinese thinking, it deserves attention. The aim is to counter the sense of superiority the Americans have, based on the United States' possession of very sophisticated conventional weapons, through the use of surprising strategies for which American forces are not prepared. Those strategies might combine advanced technology, rudimentary methods, unconventional weapons, and terrorism. In the mind of the book's authors, such warfare—the first rule of which is the absence of rules—would disorganize the American war machine and quickly reduce it to helplessness. The book, which sold well in China, primarily expresses Chinese impatience and makes the same mistake for which the Chinese criticize the

Americans: it advocates rapid and decisive operations, whereas the numerous variables in play ought rather to lead strategists to consider a long, terrible, and ultimately worldwide war.

The Coexistence of the Great Powers

For a very long time, Europe has taken from the image of the weighing of souls[5] the idea of a balance of power that would guarantee that, with no one nation enjoying a decisive advantage over the others, peace will be maintained. Peaceful coexistence, however, was not a success in Europe, where a major conflict broke out in each generation beginning in the seventeenth century. After two devastating world wars, the Europeans, recognizing their common interest in avoiding the total destruction that a new war could not fail to bring about, tried a radically different formula for relations among Europe's national components: the community, followed by the union. Speaking of multipolarity in the twenty-first century thus means forgetting the European experience in which the balance of power consistently failed and collapsed into war. The problem of peaceful coexistence arises primarily between the United States and China. Current prospects are rather dark in view of the Taiwan question. The U.S. administration believes that the policy of ambiguity is too dangerous to be continued and that it is necessary to make clear to Beijing and Taipei the redlines that cannot be crossed. The evolution of Western relations with Russia is another important unknown, because the current Russian government is traveling down a dead-end path but still has significant capacity to cause harm.

The twenty-first century will also see the appearance of new powers, like India, and we will have to consider how that country will manage its relations with China. During the Cold War, the close relations between the USSR and India depended a good deal, as Nehru himself acknowledged, on having China as a common adversary. In the last few years, following a stormy passage provoked by the Indian nuclear tests in 1998, China and India have sought closer relations by making modest advances on border questions. We can, however, expect a resumption of tension after 2008, if Chinese economic growth slows from that point on, with the social consequences that one can imagine. Bilateral problems in Ladakh, Arunachal Pradesh, or concerning Tibet cannot be ruled out. What the result might be for relations between the two most populous countries on the planet is still impossible to say, but a confrontation sooner or later seems probable. One projection for the year 2025 might envisage an economically and socially weakened China set against an India much more self-confident than it is today. Incidents between the two navies in the Bay of Bengal or fierce competition for energy resources might act as a trigger. Chinese nationalism has already reached such proportions that the Beijing government may be placed in an impossible position the day the Chinese people discover that India is beginning to emerge and that it has acquired the means to decimate the Chinese fleet beyond the Strait of Malacca. As for India, it is interesting to note that the most recent Indian works of history alter the image of Gandhi, no longer hailing him as the apostle of nonviolence. [6]

The Century of Fear?

In the early twenty-first century, we have witnessed the return of the great fears of the Middle Ages: natural catastrophes and major pandemics. The year 2005 began with the aftermath of one of the most violent tsunamis ever recorded, causing more than 300,000 deaths. The aid effort used significant military means, on the largest scale in history. At the end of summer, as though in counterpoint, the world's sole superpower was hit by a hurricane of exceptional strength, swamping New Orleans and striking a large number of victims, especially among African Americans. Emotions ran particularly high because, unlike during the heat wave that caused 15,000 deaths in France in 2003, television cameras were on the scene to record unbearable images. A large number of natural disasters are predicted in the next few decades because of climate changes that are still poorly understood. Those changes, unevenly distributed over the surface of the planet, will probably primarily affect developing countries.

As for the return of major epidemics, medical research organizations have issued warnings for more than a decade, but the shock caused by severe acute respiratory syndrome (SARS), which broke out in 2003, gave the subject concrete reality in the public mind. With contemporary international travel, the most spectacular aspect of that outbreak was its rapid spread worldwide, from China to Canada. Since the nineteenth century, it had been hoped that science would finally triumph over major epidemics. For the last ten years a new human disease has appeared almost every year, combined with the return of diseases believed to have been eradicated.

The continent most affected is Africa, whose population, armies, and police forces have been decimated by AIDS and malaria. In 2005, an epidemic of the Marburg virus, one of the most terrifying hemorrhagic fevers, killed hundreds of people in Angola.

Finally, technological advances in the realms of biology and computer science have opened up many new prospects for military applications, the discovery of the human genome being the most troubling example. And this has happened at a time when the possibility of a deliberate use of a biological weapon has increased.

Will the twenty-first century be the century of fear?

PART FOUR

BACK IN 2005

In politics, what is often most difficult to evaluate and understand is what is going on before our eyes.

—ALEXIS DE TOCQUEVILLE

CHAPTER 12

THE SCENE
IN 2005

Well? What are you going to do?
What are you going to do TODAY?

—PAUL VALÉRY

The centennial of the omen-filled year of 1905 offered an opportunity to step outside immediate circumstances to identify some major tendencies at work in the course of events. The period that for fifteen years has lazily been designated *post–Cold War*, for lack of a better term, is now over, and a name will one day have to be found for its successor. Because the date of birth of the new period has been set at September 11, 2001, one of its principal components could well be a spectacular return of violence, now that it is within the power not only of states but of small groups and even individuals to inflict serious damage. As Europe directly experienced the blind violence of international terrorism on March 11, 2004, in Madrid and July 7, 2005, in London, it no longer has any doubts about the threat it represents, including on its own territory. The times also offer an opportunity to broaden strategic vision to encompass East Asia, where there has been a troubling increase in regional tensions and a reawakening of memories of the Second World War all the more dangerous because that conflict is not yet over in that part of the world. In early 2005, however, the headlines were about neither terrorism nor regional tensions but the blows struck against authoritarian regimes in Eastern Europe, Central Asia, and the Middle East. Those were inflicted not by violent means but in a series of peaceful revolutions carried out by hundreds of thousands of individuals in the name of the fight against corruption and for freedom. In several senses, those actions were the exact opposite of the attacks of September 11, 2001. But unfortunately, few of them kept their promises even a year later, in 2006.

Within that general picture, the suddenness and the magnitude of the changes under way in Eastern Europe, the Middle East, Central Asia, and East Asia present a striking contrast to the lethargy of Western Europe, where the "pause" seems dangerously close to paralysis. It is as though the transformations the world is experiencing did not concern it. Has Europe abandoned the age-old curiosity about other regions of the planet that contributed so much to its greatness? Has it lost the sense of the appeal of freedom and democratic values of which it was the birthplace? After centuries of engaging in internal strife, the finally united nations of Europe do not seem to delight in the historic opportunity that has been offered them with no bloodshed. They do not seem to understand that the results of fifty years of constant effort may disappear, and they show little inclination to surmount their navel-gazing crisis. That myopia has already had consequences. No one claims to belong to Europe anymore, although it was Europe that created freedom as a political category, helped shape the world, and demonstrated throughout the centuries a remarkable understanding of the most distant civilizations.

It is easier to measure the scope than the real substance of the seemingly positive changes in progress, and all those movements may turn out to be flashes in the pan. Some of them, however, have confirmed an evolutionary arc that began three years ago in the former Soviet republics with Georgia's "Rose Revolution" of November 2003 and continued the next fall with Ukraine's "Orange Revolution." Following their example of peaceful popular protest against corrupt regimes, Kyrgyzstan overthrew its president in a matter of hours on March 24, 2005. Thousands of demonstrators occupied the presidential palace in Bishkek, prompting the flight to Russia of the head of state, Askar Akayev, who had ruled the country since 1990. Many of the friends of Vladimir Putin in neighboring former republics have packed their bags. Russian policy, which amounted to supporting corrupt, authoritarian politicians, has suffered failures, and unrepentantly authoritarian Uzbekistan is faint consolation. Conversely, the policy of the United States, which has not merely made speeches about freedom and democracy but has deliberately fostered the growth of many nongovernmental organizations in the countries bordering Russia[1] has been a success, however fragile and temporary it may prove to be.

In the Middle East, with the exception of Iran, where the optimistic predictions of Westerners were disappointed once again as they have been for twenty-five years, changes in the atmosphere began to be introduced in 2005. But a year later, after the electoral victory of Hamas in the Palestinian territories and the Israeli-Hizbollah fighting in Lebanon, there were reasons to be pessimistic about the durability of those changes. The election in January 2005 of a new Palestinian president, Mahmoud Abbas, made possible a resumption of the dialogue with Israel, and elections in Iraq that December demonstrated the will of the majority of Iraqis to prevail over the defenders of the old regime and the ethnic minority that had confiscated power and abused it for decades. Then, rather than a question posed to George Bush, Iraq for many seemed to turn into a power struggle between supporters of a multiethnic regime and insurgents seeking the impossible restoration of the power of a minority who, as a result, were no longer considered members of a "resistance." The outcome of that combat will depend on the solidity of the alliance between Kurds and Shiites, the continuation of the political process, and the stopping of the violence. Unfortunately, 2006 brought very bad news on the last front and was a major reason for the Republican Party's defeat in the mid-term elections.

When Syria was forced to withdraw its troops from Lebanon after making two fatal mistakes—changing the constitution in the fall of 2004 to keep their man in power in Beirut, and murdering opposition leader Rafik Hariri in February 2005—the pullout was considered a major success, and it was. After massive popular demonstrations by Lebanese citizens, and in the face of domestic, regional, and international pressure, Damascus complied with Security Council Resolution 1559 on withdrawal. Genuine elections took place in June 2005, confirming the victory of the anti-Syrian opposition. But in the summer of 2006, fighting in Lebanon allowed Syria and Iran to somehow reverse that victory and distract international attention from the Iranian nuclear issue.

Also in 2005, municipal elections were finally held in Saudi Arabia for the first time in the history of the kingdom.[2] And in Egypt, before his re-election to a fifth term, President Hosni Mubarak put through a constitutional reform instituting universal suffrage for the September 2005 elections, whereas in previous balloting he had been the sole candidate in a plebiscite.[3] The people of the corrupt police state of Egypt long for higher ethical standards in public life and their own greater integration into politics. Even if the reform is a superficial concession to the United States, it will be difficult to move backward now that a political opening has begun. Europe should participate more actively in the changes occurring in the region, which are fragile and in need of consolidation, by encouraging the redistribution of resources to support education, health, and employment for the population as a whole.

East Asia in 2005 was the region of the world from which the most troubling warnings emanated, along with the Middle East. Among them were renewed provocation from North Korea, growing anti-American feelings in South Korea, a hardening of Japanese statements on regional security, the passage by Beijing of a law authorizing the use of force against Taiwan, increased tension between China and Japan, and large-scale Russian-Chinese military maneuvers in the fall. All of those are threatening in a region in which the United States, the only real guiding force, seems not to have defined clearly its policies toward the various parties. Nor do the Americans seem to have realized that what might play itself out in the region in the twenty-first century is the belated termination of the Second World War. From that point of view, the backwardness of Asia compared with Europe is considerable: fifteen years after German reunification, we are still waiting for the reunification of Korea. One of the reasons is that there is no Gorbachev in Beijing prepared to tolerate it. The financial cost of that reunification would also be much higher than the Germans' and would risk compromising Seoul's economic success. South Korea, having made a comparative study of the subject, knows that full well.

Sixty years after the end of the war, and also unlike what happened between France and Germany, China and Japan still have not reached a reconciliation. Responsibility is no doubt shared, but the principal problem in China is certainly not Japanese school textbooks. In any contest over historical truth in textbooks, China would probably have greater difficulty supporting its positions than Japan. The atrocities committed against its own citizens in peacetime, during the Great Leap Forward and the Cultural Revolution, remain taboo in Chinese textbooks. But the way Mao facilitated the Japanese advance and never said a word about the tragedy of Nanjing is even more delicate politically. On the Japanese side, numerous apologies have been offered to the region for the atrocities committed during the Second World War, including at the Jakarta summit in April 2005 and that August at the commemoration of the end of the Second World War. We are still waiting for China to apologize to Vietnam for invading it in 1979, or to Cambodia for supporting the Khmer Rouge. What was really at stake during the patch of Sino-Japanese tension in 2005 may have been more a question of power—at a time when Tokyo was undertaking new initiatives and when its candidacy for a permanent seat on the Security Council had again come up. Finally, Taiwan has been the subject of a Chinese law justifying the use of force in circumstances that remain unclear. That may be the most dangerous strategic issue in the region, and possibly on the entire planet. Asian nations fully recognize the danger.

The importance of Asian affairs for international security—for a time obscured by the September 11 attacks and the war in Iraq—has returned in full force, and 2005 only confirmed it. Relations between Washington and Beijing will be one of the major strategic questions of the twenty-first century, along with the identity of Asia's principal regional power. Will it be India, China, or, less likely, Japan? The candidacies of Japan and India for the Security Council disturb Beijing for that very reason: it cannot accept that those two nations compare themselves to it, even symbolically. The announcement in early 2005 of a 12 percent increase in Chinese military spending should encourage thinking about the rapid modernization of the Chinese army, which began back in 1988, at about the time when China recognized that it no longer feared a major attack, as it had during the Cold War. What purpose is being served by all those military preparations? One month after the passage of the anti-secession law in Beijing, the high level of Sino-Japanese tension was a cover for fierce regional competition for energy resources. That added a troubling touch to an already gloomy picture. If history were to slip backward in the twenty-first century, East Asia would be a good candidate for the agent of that regression.

In the face of transformations that are going to decide the shape of the world in at least three regions, the European Union is bogged down in Brussels and the national capitals. With the people of the member states demonstrating little enthusiasm for their most immediate future, even those who voted in favor of the proposed EU Constitution, it can hardly be expected that they would get excited about the rest of the world. Of course, the twofold question of European borders and European identity may trouble them. The constructive ambiguity that has always guided the policies of the individual capitals and the European Commission on the question has now come up against its limitations: beyond the Turkish question, it must be clearly stated that Ukraine, Belarus, Moldova, and the Balkans may aspire to join, but not Morocco or the other nations of North Africa. Otherwise, the European project would become without definition. But Europeans are also worried about their jobs and their prosperity, and when they speak of enlargement, they emphasize its economic drawbacks—for the most fortunate—instead of grasping the historic opportunity that it offers. In a world in which their economies stand in striking contrast to the poverty and misery of others, they are unaware that the expression of those worries—seen from outside—has something indecent about it.[4]

In short, in a year that was decisive for Europe's political future, which saw the rejection of the draft constitution by French and Dutch voters, the beginning of negotiations with Turkey, a decision on the status of Kosovo, and ambiguous handling of the Ukraine question, one could see no internal dynamism and little outward generosity. Europe's plans for its nearest neighbors are muddled, and one of the messages of French voters in the May 29 referendum, even more prominent than hostility to EU enlargement, was xenophobia pure and simple. It would even be difficult to define European policy toward Russia, whose relations with the EU are considered essential. Nor can one understand why negotiations with Turkey are justified if Ukraine is turned down. Finally, five years after the Kosovo war, as the area is obviously heading toward some form of independence, there is fear of guaranteeing a situation that might anger the Russians. The Balkans cannot settle for the status quo, as the report of the Amato Commission in April 2005 showed. The entire region may plunge back into a new period of instability, or even chaos. The only solution is to open the doors of the European Union. Can that possibly be done at a moment when the European political process has stalled? Europe's affairs have for too long been the private preserve of bureaucrats. Politicians no longer have a European message for their electorates. And although the European idea still exists, it lacks strength within its own borders. In these circumstances, we should not be surprised that the voice of Europe has to struggle to make itself heard in the world.

There was another essential subject for European diplomacy in 2005: a second breakdown of the nuclear discussions with Iran, made inevitable by

the new government in Tehran.[5] The European capitals involved in negotiations with Tehran made it clear in the spring that the Iranian question
would have to be transferred to the Security Council for consideration.
The stakes are considerable for the Europeans, because an Iranian bomb
would simultaneously pose the risk of an implosion of the Nuclear Non-
Proliferation Treaty—the most important of all multilateral agreements—
and be a spur for nuclear competition in the Middle East as well as a threat
to European security. An Iranian nuclear weapon could set in motion a
fearsome arms race in a region where a regression into violence is always to
be feared, as 2006 has demonstrated. That is why the Europeans, agreeing
with the Americans on this point, have several times indicated that an
Iranian nuclear weapon is "unacceptable." Given that, what conclusions
must be drawn if the prospect of such a weapon comes closer? Contrary to
what some commentators declare, economic sanctions could be effective
against Tehran, taking into account the appalling inflation and unemployment rates in Iran and the criticism against Mahmoud Ahmadinejad's
absurd economic policy. The most effective measures would concern the
refined oil products, the much-needed investments in oil and gas infrastructure, or an oil embargo. Those are hardly attractive prospects, but a
nuclear weapon would also have an effect on oil prices, particularly if it
were followed by a Saudi weapon! In addition, beyond sanctions, there
remains little else but the use of force, or the acceptance of an Iranian
nuclear weapon, which are even less attractive options.

Even without mentioning international terrorism, although it again
cruelly struck Europe in the July 2005 attacks in London, there is therefore no lack of matters for concern. In the coming decade, the period from
2008 to 2010 merits particular attention. Russia and the United States will
both hold presidential elections in 2008. In Russia, the choice might be
between another term for Vladimir Putin—even though the Russian president has already indicated that he will not run again (he might become
prime minister with real political power); a candidate chosen by him just
as he was chosen by Boris Yeltsin; and a xenophobic nationalist candidate.
There is little likelihood in the near future of any development along liberal lines, unfortunately for chess grandmaster and presidential aspirant
Garry Kasparov and his friends. The United States will have a new president, who may confront a more dangerous situation in Asia, and probably
in the Middle East as well, a part of the world that has darkened George

W. Bush's second term. China might by then overcome its remaining inhibitions with regard to both Taiwan and Japan, after the Olympic Games and at a time when a possible slowdown in Chinese growth would pose major social and political problems. What is now in preparation would then appear in a starker light.

In that general picture, what about collective security? UN Secretary General Kofi Annan, aware of the stakes, in 2005 drew up a reform plan to bring the institution into the twenty-first century. His proposals contained important changes to the Security Council, a reform of the Human Rights Commission (which would rise in the UN hierarchy), and new criteria to govern the use of force in an increasingly violent world. But the September 2005 New York summit was badly planned and took place in the worst possible conditions. It will probably be difficult to keep an effective system of collective security alive in this century. The permanent members of the Security Council continue to set their national interests above the responsibility to work for peace and international security that justifies their privileges, notably their veto power. With the failure of the attempted reform, the ghost of the League of Nations might return to haunt us at the worst possible moment. It was in fact in the early 1930s, when the world organization was truly needed, that the League of Nations' powerlessness came to light. The same thing might happen early in the twenty-first century. The refocusing of policy on national concerns is concerted at a time when collective security has never been more necessary, considering the transnational nature of the threats. One can only regret the blindness of the United States on this question.

Finally, the year 2005 vividly demonstrated the importance of memory in the historical process. Beginning in January, a series of commemorations of the end of the Second World War took place at the sites of concentration camps, as though to force Europeans to relive the violent episodes in which their predecessors had been perpetrators and victims. In May, the celebration of the end of the Second World War in Moscow was the occasion for a painful polemic in the Baltic countries, which experienced frightful tyranny rather than liberation after 1945. A month later, the commemoration of the entry of Pol Pot's troops into Phnom Penh reminded the world of the advent of one of the most terrible dictatorships of the past century, which exterminated one-third of the Cambodian population between 1975 and 1979, to general indifference. Thirty years after the genocide, formal judgment has become possible, and many think it is indispensable for Cambodia.[6] In the Middle East, the Armenian genocide of almost a hundred years ago was once again brought up in Turkey, where authorities attempted to stifle the demand for acknowledgment with the creation of an investigative commission. In Lebanon, the Syrians' departure was the occasion for an unprecedented mobilization to discover the fates of the unknown number of Lebanese and stateless Palestinians who were imprisoned or disappeared in Syria over the last thirty years. Nor was France spared from the return of the past—in May 2005, Algeria reminded us of the Sétif massacre, which many French citizens were hearing of for the first time. In the same year, the French Parliament—and one may wonder whether it overstepped its authority here—approved a law requiring that the national education system present materials praising the virtues of colonization.

What is potentially the most explosive memory is still the one present in East Asia, as demonstrated by the events of the spring of 2005 and the commemorations of the summer. In April, the Japanese Prime Minister's speech, prepared for the Asia-Africa Conference, seemed to be a response to the violent anti-Japanese demonstrations that took place in China just before the conference. Beijing may regret having reawakened the monsters of the Second World War.[7] For Chinese memory, once reawakened, will be difficult to contain, so filled has it been with official lies and human tragedies repressed by the authorities. Among the most embarrassing lies of the Chinese Communist Party, as already stated, were the ones about the respective roles of Mao Zedong and Chiang Kai-shek in the fight against the Japanese invader. That was the subject of revelations in a new biography of Mao by Jung Chang and Jon Halliday, published in the spring of 2005: according to the authors, Mao, far from fighting against Japanese troops in 1939, and fearing a pact between Germany and Japan on the model of the Nazi-Soviet pact, collaborated with the Japanese intelligence services to weaken Chiang and secure the support of Stalin. Hence the real defender of China was the man who took refuge in Taiwan. One imagines the advantages Tokyo and Taipei might derive from those revelations.[8]

The writing of history began in Greece so that the great deeds of men should not sink into oblivion. Today, an entirely different ambition could be nourished: the ambition to preserve in our memory the always-open possibility of the return of savagery.

CHAPTER 13

RUSSIA AS IT IS

*Like mushrooms in the woods, ideologies
are always ready to reappear with the
first rainfall.*

—RAYMOND BOUDON

Since the fall of the USSR, the Western powers have based their policies
toward Moscow on individuals rather than counting on institutional
reforms or the development of civil society. Western leaders have sacrificed the principles on which their foreign relations depend for supposed
"stability" on their eastern border guaranteed by the holder of the Russian
Federation presidency, whoever he might be. As long as they got along
well with Boris or Vladimir, they saw no reason to worry. We can now
observe the results of that policy. Western influence on Russia is nonexistent. Russia's capacity to export *instability* to the rest of the world has
increased, as illustrated by Alexander Litvinenko's murder in London in
November 2006. And the country has again become unpredictable, controlled by a narrow clique with a false view of the world and of Russia. The
clique demonstrated its incompetence in 2003 in Georgia, in 2004 in
Ukraine, and in 2005 with the Beslan school hostage tragedy and its surprise at the overthrow of President Askar Akayev in Kyrgyzstan. And as far
as Chechnya is concerned, far from improving, the situation is leading to
the criminalization of Russia as a whole.

In their eagerness to discern the shape of a new world after the Cold
War, analysts presented the changes in Moscow as more clear-cut than
they were in reality. Simplification is of course an element in the effort
to explain: no analysis can be constructed entirely on the recognition of

contradictions. However, when ambiguity is inherent in a system, as in Putin's Russia, caution should be the order of the day. The externally projected image is at variance with the internal reality. We may pretend to ignore that for a while, but when the confrontation of the two realities causes a blockage, as in the Ukrainian crisis in 2005 or in the numerous political assassinations that took place either in Russia or abroad, we are faced with a serious problem. If the new members of the European Union, who theoretically have "a good knowledge of methods but also greater resistance to manipulation,"[1] were listened to more often, Western Europe might make fewer mistakes. But since the Eastern European member states are automatically assumed to be hostile to Moscow, what they have to say about Russia is greeted with suspicion.

Presidents' second terms often reveal their real ambitions. Vladimir Putin began by getting rid of all potential opponents *before* the March 2004 election. That left him alone in charge of what happened in Russia, determining both foreign and domestic policy. He should find the mistakes made costly, since they are now essentially his own. From his present solitary position, his ideas stand out with greater clarity. The Ukrainian election of November-December 2004 was a watershed. At the time, Putin's determination to restore the empire was as clear as his inability to impose that reactionary policy. Western Europe, for its part, quickly reverted to its reflexive appeasement of Moscow after initially protesting with one voice the massive fraud in the second round of balloting in Ukraine. If only the Orange Revolution would calm down quickly! If only Ukraine would not ask for too much! Above all, let it not antagonize Vladimir Putin! At the NATO summit in February 2005, new Ukrainian president Viktor Yushchenko was given an extremely cool reception by three European heads of state: the French president left the chamber after the opening remarks, the German chancellor did not open his mouth, and the Spanish prime minister, on leaving the session, said that it had not been very exciting. Since then, the president of the European Commission has been instructed to do nothing that might lead Ukraine to believe it might one day be a candidate for membership in the European Union.

The European inclination to pay court to Putin is even more surprising because the "choice of the West" he said he made after September 11 did not stand the test of reality any more than did the "European choice" he invoked in our capitals, where he let it be understood that he had been disappointed by Washington. Since April 25, 2005, when Putin, speaking before the two houses of parliament in joint session at the Kremlin in the annual presidential address to the nation, referred to the fall of the USSR as "the greatest geopolitical catastrophe of the century," one need no longer wonder about the view of the world that prevails in Moscow.

The Ukrainian episode was a reality check for Russia. Without Ukraine, it would be impossible for Moscow to resume domination over the states that emancipated themselves in 1990. Without it, Russia cannot dream of restoring the empire. Without it, finally, Russia will become a country like any other. As former U.S. national security adviser Zbigniew Brzezinski has remarked, one must make a choice between empire and democracy—one cannot have both.

A fraction of Russians, including the military and the special forces, has never been persuaded that Moscow lost the Cold War; according to them, no one gave them the chance to wage that war. The collapse of the empire, in their view, was far more political than military. Recent studies of the composition of Russian elites under Presidents Boris Yeltsin and Putin show that these elements have gained ground. The percentage of the elite with university training declined from 52 percent during the Yeltsin years to 21 percent under Putin, while the percentage in the army or the special forces increased from 11 percent to 25 percent; only 6.7 percent under Yeltsin had had military training though not currently serving in the army, compared to 27 percent under Putin.[2] The figures speak for themselves: elites are less inclined to acknowledge that the Russian Empire has definitively ended. They are the ones who have advised Putin to follow disastrous policies in Abkhazia, Georgia, and Ukraine, and above all Chechnya. Outside support for those policies can only be attributed to willful blindness. Does Europe really want to encourage Russia's dangerous illusions? On that question, European public opinion is more reasonable than European leaders, who in May 2005 at the anniversary celebrations in Moscow of the 1945 victory once again showed that they had not understood the lesson (with the exception of Tony Blair, who did not attend).

In November 2004, people had the sense that they were reliving historic scenes. The Ukrainians' democratic movement was compared to past uprisings in Poland, Hungary, and Czechoslovakia. At first, the movement had only domestic significance: it was a rejection of the massive corruption of the Kuchma regime, which had not stopped at assassination to achieve its ends. But it soon took a political stance against the entire system, including the very close ties between Kiev and Moscow. Opposition in Ukraine was intensified by the fact that Russia fully supported the corrupt Leonid Kuchma. The people's challenge thus turned into a peaceful revolution, and the old order gradually slipped away. Ukraine's Supreme Court annulled the presidential election, journalists declared that they would no longer work under orders, and 120 diplomats made public their support for a political break. For the first time in their history, before voting in a third round, Ukrainians enjoyed the right to a televised debate between two presidential candidates, during which they heard that the time had come when "the president of an independent Ukraine would no longer be chosen by Moscow."[3] Yushchenko repeated the message in Moscow in January 2005: henceforth Russia would be informed of Kiev's decisions but would no longer be involved in making them.

During this crisis, Putin, unable to adapt to an unforeseen situation, fell back on Soviet rhetoric. On November 23 in Lisbon, he denounced the observers of the Organization for Security and Cooperation in Europe, calling their reservations about the democratic nature of the election "inadmissible" even as the Ukrainian Supreme Court was nullifying the election results. A few days later, during an official visit to India, Putin denounced the "dictatorship" of the United States,[4] while accusing Europe of "openly encouraging the opposition in illegal and violent actions." In Ankara, sounding like he had gone to pieces, he warned against those who would give lessons while wearing "a colonizer's helmet." Vladimir Putin soon reverted to a more polite way of speaking, but the heated words of this mediocre leader perhaps expressed his true thoughts, normally concealed behind a cold mask and correct language.

The twenty-five members of the European Union had some responsibility for the genesis of the crisis in Ukraine: their criticism of the manipulation of the first round of the election was so tepid that the Ukrainian government felt entitled to resort to even more blatant fraud in the second round. Moreover, European tolerance of fraudulent electoral practices and press abuses in Russia for several years before that allowed the Kremlin to hope for continued silence. In the fall of 2003, in a preemptive strike before parliamentary elections in Russia, the Duma muzzled the independent press. Putin's party then used its control of the state apparatus to capture 300 of the 450 seats in the Duma in the balloting in December. The opposition had ceased to exist, and the legislature had been transformed into an adjunct of the executive. All this provoked no reaction in Europe. But in Ukraine the outrages became too big to swallow.

For Europe the real choices on Ukraine remain to be made. How should we deal with this country knocking at Europe's door? Are we to keep repeating that Kiev should remain equally distant from Europe and Russia, as Berlin says? Must we not recognize in the popular uprising of 2004 deeply European democratic convictions? Europe bears some of the blame for the results of the July 2006 parliamentary elections in Ukraine. When Moscow had to accept the Ukrainian opposition's victory a year and a half before, the chief card in Yushchenko's hand was his ability to persuade the members of the European Union to open to Ukraine; as he said in Brussels on February 22, 2005, the month after his inauguration, the demonstrators wanted to see Ukraine "in Europe," not only "a neighbor of Europe." In the summer of 2006, there was disappointment with Ukraine's Orange Revolution, after Yushchenko's party's poor showing in the July vote and the ascension to the prime minister's post of Viktor Yanukovich, the loser in 2004. One even wonders whether the Orange Revolution was really a revolution: the changes of personnel were limited, Yushchenko perpetuated the rule of oligarchs and became enmeshed with big money and the gas trade. The balance may now have shifted in Moscow's favor. But that does not negate the conviction that Europe should have supported the political events of 2004 more vigorously.

In Russia, policy continues to evolve in troubling ways. The authorities have been granted by parliament the power to shut down any press outlet whose reporting is considered "biased." In the wake of the September 2004 hostage-taking in Beslan in the republic of North Ossetia in the Caucasus, renewed centralization has deprived regional assemblies of their local legitimacy, and regional governors know as little about the regions they administer as Putin's entourage knows about Russia. The Beslan tragedy, in which Russian soldiers participated alongside the Chechen terrorists,[5] also brought to light such corruption and incompetence that the ability of the Russian state to function has been called into question. Even without addressing the energy dossier, one would have to be a blind adherent of "multipolarity" not to see all the dangerous tendencies affecting relations between Europe and Russia.

It was clear before the end of 2004, for instance, that the EU and Russia would not succeed in establishing the policy of a "common neighborhood" that was supposed to make it possible for them to work in concert in the region extending from Belarus to the Caucasus. The EU-Russia summit that began November 11 in The Hague had previously been postponed at Putin's request because of important disagreements between the two sides on questions of freedom, justice, and external security. The Russians set the rights of Russian minorities in the Baltic countries who claim ethnic discrimination against the many alleged violations of human rights in Chechnya, as though that comparison made any sense. The reality behind the Russian failure to agree on implementation of the "common neighborhood" is that Russia did not want to deprive itself of a more direct, less negotiated role or greater influence on developments in the region. The principal disagreement with the EU concerned joint actions that might be undertaken in a crisis.[6] Fifteen years after the end of the Cold War, Moscow still does not deal with Europe as a *good and reliable neighbor*. In May 2005, agreement was finally reached on the awkward formulation of *"adjacent space"*!

Another interpretation of Putin's request for a delay in the summit meeting is the rancor he harbored toward the Dutch president, Rene van der Linden, who had dared to question publicly the circumstances of the assault by Russian forces in Beslan purportedly intended to free the hostages. Beslan should have sounded an even louder alarm than the Yukos affair or the continuing deterioration of the media engineered by the government. The disastrous handling of the crisis in Beslan, which ended in the deaths of 332 hostages, more than half of them schoolchildren, and all but one of the hostage takers, demonstrated, in addition to the incompetence of the special forces and widespread corruption in the country, a contempt for human life characteristic of the worst moments of the USSR. That Vladimir Putin spoke not a single word of sympathy for the young victims and their families says more than all the investigations—or lack of them. Beslan and its Chechen hostage takers also turned the spotlight back on a frightful story that Europeans do not want to hear about: the systematic destruction of Chechnya. The Chechen war acts like a cancer on all of Russian politics and society. When they return to Russia, veterans of the war—known as "Chechens," having become identified with the people they had to fight—often engage in gangsterism, intimidation, rape, and even murder. Russian youth has partly lost its bearings in the savagery of the conflict, just as the preceding generation lost theirs in Afghanistan.

In Chechnya itself, where the population has been shattered by seven years of terror, the only result of "pacification" has been the strengthening of the most radical elements there at the expense of moderate Chechens such as Ahmed Zakaev, a refugee in Great Britain, and Aslan Maskhadov, the republic president elected under international supervision and assassinated in March 2005 by Russian special forces.[7] After that last episode, the extremists are the only ones left on either side, and Europe has its share of responsibility for the radicalization. Europeans should not be surprised if terrorist acts of Chechen origin are one day committed on their territory. Chechnya is also used to justify authoritarian and police measures taken in Russia. Because of Chechnya, Russian-speaking minorities do not return to Russia for fear that their children will end up in Grozny fighting the war. With the increasing numbers of Chechen refugees arriving on their territory, Europeans have first hand information about what is happening in that unhappy region. What are they doing about it? In Poland alone, refugees numbered 1,300 in 2001, 3,000 in 2002, 5,300 in 2003, and 7,000 in 2004. With every major crisis the spike in refugees is higher. Sometimes they journey more than a thousand miles to flee the violence that has ravaged their homeland for all but two years since 1994. The Russians let them leave, for a fee, happy to see them out of the country.

In 2006, at a time when Moscow is being celebrated for its ability to rebuild a strong state and its international stature thanks to oil and gas, the government is incapable of managing a war that is much more serious for it, and immensely more cruel for its people, than is Iraq for the United States. Moscow does not seem to understand what is happening even in its former satellites, blinkered by the narrow view that the special forces have imposed on it and the whole country. A little tact and intelligence would have made it possible to maintain good relations with neighboring countries. In the de jure autonomous Georgian republic of Abkhazia, a month before the demonstrations in Kiev, Vladimir Putin showed himself to be so brutal that his candidate was beaten. In Georgia in 2003, the defeat of Russian interests in the "Rose Revolution" was total. A few months after Ukraine, Moscow's protégé in Kyrgyzstan, Askar Akayev, was overthrown in the space of a few hours. Large demonstrations took place in Uzbekistan, where the government of President Islam Karimov resorted to brutal repression. The Russian republic of Ingushetia, located between North Ossetia and Chechnya, is said to be in a prerevolutionary ferment.

Belarus is still holding out determinedly but with such outdated methods that one wonders whether the regime can last. In theory, President Alexander Lukashenko won the right in a 2004 referendum to remain in power indefinitely, but the 2006 election stirred up popular opposition. Elected in 1994 to combat corruption, Lukashenko soon evolved into one of the most repressive rulers in the entire former Soviet bloc. In 2002, he went so far as to issue a decree requiring political information sessions. In 2004, he attacked the University of European Studies in Minsk,[8] dispersing professors and students: the education being offered there was beginning to be seen as a danger. During the same period in Russia, Interior Ministry forces raided the offices of the British Council. Had Western culture become a threat in Moscow as well as Minsk?

The current self-destructive phase in Russia is the direct result of the mediocrity of those who wield power in the country and the psychological depression that followed the failure of the 1990s. But its main roots are to be found in the terrible tragedies of the last century, which have witnesses in every family. The return of Stalinist imagery in Russia today can hardly be interpreted as a simple desire to return to the past. The spirit of revenge abroad in the land is symptomatic of a traumatized country in the process of extreme regression. But inspiring fear in one's citizens is no longer enough to establish a strong state. Yuri Andropov's methods as Soviet general secretary in the early 1980s were those of the end of a reign, and the return to them provides further evidence of the reactionary character of the regime in place in Moscow. Such methods may crush countervailing powers, but they produce only destruction. Russia is ruled by the most unpredictable and corrupt sector of the special forces. Its former elites, more enlightened and open to the world, are removed from the president, whom they despise. The Russian special forces who hold power have also been corrupted and now more resemble the villains in a pulp novel of Cold War vintage than the nuanced adversaries in the acclaimed works of John Le Carré.

In December 2003, Nikolai Petrov, a researcher at the Carnegie Moscow Center, described how the *siloviki* took power:

It took Vladimir Putin some time to bring his associates into the government. The first important step was the appointment of Boris Gryzlov to the ministry of the interior, followed by that of Sergei Ivanov to defense. Trusted associates were discreetly installed in every administrative sector. They learned and practiced for nearly three years. They are now ready to take their places in politics and business.[9]

As the fall of Mikhail Khodorkovsky illustrated in October 2003, the special forces are not indifferent to business matters.[10] The pull of money and the corruption rife in their ranks explain why they became involved in such activity. Most observers came to view the Yukos affair as the beginning of the reconquest of economic power by the secret services. In many respects, Russia has become a gangster state in which the only thing that counts, after nearly a century of communism, is who owns what. It is a country controlled not by warlords, like Afghanistan, but by financial lords. The secret services seek control in every area, particularly when it comes to the economy, but legitimate business is irritating because it does not lend itself to such control. Those in power thus nourish fond dreams of a totalitarian capitalism, recalling the end of the Soviet New Economic Policy in 1924, and providing yet more evidence of the regressive nature of the Putin regime. Since the Khodorkovsky affair, many have been wondering if and when, as liberal entrepreneur Oleg Kissilev put it, "another plane is going to hit another skyscraper of Russian business." Exhausted by more than ten years of fruitless reforms, the Russian people have long given the government a free hand. Since the oligarchs were seen as bandits—evidence that they were was not hard to find—the measures the government proposed were often as popular as they were ineffective, with the suggestion of a return to Soviet-era practices. On the other hand, the period of decadence may continue for some time because the political alternatives involve much more nationalistic elements.

Analysis of the current Russian bureaucracy should be given more attention in the West. The Academy of Sciences' study of elites previously referred to, which incorporates the biographies of 3,500 high-level Russian officials, finds that more than half come from the secret services, the army, or the police. The study's author, Olga Krishtanovskaya, asserts that

Vladimir Putin now directly controls 17 "power" ministries (public prosecutor, police, treasury, customs, taxes . . .). That means in practice that when a political decision is made, the FSB [Federal Security Service, the successor agency to the KBG] implements it by transmitting information to the public prosecutor, who then calls on the militia. Justice is all carried out at the lower levels. In this system there is no countervailing power.[11]

In these circumstances few could change the direction of society, and even when out of the country, they are afraid to say what they think. The question of who will replace Vladimir Putin in 2008 is already on the table, and there can be no doubt that his succession is already the explanation of the current ferocious power struggle taking place in Moscow. One person often mentioned is Sergei Ivanov, whom some feel has the advantage of offering a good deal of continuity. But a relative unknown such as Vladimir Putin himself was in 1999 is also a possibility, and the current president of the Russian Federation may also find ways to transfer most of the political power to the prime minister, a position he can pretend to assume. What is certain is that once the candidate is chosen he must win, and to accomplish that, anything can be considered, including terrorist attacks—like those which killed more than 300 people in 1999—and assassinations.

Since the end of the Cold War, Western countries have gradually lost their expertise on Russia, laboriously acquired over several decades. This expertise should be rebuilt and renewed now, since Russia and the surrounding areas have undergone great change since 1991. Moscow's politics, often out of touch with reality, now involve risks that have nothing to do with the surprise attack anticipated during the Cold War. After fostering hope for a slow rapprochement with Europe, all indications show, to the contrary, that Moscow has been moving away from Europe for the last few years. In February 2004, the European Union did acknowledge that its policy toward Russia was "ineffective."[12] What else could it be, since it is based on neither accuracy nor justice? The only way to change it would be to demand more accountability from the EU's authoritarian, repressive, and, above all, enormously corrupt neighbor.

The greed rampant at all levels of the Russian bureaucracy is now more troubling than the new missiles coming out of Russia's arsenals. For it is this that may lead official or unofficial bodies to sell to the highest bidder the countless weapons and military-related matériel, equipment, and technology developed in the USSR and later in Russia. The channels used for such transfers often have direct links to organized crime, as is the case for instance in the North Caucasus. But arms sales also affect wider power relations. Iran in 2006 continues to benefit from Russian arms sales, including air defenses and cruise missiles. The modernization of the Chinese army, among others, is being carried out largely with Russian matériel, and the official portion of sales, which is supposed to enable the Russian weapons industry to survive, and involving Sukoi planes, air-ground defense systems, and Kilo-class submarines, is only the tip of the iceberg. One of the main objectives of Chinese espionage in Russia concerns ballistic missiles with sophisticated maneuvering capabilities that were scheduled to be put into operation in 2005. The idea of a strategic alliance between Russia and China appears to be a fantasy, even though 2005 was the occasion for the two to conduct joint military maneuvers, including amphibious landings and underwater operations. Nonetheless, the Russian contribution to China's increasing power is real and adds to legitimate worries about internal developments in Russia and their consequences abroad.

One should recognize that both the Russian Empire and the "special path" for Russia are over. And we should also recognize that for nearly three centuries now Russia has been involved with the West. Just as the end of Nazism was a salutary catastrophe for Germany, the end of the USSR has presented Russia with the possibility of joining Western democracy by definitively abandoning dreams of imperial restoration that are doomed to failure in any case. But since the Russians associate the very idea of democracy with the savage privatizations and the corruption of the Yeltsin era, dreams of empire have not collapsed. Disintegration proceeds and the Russian catastrophe has not yet come to an end. And those who now believe that oil and gas represent an answer to Russia's crisis should read more history books.

CHAPTER 14

THE TWO CHINAS

It has been more than a century now that the supporters of Realpolitik, lost in their exotic dreams, have been making the same blunders about China.

—SIMON LEYS

Foreign policy deals with many peripheral subjects, but it sometimes seems to lack a center. Here is one: *Taiwan is the Alsace-Lorraine of the twenty-first century.* Beijing has often used this parallel, especially when trying to charm French interlocutors. One of the great strengths of the Chinese, in fact, is the very clever way in which they pay court to the elites of countries in their sights, particularly to diplomats. Instead of touching a displaced national sentimentalism in France, however, China's parallel of Taiwan with Alsace-Lorraine should frighten us. Better than anyone, the French can imagine the blind fury that national cause of China's could justify. Chinese officials, even ones who are moderate on other subjects, are convinced that the recovery of Taiwan could justify anything, including jeopardizing decades of economic growth—even risking a new world war. Westerners listen in disbelief, rejecting the possibility that such folly could be committed for an island that already has all the attributes of independence: president, parliament, army, political parties . . . But those bystanders fail to take into account a historical truth iterated down through the centuries: conflicts seldom begin for rational causes.

Chinese Premier Zhou Enlai back in the 1960s had already invoked the comparison with Alsace-Lorraine in a conversation with the author and politician Alain Peyrefitte. The parallel is stretched. Taiwan is not occupied by a foreign power, and a large majority of the Taiwanese do not want to return to a continental embrace that would crush them.[1] Most importantly, Taiwan has its own historical roots. Europeans were the first to take an interest in the island; the Dutch East India Company was followed by the Spaniards, and Japan intervened only at the end of the nineteenth century. For four centuries Taiwan has been populated by Chinese fleeing the arbitrary rule of the empire. It was governed by continental China only between 1945 and 1949.[2]

The real similarity between Taiwan and Alsace-Lorraine is that Taiwan is no more an internal question than those provinces were in 1914. It is an international question that must be treated as such. The defense agreement between Taiwan and the United States would transform any confrontation between the two Chinas into a worldwide conflict, with an awareness on both sides from the very beginning of hostilities that they both possess nuclear weapons. In fact, the risk that nuclear weapons could be used in a conflict is greatest precisely in this area of the world. Recognition of that fact should be enough to heighten awareness and encourage caution in dealing with the issue of Taiwan. Caution, however, does not mean leaving China master of the situation, selling it weapons, or refusing to sell them to Taiwan. On the contrary, the more China has the feeling that it can attack the island with impunity, the greater the temptation for it to do just that. Beijing has never renounced the use of force against Taiwan. It would hope, if it decided to attack, that the rest of the world would treat the decision as an internal affair, as it has treated Russian intervention in Chechnya. The two countries, which have good reason to mistrust one another, understand each other perfectly on that point.

China's arguments on Taiwan have changed little over time. During the presidency of Richard Nixon, when the question of a rapprochement between China and the United States arose, Zhou Enlai had the habit of counting out on his ten fingers the assumptions of mainland leaders that would have to be accepted: 1) The government of the People's Republic of China is the only legal government representing the Chinese people. 2) Taiwan is a Chinese province. 3) Its liberation is an internal Chinese problem. 4) No foreign intervention can be accepted. 5) To say that the status of Taiwan is not settled is erroneous and absurd, since the province was returned to its homeland as soon as the war with Japan ended in 1945. 6) Its status was settled at that time once and for all. 7) China is firmly opposed to the "two Chinas policy," a continental China and a China on Taiwan, or any similar maneuver. 8) China is equally opposed to any movement for Taiwanese independence, manufactured abroad and manipulated by foreign interests. 9) The United States must withdraw all of its armed forces and military bases from Taiwan and the Taiwan Strait. 10) The defense treaty between the United States, Taiwan, and the Pescadores, signed by U.S. Secretary of State John Foster Dulles and Taiwanese President Chiang Kai-shek after the Geneva Conference in 1954, is illegal and void. China will not be a member of the UN so long as the question of the two Chinas remains open.

Since Beijing replaced Taiwan at the UN in 1971, the rhetoric to which all Western countries have submitted has introduced a major ambiguity: If Taiwan is recognized as part of China, how is it possible to challenge the claim that any aggression against the island is a purely internal matter? That is why Beijing has always considered recognition of the "one China" concept crucial and why it asks all foreign dignitaries to perform a ritual: not to prostrate themselves before the emperor as in bygone days, but to mutter, if possible as soon as they get off the plane, some sentence about the unity of China. Even though the assertion has less and less relation to reality as time goes on, everyone mouths it willingly. It is not certain that peace is helped by the process, for a gulf between diplomatic declarations and reality is dangerous. If Taiwan were recognized as a sovereign state, any offensive action would be identified as an attack and so condemned by the UN—which would give the international community superior resources to prevent such attacks. In 1966, Italy introduced the idea that China could have dual representation at the UN, through both Beijing and Taipei. Unfortunately, a resolution by pro-Communist Albania proposing that Beijing replace Taipei won out, and it became a fait accompli in 1971, with China being given a Security Council seat the following year. Since 1977, Taipei has sought the same status as the two Germanys or the two Koreas—indeed, why not?— but no one now wants to reconsider the 1972 Shanghai Agreement signed by Nixon that laid out the "one China" policy. France played a pioneering role in the matter. As early as 1964, after a mission to China, former French premier Edgar Faure advocated Taiwan's replacement by mainland China at the UN Security Council. Raymond Aron remarked at the time that the risks of the operation—the replacement of Taiwan by China at the UN— would have been lower if relations with America had been better. In a

January 31, 1964, press conference, President Charles de Gaulle at least pointed out that since human life and fundamental values were not respected in China, the attempt should be made to avoid a break with Taipei. Nevertheless, a break occurred, and France confessed that it was settling for seeing "the world as it is"—a formulation all the more ambiguous because the world can be described in all kinds of ways.

Jean de Broglie in 1965 phrased the truth more directly: the French government recognizes only states. That position is based on the principle of the continuity of the state, which holds that internal changes have no influence on the international standing of a state. In the name of that principle, France did not acknowledge the crimes of Vichy until President Jacques Chirac did in 1995—until then, under President François Mitterrand, for instance, Vichy was supposed to represent a *discontinuity* of the French state. Beijing could be allowed to sit on the Security Council even if its policies have not been approved—after all, that was already the case for the USSR. But in 1964 France abstained on the question of the Chinese seat, and General de Gaulle was strongly tempted by the theory of the two Chinas. We have traveled much further since then. The 1994 Franco-Chinese communiqué accepted the exclusivity of Beijing's authority. Under those circumstances, would France relinquish the right to condemn an act of aggression? The question is legitimate, especially because ten years later, on January 26, 2004, Jacques Chirac criticized Taiwan for "upsetting the status quo with a destabilizing unilateral initiative" by putting on the ballot in the upcoming Taiwanese elections a referendum calling for a peaceful resolution in the Taiwan Strait, and of "assuming heavy responsibility for the region." Worse, France participated in Chinese naval maneuvers in the Yellow Sea five days before the voting in Taiwan. The maneuvers had of course been scheduled far in advance, but in light of the political circumstances it was hard to complain when everyone viewed them as "manipulation of France by Beijing." That is exactly what they were, and Chen Shui-bian could not restrain himself from comparing them to the Chinese missile tests near Taiwan during the island's 1996 elections, which Beijing staged to intimidate Taiwan. Paris feigns ignorance of the democratic development of Taiwan and has given Beijing leave to do as it will on human rights. China is frequently described as a "major and responsible actor" and praised for its "peaceful" rise to power, despite the magnitude of its military preparations.[3] One of the first utterances by the president of the French Republic when he set foot on Chinese soil in October 2004 was a diatribe against Taiwan. But the more Beijing has the feeling that aggressive acts on its part have no consequences, the greater the risk of conflict. China's worst mistake would be to believe that the United States would not intervene in such a situation. A miscalculation of that kind is one of the most common among America's adversaries. It is the mistake Saddam Hussein made in 1990 and repeated in 2003. It is the mistake Serbian President Slobodan Milosevic made in 1999. It is a mistake Beijing may make in turn, especially if it thinks it can split the United States and Europe on this question that it considers vital.

Chinese patience is often praised, but the most distinctive characteristic of China over the last few years has been, in fact, its *impatience*—the feeling that it must soon reach its goal and the arrogance that goes along with it. Some observers expect a crisis as early as 2007 or 2008, during the last stretch before the Olympic Games and at the end of Chen Shui-bian's presidency. Chen has promised greater autonomy for Taiwan before he leaves office and that will be the last opportunity to fulfill the promise. The approach of the Olympics in Beijing may lead Taipei to believe that a declaration or a change in Taiwan's constitution—for example the sovereignty clause—could be made, with Beijing in a sense paralyzed in the spotlight. China is already doing everything possible to isolate Taipei and to win symbolic or legal victories over it. There might also be, more likely, another crisis later on, comparable to the one in the Taiwan Strait in 1996, which led the United States to send an aircraft carrier to the area. That incident was the only real show of force that President Clinton risked during his two terms. In fact, the period from 2008 to 2010, when the United States will have a new president that China may attempt to test, seems more dangerous, particularly if the Chinese economy, often criticized for overheating, experiences difficulties that increase the current social unrest. That unrest is greatly underestimated in the West, where it is not understood that the poverty of peasants and workers, when they are confronted with the corruption of many bureaucrats, is increasingly hard to bear. Facing internal tension, China might embark on dangerous initiatives abroad. Despite the claims made for it, Beijing's foreign policy is often lacking in subtlety, and at times commits serious blunders. An illustration of that was the passage of a law in March 2005, at the worst possible moment, authorizing the use of force against Taiwan in poorly defined circumstances.

For years the entire region has been preparing for a serious crisis. That, along with yet broader concerns, has led Japan to modify the limits of its defense policy. In September 1997, a clause was added to the security treaty with the United States allowing Japan to move from "passive defense" to "active participation" in "regional affairs." Japanese defense forces can now provide logistical support to the American army in case of an event that "risks seriously affecting stability and peace around Japan." Taiwan is, naturally, an element in such scenarios. After the September 11 attacks, Japan crossed another defense threshold, adopting three antiterrorist laws authorizing the dispatch of troops to foreign conflict zones. Tokyo's decision to send soldiers to Afghanistan and Iraq to help with reconstruction shows its determination not only to participate in peacekeeping operations but to resume a normal defense posture fifty years after the end of the Second World War. Then, Defense Minister Shigeru Ishiba pointed out that it would be "absurd to leave Taiwan out of discussions on the security of Northeast Asia." It was the first time a member of the Japanese cabinet had spoken so clearly in favor of Taiwan on this delicate issue, which shows the importance Japan accords to stability in the strait. In January 2003, a reserve officer was named to the Japanese bureau in Taiwan, which made it possible to increase the level of bilateral military exchanges. In February 2005, a Japanese-American statement publicly affirmed the two powers' joint protection of Taiwan against possible Chinese aggression. Tokyo could not in fact remain passive in that eventuality: a blockade of sea lanes between Japan and the Middle East would be catastrophic for the supply of raw materials Japan must import. Finally, new Japanese prime minister Shinzo Abe has generally taken a hard-line stance on regional foreign policy, and he is particularly respected in Taiwan for historical reasons: his great-uncle Eisaku Sato was the last prime minister to visit Taiwan while in office.

Taiwan is a democratic country—it has had three direct ballot presidential elections with peaceful transfers of power, 80 percent participation in the March 2004 elections, and 99 registered political parties—demonstrating that Asian values are in no way opposed to the development of civil liberties. Freedom of expression and freedom of worship, the holding of free elections, and political reforms have all been gradually won by the Taiwanese. The notion that China and Taiwan are separated only by their economies and standards of living, as we are sometimes asked to believe, is absurd. What most deeply divides China from Taiwan is politics. But one sometimes feels, here as in Ukraine, that France fears democracies more than it supports them, and that the "right choice" is finally that of the authoritarian countries, Russia and China. It is an old French tradition, and it would be desirable if Europe were finally to rid us of it. Beijing's contempt for human rights and human life, which caused Fernand Braudel to say "Man is worth so little in China," has obvious effects in security matters. The authorities will not refrain from sacrificing millions of people if they consider the sacrifice necessary for their ambitions or their survival.

How, then, should the question of Taiwan be approached, while preserving all chances for a peaceful resolution? If the question is primarily political, that is the ground on which we should stand. A good beginning would be to stop repeating Beijing's propaganda. The Republic of China is a de facto sovereign country, and neither side of the strait belongs to the other. "One China" is therefore a unilateral definition by Beijing that, furthermore, is abstract in nature: the Taiwanese will never accept the formula "one country, two systems," as Hong Kong has, particularly after the political restrictions gradually imposed on that territory in contravention of the agreements signed before Great Britain handed it back in 1997. If a referendum in Taiwan on independence is dangerous for Beijing, it is solely because the fiction that only a minority of the Taiwanese favor independence must be maintained. The equilibrium established by the Shanghai Agreement could be called into question. The "One China" policy is incoherent, ignores real developments on the island, and encourages the mistakes in interpretation by the principal players that have already been mentioned. It would be in Washington's interest to end the ambiguity by regularly reminding Beijing that it would intervene in case of a use of force. But Washington also has to make Chen Shui-bian see reason: "Do not think that China will not intervene. Remember 1989 and the student movement."

The first order of business is to avoid driving the two sides to the breaking point, as with France and Germany before 1914. Fear of what has already become reality—the existence of two Chinas—prevents diplomats from seeing the obvious: that the lack of diplomatic recognition may drive Taiwan to take dangerous initiatives that China might interpret as movements toward independence. In light of the anti-secession law passed in Beijing in 2005, no one knows where that interpretation might lead if

China considers conditions ripe for an attack on Taiwan. Conversely, recognition of Taipei would be the equivalent of a declaration of independence for the island, but it would prevent hostilities. Out of it would come a diplomatic crisis with Beijing that could not develop into an armed conflict. To help the two countries out of the dead end in which they find themselves, this path, revolutionary in form but peaceful in substance, deserves consideration. It seems audacious only to those who have not thought out the frightful price of a conflict on this question and in this part of the world. The First World War was triggered "by a kind of 'mechanism' *in the face of which statesmen were helpless.*"[4] The Third World War—or, rather, the final act of the Second—could have the same kind of beginning. Europe has a moral responsibility in the matter because it knows better than anyone the fatal logic that leads to suicidal confrontations. It could take the initiative in a campaign for the recognition of Taiwan, especially because Beijing's legal arguments for claiming the island have always been weak and have been strengthened only by acknowledgment of the relative power of the two entities, which has nothing to do with the law.

For the moment, however, Europe has taken the exact opposite path by paying court to Beijing in a manner both absurd and dangerous.[5] It is hard to understand why Greece, a member of the EU, lowered itself in 2004 by going along with the decision to deprive Taiwanese athletes who won gold medals of the right to their flag and their national anthem. What precedent do these actions set for the Olympic Games to be held in Beijing in 2008? It is even harder to understand why the duo of France and Germany thought it had to take the lead in a movement to lift the arms embargo against China. Germany tells anyone who wants to listen that it does not sell weapons, and France has never stopped saying that lifting that embargo would change nothing in the current situation. In such circumstances, why engage in frantic activity only to fail in the end to lift the arms embargo? Moreover, why backtrack under pressure from the United States instead of changing one's mind after taking into account the serious security problems troubling East Asia? As long as policy makers lack this strategic insight, the question of arms sales will be raised again every year.

The arguments put forth for lifting the embargo are as numerous as they are unpersuasive, the one no doubt explaining the other. First, the embargo is said to be obsolete twenty years after the Tiananmen crackdown, and its effect is alleged to be primarily political, because the

Europeans are in fact not considering any weapons sales. Beijing obviously does not have the same concept of time that Paris does. Fear of demonstrations on the death in 2004 of the only Chinese politician who had opposed the use of tanks against the peacefully demonstrating students at Tiananmen produced such a large deployment of police in the square that it seemed the events of 1989 had taken place only the day before. China has never agreed to reconsider its interpretation of those events, nor to condemn the ferocious repression that came down on the heads of the demonstrators. So there is nothing *obsolete* about the situation. Quite the contrary. Many of the Tiananmen protesters are still in prison, and Jiang Yanyong, the military doctor who broke the silence about the severe acute respiratory syndrome (SARS) epidemic in China in 2002-2003, was arrested in June 2004 for declaring that the repression unleashed at Tiananmen was not a response to a "counterrevolutionary" plot but a massacre of unarmed students. Official confirmation of his fate after his arrest gives a good picture of the progress of human rights in China: "Jiang Yanyong has recently violated the army code of conduct. Officers are striving to help him and to complete his education." It sounds as though we are back in the time of the Cultural Revolution. Testimony like that of Harry Wu, who spent nineteen years in labor camps as a political prisoner, indicates that the Chinese gulag is growing rather than shrinking. Christians and nongovernmental organizations are still persecuted. But none of this is ever denounced by the UN Human Rights Commission sitting in Geneva, either because of the no-action motion used each year by Beijing, or because of the lack of interest in Western capitals. Should we say to those who are persecuted in China that the Europe of "values" cares no more about what has been inflicted on them than it does about what will happen to them?

The second argument that proponents of lifting the arms embargo use is the growing importance of China on the international stage. The unhealthy fascination that surrounds power urges this, and the formulation "You can't treat China like Zimbabwe" is frequently trotted out. But as it happens, the relevant difference between China and Zimbabwe is that the latter does not threaten its neighbors and, above all, has no chance of unleashing a world war. We can easily conclude from this that we should be much more cautious with China.

The third argument is just as strange: We must "modernize" relations with China.[6] That may well be true, but why should modernization of those relations take place through arms sales? The reason is hard to grasp, unless we are talking about the modernization of the Chinese army. Progress in the region by means of arms sales to China is really more open to question than "the imposition of democracy from outside," which elicits so much mockery in discussions about the Middle East these days.[7] Montesquieu remarked that "it is a constant experience that those who hold power are inclined to abuse it: they keep going until they come up against limits." That is in fact precisely the problem of China in the twenty-first century, and it is an excellent reason for not providing China with the elements of advanced technology that its avionics or its satellite capabilities lack. Moreover, it is preferable that China come up against those limits in a time of peace rather than in circumstances more difficult for the West.

The fourth argument is rarely made publicly, but it is familiar to anyone interested in European military strategy: we have to balance U.S. arms sales to Taiwan with European arms sales to China. Aside from being based on a curious concept of the European alliance with the United States, and even of European interests in case of a conflict between China and the United States, this argument leaves out the strategic realities of the region. With more than 600 M9, M11, and DF21 missiles aimed at Taiwan from four Chinese provinces, one wonders what kind of balance we can possibly be talking about. In the most pessimistic scenario, any anti-missile defense, even if it functioned, would soon be saturated by a Chinese assault, not even giving the United States and Japan time to intervene. Thus hypocritical arguments lead to an extremely hypocritical conclusion: it is better to sell arms to China than to have China produce them itself. Aside from China's notorious expertise in copying manufactures and pirating technology, that conclusion contradicts the argument that lifting the embargo will change nothing since we will sell nothing. And finally, since the Europeans do not have the slightest idea what they would do in the event of a conflict over Taiwan, the entire discussion is taking place among irresponsible participants.

Is another policy possible? It certainly is. Europe could begin with a complete assessment of the arms embargo as it has been conducted since its imposition in 1989. The first step would be compiling a list of what the various European countries have sold to China since that date in the way of military matériel. There has never been an agreement among the European nations spelling out what is barred from sale, and the only collective measure has been consultation among EU members about supplies and equipment already rejected by one of them. The list might, therefore, reveal some surprises. Beijing claims that the embargo is a "relic of the Cold War," but the weapons it covets are those of the future rather than of the past.

In the second place, since Beijing has asserted that the international community should include only countries that "respect history" and that "assume their responsibility in the face of history,"[8] Europe could encourage acknowledgment of the crimes the Communist authorities have committed against the Chinese people since 1949. It is past time to undertake that effort of memory, owed to the millions of the dead who have never received the attention granted their companions in misfortune in the Russian gulag. Moreover, securing from the Chinese authorities more humane treatment of miners or of the hundreds of thousands of people victimized by a despicable system for the selling of blood in the 1990s[9] seems highly unlikely while China continues to keep the past immured behind a wall of silence.

We should also try to understand why so many countries are worried by the changes taking place in China. Thus we must begin a strategic dialogue on security questions in East Asia with the United States, and with Japan, India, Indonesia, and Australia. Perhaps then we will discover the reasons developments in Beijing trouble many countries. On April 29, 2005, India and Japan decided to open discussions on regional security, and they announced this publicly. The strategic dialogue could also be an opportunity to assess the consequences for the European continent of major troubles in Asia. It would finally be normal to stop repeating on all occasions that Taiwan is a Chinese province, paying no attention to history, and also to support the democratic China that has demonstrated that our values have also their place in its part of the world. Conversely, it is dangerous to allow Beijing to believe that it can do anything it wishes—for example, tolerating vandalism against Japanese property. There is in fact a risk that Japan will not be the only victim of Chinese nationalism. Japan knows this better than anyone, because China's ambition now is the same as Japan's at the beginning of the last century. The only difference is the scope of the vision, proceeding from the image that China has of itself as the absolute center of world affairs.

In the spring of 2004, Francis Deron published a remarkable article in *Commentaire* on the year of China then being observed in France. To conclude this chapter, we will quote that journalist with a noble sense of his calling:

In January 2004, a wave of delirium struck Paris. In honor of the Chinese New Year, the Eiffel Tower was illuminated in red, the People's Republic of China having asserted a kind of worldwide monopoly on the color that used to be Communist, and no one cared to find out why. On the Champs-Élysées, there was a parade sponsored by the municipality of Beijing. This parade was a distant revenge against the bicentennial of the French Revolution on July 14, 1989, when members of the Chinese opposition fleeing the repression of the Tiananmen uprising had on the same spot beat the drum for the glory of human rights. Even more incongruously, the façade of the Hotel Meurice was also illuminated in red, on the grounds that the delegation of the chief dignitary from Beijing, Hu Jintao, was staying there. No one had the right to an explanation of the reasons that had driven the nominal head of the regime in Beijing to take up residence in the former headquarters of the German Kommandatur during the occupation. On top of everything else, Jacques Chirac decreed, to widespread surprise, that Taiwan, the only Chinese territory living more or less under democratic rules, had no right to conduct a referendum on its territory inhabited by 22 million people.[10]

CHAPTER 15

North Korean Blackmail

In politics more than anywhere else,
everything begins with moral indignation.

—Milovan Djilas

The problem with totalitarian regimes is that they have a habit of lasting a long time. Before collapsing, they can cause unimaginable suffering in their own countries as well as the rest of the world. And when they assume a form as surprising as the regime of the Dear Leader Kim Jong Il in North Korea, all predictions are futile. One can only point out the degree to which since 1992 the position of the world with regard to Pyongyang has been aberrant. Political elites have failed utterly, allowing a small ruined country that torments its people to continue blackmailing the rest of the planet. One day North Korea issues a declaration on the reprocessing of nuclear fuel to get plutonium. The next, there is talk of possessing nuclear weapons. The day after that, talk of ending the moratorium on ballistic missile tests. Then there is talk of a sale of nuclear materials and weapons to "friendly nations" or even terrorist organizations. And finally, there is an actual nuclear test. On every occasion commentaries proliferate, with little action to prevent further and even more dangerous steps.

It is worth asking two questions: Has the regime finally reached the point of exhaustion? And most important, what would happen to the North Korean threat if China were to abandon Pyongyang politically and economically? The first question is more difficult to answer. There are many indications that Kim Jong Il is in difficulty and might be in his last days. The *Sunday Times* reported on January 30, 2005, that "the population that had been living in terror now dares to speak of escaping the country" and that "the regime has practically given up trying to stop them." There is conflicting evidence on the condition of the absurd government oppressing North Korea and observers have often been wrong about its capacity for survival, but the October 9, 2006, nuclear test may prove to be the excess that will put an end to Kim's power. Because it is easy to answer the second question: without China the regime would no doubt collapse and Beijing now appears seriously upset with the current leader. It would probably like to prolong the regime with more reliable interlocutors: perhaps a group of North Korean generals?

Korea has sometimes been compared to Poland as a victim of the great powers surrounding it. Before becoming a major focus of disputes between the USSR and the United States, and then between China and Japan, the Korean peninsula was coveted by Moscow and Tokyo, and it was in fact one of the principal stakes in the Russo-Japanese War of 1904–1905. After the Japanese surprise attack on Port Arthur, the weakened Russian Far Eastern fleet was soon defeated at sea, while the Baltic fleet was iced in; Russia was also defeated on land in the battle of Mukden in 1905, at the cost of ninety thousand killed. The Japanese then landed in Korea, where Russia was forced to recognize Japanese freedom of action by the Treaty of Portsmouth. Japan took control of the peninsula in November 1905 and maintained it until the end of the Second World War. After the Japanese defeat in 1945, Korea had little time to enjoy its restored freedom. The advance of Soviet troops in the north led the United States at Yalta to accept division of the country at the 38th parallel. The deterioration of relations between East and West in 1947 saw the establishment on the peninsula of two rival regimes controlled by the new superpowers, followed by Kim Il Sung's invasion of the south in June 1950, with Stalin's reluctant agreement. When the bloody war ended in 1953, after millions of military and civilian deaths, the division of Korea was just about the same as it had been at the outset.

One of the most interesting elements in the Korean War, in which opposing forces repeatedly advanced very quickly only to retreat to their previous positions, is the numerous mistakes in judgment on all sides. Stalin was convinced that the United States would not enter the war—which was why, after forty telegrams from Kim Il Sung, he finally agreed to the invasion and the plan of attack. Stalin thought the United States would stay out because he interpreted Mao's victory in China as a sign of American weakness. Nor did Mao believe that the United States would intervene: taking risks for a territory as small as Korea seemed to him absurd, and for its part, Washington—Secretary of State Dean Acheson as well as President Harry Truman—never thought China would be so reckless as to intervene only a year after the revolution and the establishment of the new government in Beijing. General Douglas MacArthur wanted to attack Chinese territory and even use atomic weapons; his eccentricities finally led to his being replaced. As for Kim Il Sung, father of the current potentate, he was convinced that he would be greeted with flowers in the southern portion of the peninsula, which was one of the arguments he made to Stalin. In short, everyone was mistaken in this first confrontation between East and West, which had many observers living in the shadow of the Second World War, fearing that a Third World War would break out, this time in Asia. Although the conflict did not spread, its human costs were frightful. It was during the war that we first caught a glimpse of North Korean concentration camps, which are only now, fifty years later, beginning to be talked about. In fact, a French diplomat, an embassy secretary, Georges Perruche, was held prisoner by the North Koreans for the duration of the fighting and gave an account of his captivity in a mission report to Georges Bidault in July 1953.[1]

In the armistice signed on July 27, 1953, which was not followed by a peace treaty, Korea remained divided. When Germany was reunified in 1990, a few eyes turned toward the "last Cold War division in Asia." No one then—the United States least of all—seriously believed that North Korea could long resist the spirit of the age or survive the catastrophic way it was being governed. The death of Kim Il Sung in 1994 provided an opportunity for new wagers on how long the regime would last: when the United States signed the nuclear freeze agreement with Pyongyang in October 1994, American officials firmly believed that in ten years there would no longer be a North Korea. The promise to provide nuclear reactors was therefore considered to be of little import. We have to admit that this expectation was mistaken for the simple reason that no one really wanted a rapid reunification of the peninsula—South Korea because of the cost, not comparable with that of the two Germanys; Japan because of the competition of a united neighbor and fear of an unprecedented wave of immigration; the United States because it would have to deal with the question of its troops stationed in South Korea; and China because reunification would only be acceptable on its terms, that is, when Beijing could be certain that it would not benefit the United States.

The last Chinese condition seemed almost impossible to meet ten years ago, but anti-American sentiment these days is so strong among young South Koreans, who sometimes even express admiration for the way Kim Jong Il stands up to Washington, that time may well be on Beijing's side. In light of this, the arrival in South Korea of an unusually large number of defectors in 2004 (around five hundred)[2] by way of Vietnam is not necessarily a prelude to coming reunification, as a superficial analogy with Eastern Europe in 1989 might suggest. As just pointed out, not only do China and North Korea not want to hear about unification but they are joined by South Korea, which fears the effect that 23 million poverty-stricken North Koreans might have on an economy that is currently sustaining 48 million South Koreans.[3]

Sometimes, however, Korean nationalism is awakened throughout the peninsula, at China's expense. Pyongyang and Seoul were united in opposition in 2004 when Beijing decided to rewrite the history of the ancient kingdom of Koguryo, founded two millennia ago in the Tongge River basin in what is now North Korea and which at its apogee included a large part of Manchuria. The question raised by the Chinese revisionists was whether this kingdom was Chinese or Korean. The rewriting of history, supported by the Chinese Foreign Ministry, was a preparation for the future. In case of a sudden reunification, a possible modification of borders would be an additional pressure on the Koreans, who do not have the means to oppose Beijing.[4]

For China, the peninsula is a backyard over which it can never lose control. It is also a card in its main game against Washington—over the fate of Taiwan. The link between those two questions is as old as the Chinese Communist regime. Soon after the 1949 revolution, when China had to take a position on the Korean War, Premier Zhou Enlai declared his hesitancy because the regime was so new and because Stalin was not in support. Mao Zedong, on the other hand, had not the slightest hesitation: if China did not intervene on the side of Pyongyang, it would have no chance of recovering Taiwan.

Today, the situation has evolved considerably but the two Koreas are still divided and Taiwan has maintained its autonomy. Beijing's determination to do everything in its power to "recover" Taiwan has if anything grown stronger in recent years. China's tolerance of its turbulent little neighbor has no other explanation: North Korea is a thorn in the side of Washington and Tokyo with its missiles and unconventional weapons, with which it periodically threatens both capitals. It tests Washington and Tokyo at regular intervals with new provocations to see how they react.

The game has become dangerous because Pyongyang has the ballistic and nuclear resources to play in the major leagues. One of the principal lessons of the Cuban missile crisis was that the essential peril came not from Moscow but from Cuban President Fidel Castro, who was prepared to incinerate the planet rather than accept a compromise. That is an excellent reason to discipline Kim Jong Il before he becomes completely uncontrollable, or to replace him with a more predictable government. Some Chinese experts on defense questions are aware of the dilemma, yet the authorities in Beijing have not put serious pressure on Pyongyang thus far. North Korea's ties to Islamabad, its missile dealings with most countries in the Middle East, and its threat in May 2005 to sell nuclear weapons to terrorists have all given this small country a great deal more power than it really represents on the international stage. North Korea provides one of the best illustrations of the imbalances with which the twenty-first century will have to deal, in striking contrast to the celebrated balance of power between the two blocs in the Cold War. Korea was no doubt a victim in 1905, but a century later it has become a major disruptive force, especially if the prospect of a unified nuclear Korea is no longer pure fantasy. Seoul's embarrassed revelations about undeclared experiments conducted in the 1980s, prohibited by its international agreements, show that scientific curiosity was not the sole motive behind the tests. The extent of the nuclear activities carried out by South Korea was underestimated in the reports of the International Atomic Energy Agency, perhaps under American pressure, but the program was relatively sophisticated particularly with respect to enrichment.

As for North Korea, it is absurd to think that a country that behaves so brutally toward its citizens would keep its word to the rest of the world if it received a little encouragement from the West.[5] Like his father, Kim Jong Il is one of those men who give the lie to anyone who claims that there always comes a moment when tyrants grow weary of their tyranny. His only problem is to avoid any possibility of "perestroika" that might put an end to the Kim dynasty. Only Beijing may be in a situation to settle this by offering him a deal: leave the country and enjoy life.

Kim Jong Il's fear of reform is matched only by his love of ritual. When, for example, he plans to meet with a foreign dignitary visiting Pyongyang, a room is chosen from among the forty in the palace reserved for foreigners. Just before the visit, a military vehicle arrives with a team of specially trained soldiers who remove all furniture from that room, including the carpet. A second vehicle brings replacement furniture, Kim Jong Il's personal desk, his personal effects, and baskets of flowers. The "Dear Leader" arrives, engages in friendly conversation in this setting for 10 minutes, then withdraws, and the two vehicles return to remove the furniture and bring back the originals.

Even Stalin does not have such tales in his biography—perhaps he was less beloved by his people than Kim Jong Il. The greater the love others bear toward you, the more cautious you need to be. And for a figure who, according to stories told to the children of the country, managed to sink his ball in five holes with one stroke in his first time on a golf course, an occasional change of furniture is of no great moment. There are reports that the government even asks North Koreans to keep a special cloth to dust off pictures of him and of his father. When a train exploded in Ryongchong in April 2004, killing hundreds, the North Korean propaganda machine put out articles daring to claim that mothers had dived into the flames to save those precious pictures rather than their children.

Economic reforms that Pyongyang finally undertook in 2002 were carried out only after a formal promise from Beijing that the regime would not be in danger if Kim Jong Il followed China's example. So far, the reforms have succeeded only in causing inflation, further increasing the misery of the population. A comparative study of the physical condition of the citizens of the two Koreas, conducted with the support of a Korean foundation, came to the conclusion that North Koreans' diet had prevented them from experiencing the increase in height recorded in the South in the second half of the twentieth century. In the developed world as a whole during this period, there has been an increase in height of one centimeter per decade as a result of enhanced nutrition, elimination of most epidemics, improvement in medical services, and urbanization. Because of the impossibility of reaching the people living in North Korea, researchers could only look at data from the North Koreans who have escaped to the South, who often come from the most educated segment of the population, which would tend to fare better economically. The conclusions are stark: the difference in height between North Koreans and South Koreans twenty-five to thirty-five years old is six centimeters (almost 2.5 inches).[6]

And these were the North Koreans who were not prisoners. On the day that North Korea collapses we will discover a merciless concentration camp system, one of the worst in history, with survivors whose stories will shame the free world. And we will wonder why the available information did not lead to a break in diplomatic relations and calls to hold Pyongyang accountable. Dissemination of the documents available about the camps, satellite images, and accounts of former prisoners and guards should receive more attention than Pyongyang's blackmail with its supposed weapons. The blackmail has paid off: the regime has obtained supplies, credits, and fuel oil for years and once again in the summer of 2005 owed its survival to massive aid from South Korea.[7] It has sat at the table with the Chinese, the Russians, the Americans, the Japanese, and the South Koreans for discussions that have never had any result but to provide more opportunities for blackmail. During that time, the camps continued to torture and kill political prisoners—three generations of them—and escapees to China who had been turned over to the authorities in Pyongyang. The Western press has published too much on the subject for anyone still to feign ignorance.

North Korea, as pointed out, plays an ambiguous role in Chinese strategy. Without Beijing's complicity, Pyongyang's blackmail would be impossible, for the country survives on Chinese aid and only on Chinese aid. In a recent article in the *Far Eastern Economic Review*, a Chinese researcher close to the government contradicts Beijing's official line that Pyongyang's possession of a nuclear weapon would not be a strategic problem for China. Beijing will never be a target of its protégé, but in case of a conflict with the United States, Beijing might use North Korea against Japan as it uses Pakistan against India. But Beijing certainly wants to choose the time of the crisis and not be hostage to Kim's provocative policies.

The path the West should follow is exactly the opposite of the one traveled up to this point. We must increase the diplomatic isolation of Pyongyang, which is a possible interlocutor only for hoodlums and criminals, and force Beijing to take the North Korean problem in hand or pay the price for the regional effects of the increasingly unbearable blackmail by Kim Jong Il. A victory over Pyongyang would be one way of decreasing the risk of conflict in East Asia and reducing the unknown factors in a conflict over Taiwan. Finally, in case of the sudden death of Kim Jong Il (if he is not deposed by Beijing in the coming months or years), Japanese military forces might well be placed on immediate alert because of the unpredictable nature of the North Korean army. That army might see such a step as a provocation to which it would respond by firing missiles. What would happen after such an event, which is far from improbable, is left to the reader's imagination.

CHAPTER 16

The Choice of the Peoples

We, the peoples ...

—United Nations Charter

The order of the twentieth century was often unjust and oppressive, and in a large part of the world it was based on excessive power of the state. In the name of realpolitik, this *order* subjected many of the peoples of Europe, Asia, Africa, and South America to regimes that violated all the founding principles of democratic societies. Stability was the key word in Cold War diplomacy; countries waiting for help behind the iron curtain met with indifference. The West preferred injustice to disorder. We Europeans had to wait until 1989 to learn that Prague was a one-hour flight from Paris and that for a time the French embassy in Poland prohibited any contact with Lech Walesa or his supporters. Nor was support lacking for dictators and authoritarian regimes in the other camp (Indonesia is a good example), in the name of the fight against communism.

The preference for order over justice in foreign policy should have died after the fall of the USSR, but the West has persisted in the habit. Thus it has refrained from asking Moscow questions about the lack of an investigation after the suspicious explosions in Russian cities in 1999, or about the kind of gas used by troops in storming the Moscow theater in the 2003 incident in which 129 hostages died, or still more about the special forces in Beslan in 2004 *liberating* a school full of children with tanks and flamethrowers.[1] That stance of the West's also explains the complacency about China: foreigners in general and Western countries in particular convince themselves that there has been progress on human rights there, but the Chinese know that progress has been essentially on paper. And finally, preference for stability over justice also explains the failure of the EU's "Euro-Mediterranean partnership" with Middle Eastern and North African countries, known as the Barcelona Process, whose tenth anniversary was celebrated in 2005: despite an investment of 21 billion euros over that period, results are nonexistent, largely because of the EU reliance on governments rather than on civil society.

Upon the Tiananmen massacre in 1989, protests by governments raised hopes that there would be a change of attitude in favor of peoples. A breath of freedom had been blowing through Eastern Europe, not many months before the fall of the Berlin Wall, and people had come to the fore with a series of peaceful demonstrations. It was then that the massacre of students occurred in Beijing, as frightful as the movement was harmless, so timid had been the students' demands. The Chinese authorities wanted to show the rest of the country and the world that Beijing would brook no opposition. International reaction was strong and unanimous—except for countries like Burma, which was dealing with its students in a similar way. It was then that the Parisians saw Chinese dissidents parading down the Champs-Élysées in support of human rights for the bicentennial of the French Revolution on July 14, 1989. How distant that now seems! To erase that bad memory, the city of Beijing organized another parade down the same route in January 2004, from which it excluded anyone not strictly under its control, with the support of the French authorities. In that manner it inaugurated the Year of China—certainly not the Year of the Chinese. There was no longer any mention of human rights: the two states offered each other mutual congratulations, and that's where we are now. Popular demonstrations continue to proliferate in rural China protesting corruption and the arrogance of government officials in a country where many peasants are again hungry. It is well known that the most important cause of inequality in China is now the urban-rural income disparity. But the majority of the people are denied access to affordable housing, health care, and education. Petitions to the central government increase 50 percent each year, but only 1 percent are dealt with to the satisfaction of the petitioners. In November 2004, 100,000 peasants from the province of Sichuan took over municipal offices before being driven out by paramilitary forces. Repeated incidents have gradually weakened the local authorities and the national government as well, a phenomenon to which the outside world has paid no attention. It will probably take a serious economic crisis and social unrest on a much larger scale for the world to begin to take an interest in such developments. China faces enormous social and political challenges in the decade ahead and rosy predictions about its future require some dose of skepticism. Western financial interests in China may well be affected, and social upheaval could have serious regional strategic consequences. The resulting decline in foreign investment, if it happens, would further aggravate the crisis. The Chinese economy is the only aspect of China that is closely followed in Europe, but mostly with straight-line projections, without taking into account the need for China to dismantle the monopoly of the state in key industrial sectors. In principle, the articles that have begun to appear in recent years on the numerous uncertainties weighing on Chinese growth have more likelihood of capturing the attention of politicians than any repression of workers or peasants, even of massive proportions, but most of the time they prefer fairy tales in the economic domain as well.

Ten years after Tiananmen, in 1999, public opinion in Western countries forced governments to intervene to protect the civilian population of Kosovo, where ethnic cleansing was taking place. The idea that limits should be imposed on the power of leaders has made inroads and is now an element in many diplomatic speeches. In reality, however, as the tragedy of Darfur has demonstrated for now many years, Western countries still refuse to intervene in danger zones when their security interests are not directly threatened, a view that not only ignores recent recognition of the "transnational" nature of contemporary threats, but also of the "responsibility to protect." To put it plainly, the Western countries no longer want to intervene in Africa. The need for order continues to be seen as superior to the need for justice, and the survival of states is always more urgent than the survival of the populations in their charge. If the people are more important than the state, as the United Nations, whose first words are "We, the peoples," proclaims, which states are prepared to make this proclamation a tenet of international relations? Raymond Aron tried to reconcile political realism and concern for the peoples of the world by asserting that caution did not always mean indifference to or even less complacency about the regimes ruling states. Governments are still, however, primarily defenders of sovereignty, and among European countries such conviction is perhaps particularly true of France. That conviction manifested itself in Paris's disregard for the tragedy of the Algerian people, the deaths of 150,000 civilians under suspicious circumstances, in order to keep up good relations with Algiers, which played a role in the massacres; in the handling of the ethnic conflict in Rwanda that took around a million lives, where the desire for influence and *francophonie* won out over the protection of people; and in France's reaction to the 2004–05 Ukrainian political crisis, which showed that we Europeans continued to think that while Moscow might no longer make the rules in Kiev, Kiev for its part could not possibly oppose Moscow, which must not be "humiliated."

In principle, a state that does not fulfill the most elementary of its duties, to protect its citizens, thereby loses its sovereignty. And order is a value only to the extent that it is a condition for justice. Saddam Hussein and Slobodan Milosevic could not refer to international law as justification for their rule in Iraq and the former Yugoslavia. The former made light of it for a dozen years after the 1991 Gulf War, flouting the UN and the IAEA, in addition to ordering the massacre of his Kurdish and Shiite subjects and using chemical weapons prohibited by international law. The latter put the Balkans to fire and the sword for eight years. Both have been put on trial for their crimes. As for disorder—or even war—it is sometimes necessary to make justice possible. This truth is part of European history. No one could criticize the Third Reich or Stalin's Russia for not loving order. But how can one justify the support those two regimes received outside their borders?

The disturbances in the early 1990s in Europe made the reunification of the continent possible. Thus instead of systematically favoring stability, we ought to acknowledge, unless we are lacking in historical sense, that the support of dictatorships exacts a very high price in security and that the fall of worm-eaten rulers—for instance, Erich Honecker shortly before the end of East Germany—should be encouraged.

The idea of a link between security and human rights has a longer tradition, but the Second World War gave the best demonstration of its power. In his 1941 State of the Union address, Franklin Delano Roosevelt proclaimed the four freedoms: freedom of speech and expression, freedom of worship, freedom from want, and freedom from fear. A few years later these freedoms became the fundamental principles of the United Nations Charter. The founders of the United Nations recognized the interdependence between the security of individuals, the security of the state, and international security. The connection operates in both directions: international events affect societies and individuals, and societal phenomena have international ramifications. Over the years, the fundamental principles of the Universal Declaration of Human Rights, promulgated by the UN Commission on Human Rights in 1948, have become principles of customary international law. The Universal Declaration was reaffirmed in 1966 by the General Assembly's adoption of two legally binding international covenants, one on civil and political rights, the other on economic, social, and cultural rights. As of today, 140 countries have agreed to be bound by the two pacts. These two instruments and the Universal Declaration constitute the Universal Charter of Human Rights and are the basis of international law on human rights. That law applies to everyone at all times.

Many threats may also weigh on the security of populations without concerning either the rulers of those populations or the rulers of neighboring states. That is true of poverty, pollution, and threats to health. The International Commission on Intervention and State Sovereignty forcefully reiterated this idea in its 2001 report.

The traditional, narrow perception of security leaves out the most elementary and legitimate concerns of ordinary people regarding security in their daily lives. It also diverts enormous amounts of national wealth and human resources into armaments and armed forces, while countries fail to protect their citizens from the chronic insecurities of hunger, disease, inadequate shelter, crime, unemployment, social conflict, and environmental hazards.[2]

Europe is, however, increasingly aware that in the absence of a policy of more targeted and more conditional aid for developing countries, particularly those bordering its territory, it will in coming decades face political troubles and immigration that will be difficult to contain or manage.

For forty years, the great powers have relied on a balance of power between states to guarantee the security of their people, and to some degree, the security of the world. They neglected the protection of individuals in favor of a nearly exclusive focus on the state, and that was just as true in the West as in the East. The West was predisposed toward caution and realism, while the Communist world was never based on the idea of justice. As the Polish philosopher Leszek Kolakowski has pointed out, Marx did not approach social problems from a moral angle. He never said that capitalist society should be condemned because it was unjust or because the revolutionary struggle had justice as a goal. It was historical laws, not injustice, that would bring down capitalism. The first human right in the USSR was thus the right to work, and it soon served as the Communist regime's perverse justification for opening the gulag. The denunciation of dictatorships should be routine politics in the post–Cold War world, but it is far from being the case. More attention is still given to states than to regimes, and to governments than peoples. That is because dictatorships raise troubling questions for democracies, the first of which concerns their capacity to effectively resist political cynicism and brute force. The historical experience of the twentieth century, rich in dictatorships, has not put paid to the legendary ineptitude of democratic regimes in the face of the most aberrant forms of political power. Dictatorships should not be considered regimes of another era; they exist in every era. Confronting them, democracies constantly forget that they bear within themselves the recognition of the unity of the human race above and beyond the world of nations.

CHAPTER 17

The Unity of the Western Camp

*Whenever my thoughts grow too dark
and I despair of Europe, I find some hope
again only by thinking of the New World.*

—Paul Valéry

Valéry's hopes turned to the New World in 1938, at a moment when it seemed possible that European culture might vanish in the "fury of war," along with European cities, universities, and museums. The thought that the New World, as Valéry still called it, could bring "the unhappy Europeans" back to life with a new existence on the other side of the ocean was consoling, but the poet did not know how great the debt of Europeans to America would be. Countless exiles would owe their lives to taking refuge across the Atlantic, and America's entry into the war would be decisive for the eventual Allied victory. Nor did Valéry foresee that, having done so much for the liberation of Europe, America would ensure the recovery of the old continent and then guarantee its security for nearly half a century.

During the present difficult period for transatlantic relations, created by misunderstandings that we tend to think of as entirely new, we forget that the misunderstandings began very soon after World War II. Current evocations of transatlantic relations during the Cold War are like the reminiscences of old men about their far-off youth—everything is prettified. We recall that the strategy established in 1945 responded to the decline of Europe and to America's rise to power, attempting to fit the Western "bloc" to meet the coming storms. We speak of the common enemy, of the great moments of NATO, and of transatlantic friendship. That attitude requires forgetting how difficult, contested, and thwarted the alliance was, and how many major crises—for instance, Suez in 1956—it went through. It forgets the importance of the Communist parties in France and in Italy, which followed Moscow's policies; the pacifist parties in Germany, which complicated the defense of the alliance; and the reluctant or even difficult allies, as the French always were. The union was never as strong, as durable, or as firmly supported throughout Western Europe as it is painted.

Considering the negative talk about the American empire which began back in the 1970s and swelled after 1989, we might wonder whether the post–Cold War world is really that different, and whether the disappearance of the fear of the Soviet threat has had effects nearly as significant as has been claimed. It is true that Europe no longer feels threatened and wants to enjoy the "peace dividend," but then, many Europeans never believed in the reality of the threat during the Cold War—at least of the threat from Moscow and the Warsaw Pact. Even then, many believed that the biggest threat came from Washington! Similarly today, a number of Europeans prefer Vladimir Putin to George W. Bush. During the Cold War, Europeans harbored contradictory fears: of not being in a position to defend themselves against Moscow (hence the fear of American withdrawal) and of being the losers in an understanding between the two superpowers (hence the talk of a "condominium" between Washington and Moscow).

What is not open to question now is that Europe is no longer the center of gravity of world strategic affairs; Asia is. We Europeans should be pleased at that major shift, because it enabled Europe to unify after decades of division, but also because if a major conflict broke out, it would no longer be on European soil. But far from giving Europe permission to go on a sort of holiday from history (the famous peace dividend), the current respite ought to enable it to assume once again its responsibilities in the world.

Of the two priorities identified in U.S. defense policy—international terrorism and Asian security—the first is a threat to Europe as well, and a serious crisis involving the second, despite European strategic myopia on the subject, would soon have consequences for European countries. If we take globalization seriously, we must acknowledge its effects in the realm of security. Containing conflicts now is even more difficult than it was in the last century, which saw all too much what globalization of wars actually meant.

Analysts differ in their assessment of threats and in their advice about action to be taken. In the case of international terrorism, there was remarkable unity of purpose in the immediate aftermath of 9/11, in the Security Council as well as the General Assembly, in NATO as well as the European Union. The desire to unite to lessen the chaos that threatened world security at first seemed quite real. But several years later, despite the 2004 attacks in Madrid, the 2005 attacks in London, and the 2006 foiled attacks against ten transatlantic planes, Europe is still convinced that it is less threatened than the United States. As a result, European governments, with the notable exception of the British, have not presented the terrorist threat to their people.[1] The behavior and dignity of Londoners after the 2005 subway and bus attacks was a result of the psychological preparation the government had undertaken during the previous several years under the rubric of *resilience*. One wonders whether the assessment of the threat in most European countries is still not a function of the budget allotted to deal with it rather than the other way around. By this measure, Europeans may claim that the United States is exaggerating the danger, but they probably underestimate it on their side.

With regard to Asia, Europe has yet to spot that immense territory on its strategic radar screen, despite the fact that it has territorial continuity with it. What the Europeans might do in the event of conflict on the Korean peninsula has not been thought of, although some European nations, France included, were signatories of the 1953 armistice. Nor has anyone thought about what Europe would do in case of a conflict between the United States and China over Taiwan. The Germans see China essentially as a major market and the French see it one of the principal actors in an ill-defined "multipolar" world, while the British long confined their consideration of China to the problem of Hong Kong. In the *European Security Strategy* published by the European Council in December 2003, Asia appears at the very end, and then only in the context of a general discussion of "strategic partnerships" of the European Union, where one finds, in no particular order, China, Japan, and India. That document is an indication of how limited thinking has been: none of those three countries are comparable in terms of security and none has a strategic partnership with Europe worthy of the name. The document is thus devoid of meaning, despite its very general acknowledgment of "global challenges."

At the turn of the century, the United States produced an impressive study on Asia in 2025, which considers the conclusions that ought to be drawn from developments on that continent in demography, energy, and the military. It looked at different scenarios, emphasizing the numerous possibilities for strategic surprises from that part of the world, whether in South Asia, East Asia, or South East Asia. In Europe, on the other hand, lack of understanding of these problems from a security viewpoint is almost total. Without discussions on China's rise to power between Europe and America, and Europe and Japan (which might give substance to the strategic partnership that has been talked about), it will be difficult to have any substantial Western solidarity in the twenty-first century. Some observers on either side of the Atlantic are worried about the appearance of "two Wests."[2] Divisions arise because the American power that once protected European weakness now worries it, because Europe has become a significant economic force while having no desire to play a role in strategic affairs, and finally because European and American analyses of threats coincide only in part.

Those different judgments are grounded in a deeper, historical crisis due to the coinciding of the apogee of American power with the unification of Europe. Unification ought to have gone hand in hand with a change in strategic status but has not, for the excellent reason that most Europeans have no desire for a return to power politics. The problem here lies in a narrowing of Europe's traditional openness to the world, demonstrated throughout its history, which made it one of the richest civilizations on the face of the earth. History seems to have been forgotten at the very moment when territorial unity has been achieved. Conversely, the United States, whose interest in the world is more recent—dating from the end of the nineteenth century, when the Spanish-American War gave it control over Cuba and the Philippines—has continued to broaden its horizons. Necessity guided it, not self-seeking ambition. Thus it fought and emerged victorious from two world wars, and then the exceptionally dangerous Cold War confrontation, in which Washington for the first time bore the principal strategic responsibility in the West.

Sixty years after Pearl Harbor, on September 11, the United States received another shock from the outside world, but this time the blow struck at the heart of America. The result was a feeling of urgency, a recognition that the country could not be satisfied with upholding the established order or depending on containment for its security. American support for regimes that seek only to last had become a potential danger rather than a guarantee of stability.

European thinking has followed a different path. The transformations Europeans have seen on their territory since 1989 are so numerous that they often dream of stability in the rest of the world. The debate on the proposed European Constitution showed that members have not yet even accepted enlargement, which is seen not as a remarkable success after decades of painful separation but as a disturbance of the economic life of Western Europe by the arrival of new states.

For most observers in the outside world, the United States is the primary representative of the West, having taken the place of Europe, which occupied the front rank only a century ago. The mistake would be to think that this demotion of Europe's will protect it in any way from the twenty-first century's turbulence. In the minds of America's enemies, the distance separating it from Europe is not as great as has been claimed. The English speak ironically of the Atlantic Ocean, calling it "the pond." Europeans and Americans may delight in commenting on how different their political, social, and military choices are. But America's most dangerous enemies also see the Atlantic as a pond, both of whose shores are populated by "infidels," or simply "Westerners." As good tacticians, they attempt to separate the two sides of the Atlantic. But the Western world—though we who live there often refuse to recognize it—is seen as one world by the enemies of America, who are equally willing to attack Europe.[3] That is one of the lessons of the Madrid and the London attacks, but also of the attacks on German tourists in Tunisia in 2002, or against French interests in Yemen and Pakistan in 2003. It is also the lesson of the three warnings that France received from Al Qaeda: first in November 2002, then after the law on the veil was passed, and finally in October 2004. The attacks and warnings should put an end to the illusion of a people *retired from history*, a position Europeans would be happy to fill because of the general unwillingness to see the world in terms of power relations. As Leon Trotsky put it, in one of his striking expressions, "You may not be interested in war, but war is interested in you."

The current U.S. policy of intervening in world affairs to shape the world resembles Europe's past policy—while Europe's current policy resembles that of a bygone America—stay home and develop a model.

Thus each power is somehow irritated by the image of itself presented by the other. But the truth is that the two need each other to confront the century's challenges, just as the world needs their common contribution. The paradox is that Europe now contains only democratic countries whose values are close to those of the United States. As indicated earlier, the 2003 European Commission document *European Security Strategy* expresses a provincial view of the world, with the Balkans, Russia, and the Mediterranean presented as the only truly relevant areas. And even in those three areas, points of convergence for a number of thorny issues, the Union has no real strategy. Europe, however, seems to be unaware that in the event of an attack on its territory or its strategic interests (oil, for example), neither its own resources nor the UN will be sufficient to defend it.

In the meantime, the United States circles the world, often without knowing it and does not always understand the difference between winning battles and winning wars. It is often said that it does not have the same view of the future of the West that Europe does, but that remains to be seen. Only the first great test will reveal the truth. At that moment, unity will perhaps be restored. The question is whether it will not be too late then, military resources and doctrines having grown too disparate to work effectively together. Comparisons of the wars in the Persian Gulf, Kosovo, Afghanistan, and Iraq demonstrate very significant developments in American defense doctrine, with an exceptionally rapid and effective implementation of the revolution in military affairs. U.S. forces use information technologies at qualitative and quantitative levels that no European forces can hope to reach. We are told that we have to follow the same path. That may well be, but it is also true that we do not have the means to do so with the defense budgets that are currently accepted in Europe. In addition, due to inefficient spending, the Europeans lack both the concentration of power and the economy of scale that the United States does. The risk is that we will no longer be able to fight together, even if we decide one day that it has become necessary.

Agreement between the two sides of the Atlantic is a guarantee of success, as the renewed unity at the time of the Ukrainian elections demonstrated in 2004. It was not possible for Moscow to pursue the dangerous course of counterdemonstrations, which might have given rise to violent confrontations. Similarly, during the same period, the Franco-American–sponsored Security Council Resolution 1559 on the withdrawal of Syrian troops from Lebanon bore fruit within a few months, when in April 2005 Syrian troops and the Syrian secret services withdrew from Lebanese territory. More generally, the global responsibilities of the two Wests are crushing and can only be assumed together. The two approaches therefore must be harmonized, with the conviction that it is not necessary to do everything jointly or in the same way but that it is imperative to work toward the same ends. Europe and the United States no longer make up what was called during the Cold War the *Free World*, but they continue to have very similar objectives and security interests.

In peacetime bonds tend to loosen, and that is what is happening today. Relations between Europe and America have been on a downward spiral since 2002. But considering the resources Europe will have available for its defense over the next two decades, it will be unable to confront a serious threat. Washington has never relied on the goodwill of other nations to guarantee its security, and it has always thought it should be prepared to act alone.[4] What constituted a veritable revolution for American security in the twentieth century was the recognition that events occurring in Europe had an impact on the security of the United States. The possibility that a single power could have a stranglehold on Europe was a considerable threat. Theodore Roosevelt, president from 1901 to 1909, already thought so, and both his diplomacy and his naval policy were aimed at preventing it. Later, after the First World War, Woodrow Wilson thought the threat came from a lack of democracy. Today, the Americans may be as close to Wilson as they are to Roosevelt. But the biggest difference between contemporary Americans and Europeans when it comes to strategy is that the Americans have many more choices, while in Europe, on the contrary, possibilities tend to grow narrower.

On both sides of the Atlantic, the West is seen by the rest of the planet as living through the historical problem of a world in decline. That is truer of the old continent of Europe, which for centuries played an exceptional role in the history of humanity but now seems worn out by that long history. America has preserved its extraordinary talent for drawing the bulk of its energy from the future, but it is probably on the way to extending its power too widely around the world. Hence for opposite reasons—withdrawal on one side, extension on the other—both sides of the Atlantic are threatened by decline. The conviction that both are vulnerable makes attacks against the Western world both probable and dangerous, for it is always in periods of decline that enemies take off their masks. In the struggle, Europe ought not to forget that the strength of America is its own, whereas its weakness is shared by the West as a whole.

CHAPTER 18

RETHINKING NUCLEAR WEAPONS

Next time we won't be so lucky.

—NIKOLAI S. LEONOV, head of Cuban affairs in the
KGB during the 1962 missile crisis

In the nuclear realm, the pessimism of a few cool observers in the 1950s did more for peace than all the arguments about the gradual advance of liberal ideas in the world. The fear of total destruction, and that alone, made leaders think long and hard and gave deterrence a major role in the prevention of a new world conflict after the Second World War. But the very success of the enterprise,[1] manifest at the end of the Cold War, somehow undermined its principal gain: since a nuclear exchange had *not* taken place, the notion of survival lost a good deal of force and sense of urgency. And the absolute necessity of mastering violence between states receded in our thinking. Humanity doesn't learn very much from events *that do not happen.* It needs to make mistakes, and even sometimes to live through catastrophes, to force it to go down different paths and change its course. If things worked out well enough during the Cold War, future generations are not guaranteed that kind of phenomenal luck. After all, the non-use of an available weapon is more the exception than the rule throughout history. The continuation of that luck beyond fifty years requires such a combination of favorable factors that it hardly seems probable.

The use of nuclear weapons, although less talked about nowadays, has in fact become less unthinkable than during the second half of the twentieth century. The increase in the number of nuclear powers has increased the risks. Qualitative factors also play a negative role: for instance, new nuclear powers, with no experience of deterrence during the Cold War, seem not to grasp that between countries with nuclear weapons, it is not only nuclear conflicts that must be proscribed but all forms of conflict, since the situation most likely to lead to use of nuclear weapons is the loss of control of a conventional conflict.[2] Finally, for countries building up their militaries, since nuclear weapons cost much less than sophisticated conventional weapons, the temptation is very strong to respond to the revolution in military affairs with a "revolution in violence" and the acquisition of weapons of mass destruction.

We must keep in mind that any use of nuclear weapons now would take place in conditions very different from those of 1945, when there was only one nuclear power and when long-range missiles did not yet exist. Nor would the situation be comparable to that in 1953, the year of publication for Robert Oppenheimer's far-sighted article in *Foreign Affairs*, when the proliferation of nuclear weapons and ballistic missiles had not yet begun. The principal warning in that article, which dealt with the survival of humanity, remains strikingly pertinent today. It is a safe bet that if Oppenheimer could speak about the contemporary world, where unscrupulous individuals sell all the elements needed to make a nuclear weapon through clandestine networks, he would not attempt to reassure us. Instead he would probably, like Schopenhauer, propose that we imagine the world we are preparing for future generations by allowing a multiplicity of nuclear powers to appear on the world scene, particularly in regions that are in a constant state of tension, such as the Middle East, South Asia, and East Asia.

Far from abolishing the nuclear threat, the fact that European soil is no longer the epicenter of a possible nuclear exchange has merely *displaced* and *complicated* it. That nuclear weapons are no longer central to global strategic balance has changed deterrence in some of its crucial aspects. The division of the world symbolized by the iron curtain may have been unfair and painful, but it had the enormous advantage of clearly delimiting the two camps. No such clarity exists today in the three regions mentioned above, in which there is nothing that can properly be called a status quo.

In South Asia, the northern borders of India with Pakistan and China are not even fixed and are still called *lines "of control" or of "actual control."* In the Middle East, several nations do not recognize Israel—Iran even wants to "wipe it off the map"—and have territorial disputes with each other. In East Asia, tension and passion are fostered by the prospects of Korean and Chinese reunification. No one today can make reasonable guesses about the way in which either question will be resolved, but the chances are great that the price will be much higher than was the case for German reunification. Moreover, the West may have been mistaken in believing that it understood the Soviet world, but it certainly misunderstands new nuclear actors. It would be extremely difficult, for instance, to find any studies of North Korea or Iran on par with those written on Soviet strategy. Misunderstanding of adversaries is always serious in military matters, but it can quickly turn fatal when nuclear weapons are involved. Finally, no one knows how to deal with a world in which the Middle East might contain four or five nuclear powers within twenty years, and the continent of Asia a comparable number.[3]

Any use of nuclear weapons anywhere in the world would call into question a taboo that has been observed since 1945. In addition, consequences of the escalation of violence are even more unpredictable now than during the Cold War. In a way, the "balance of terror" has given way to the "imbalance of terror," its exact opposite.[4] And situations of imbalance may create fears just as acute as those of the past, by spreading a general feeling of vulnerability, including among the most powerful nations. Surprise attack, which was the main fear during the Cold War, the one all diplomatic and military measures were designed to counter, is again on our minds, but this time from enemies who sometimes allow for no political dialogue, as in the case of Pyongyang. This may still increase the risk of misunderstanding that was referred to earlier. If this feeling of uncertainty and this fear of "surprise" is so strong at the beginning of the twenty-first century, what will happen in twenty years if the tendency is not reversed? Today, it may still be possible to argue that this is a messy but necessary transition period, and that stability will eventually come. But such hopes hang on a thread; peace will not preserve itself; it needs human action. If there is no reason to panic in 2006, there is reason to recover what actually proved far more important than our warheads and missiles during the Cold War: self-confidence and determination. Today, the West looks and *is* demoralized. As a consequence, it is also discredited and vulnerable.

Although the end of the USSR was hardly unforeseeable—some acute minds pointed out fairly early on that we were seriously overestimating the power of the enemy—it was rarely considered *possible*. It was as though until the late 1980s we Westerners were afflicted with a form of voluntary submission to a system that was contrary to everything that Western societies represent. We are now confronting a comparable problem with much smaller nations, like North Korea, but also with China, the only country with which a major nuclear crisis is to be feared in the twenty-first century.

There was one major nuclear crisis during the Cold War, the Cuban missile crisis in October 1962. It can now be analyzed in detail, after the Cold War's end allowed for declassification of the principal documents and the bringing together of American, Russian, and Cuban officials at many seminars on the subject. The essential lessons are clear. Although the episode was long considered a model of deterrence, with President John F. Kennedy's determination making the Soviets back down in a duel, the reality is more complex. It was not the hostility of the two principal leaders but a foolish Cuban initiative that nearly unleashed catastrophe and could have begun a third world war.

The crisis, which lasted thirteen days, started when the president's national security adviser, McGeorge Bundy, informed Kennedy that photographs of the island of Cuba indicated the presence of Soviet nuclear missiles. Once operational, these medium and intermediate range missiles, capable of reaching all the major cities on the East Coast, would have endangered 100 million Americans. The news was a complete surprise to the United States, since Foreign Minister Andrei Gromyko and other high-level Soviet officials had given explicit assurances that very year that the USSR had no nuclear missiles in Cuba and had no intention of deploying them in the future. That lie was the Soviets' real mistake, because it could have resulted in a nuclear exchange. As recently as the month before, President Kennedy had declared that if Soviet missiles were deployed in Cuba "the most serious consequences would ensue"; he could hardly go back on his word one month later. The Soviets, relying on shock tactics, thought that the Americans would accept these deployments, which did not really change the nuclear balance between the two great powers. Their mistake in judgment is explained by the fact that only five or six people in Moscow were aware of all the details and the Soviet analysis of the situation was rudimentary because of its very secrecy. Kennedy's immediate decision was to force the Soviets to withdraw their missiles. The problem was how to do it without starting a war.

According to Robert McNamara, then secretary of defense, the most important decisions Kennedy made at the outset were: to limit the number of senior officials who would be kept informed about the situation; to prevent any leaks to the press in order to avoid pressure from public opinion; and finally, to identify a series of possible responses to the Soviet deployment, indicating the arguments for and against each. "No later decision made during the Cuban missile crisis contributed more to the prevention of conflict than those three decisions made immediately by President Kennedy," McNamara asserted.[5] Two solutions were proposed to the president: a naval blockade of Cuba to prevent further deliveries of missiles and an air attack. The majority of Kennedy's advisers leaned toward an air attack. The president then asked General Walter Sweeney, head of the U.S. Air Force Tactical Air Command, if he could guarantee that all the missiles would be destroyed by an air attack. Since the answer was negative, the naval blockade of Cuba began on October 24. Three days later, Moscow still had not made known its intention to withdraw the missiles from Cuba.

One fundamental element of the crisis came to light only much later. The belief prevailing in Washington in 1962 was that the missile warheads had not yet been delivered but were about to be; in fact, 162 tactical and strategic warheads were already in Cuba.[6] Not knowing that, Kennedy threatened to attack and invade Cuba. Soviet Premier Nikita Khrushchev offered a compromise: if the United States did not invade Cuba, the USSR would withdraw the missiles. The crisis could be considered ended. But the next day an American U2 spy plane was shot down on Castro's orders, against those of Khrushchev. As it turned out, the third player, Cuba, was a decisive one. At a conference in Havana in January 1992, Fidel Castro stated that he would not have hesitated to unleash nuclear war if an invasion had taken place. And since the presence of the warheads was unknown to the United States, deterrence could not operate—even if the obvious consequence of Cuba's use of the weapons would have been the destruction of Cuba. There is a major lesson in this story: today, we will probably have to deal with more Castros than Kennedys or Khrushchevs.

This crucial episode of the Cold War also illustrates the danger of having not two but three actors in a nuclear crisis. If two of them behave wisely but the third behaves foolishly, war may break out even if the third player is the least important of the three. The introduction of nuclear weapons into Cuba, which reduced Soviet launch time to seven minutes, significantly shortened or even eliminated the time needed to evaluate nuclear alerts. For a brief moment, the magnitude of the anticipated attack, the impossibility of determining with precision when it would occur, and the third actor's lack of restraint put the lives of millions of people in danger. That is the recently expressed conclusion of Nikolai Leonov, who in 1962 was head of the KGB's department of Cuban affairs:

> A single error at the wrong moment in October 1962 and everything might have been lost. I can hardly believe that we are here today to discuss that crisis. It is almost as though there had been divine intervention to save us from ourselves, but with this warning: you must never again come so close to catastrophe. Next time we won't be so lucky.

Those remarks will be greeted with spontaneous assent from anyone who has followed the twists and turns of the Iranian nuclear saga, North Korean blackmail, or tension in the Taiwan Strait. Nuclear weapons are, to be sure, less numerous today than during the Cold War in the two most significant arsenals, and they no longer govern strategic relationships. But nuclear deterrence worked because there was a clear division of the world and not much was asked of it beyond preservation of the status quo. Nothing of the kind exists in the three regions we are discussing.

The other condition for deterrence was, of course, mutual vulnerability. In the case of a possible confrontation between the United States and China, is that still true? Western countries, including the United States, would be unable to "swallow" what China can absorb. Chairman Mao was already very aware of that truth when he made provocative statements about China's ability to absorb a nuclear strike, demonstrating once more its contempt for human life. In a sense, one can argue that there is no real mutual vulnerability between the United States and China, because of different scales but also different feelings regarding casualties—a huge change from previous situations. Furthermore, the nuclear danger today is much more diversified and difficult to grasp. As already stated, Iran and North Korea are actors about whom we in the West know almost nothing. The former always has three or four different policies in mind, and the latter is recognizable only by its dramatic and provocative gestures. More than governments, Tehran's and Pyongyang's regimes look like conspiracies.

The question remains as to whether the nuclear peril is behind or before us. Behind us, say the strategists of the Cold War. Before us, retort those who have been following nuclear proliferation. The former can argue that nuclear weapons will never again play as important a role in world affairs as they did between 1949 and 1989, and that is indeed so. But the latter will demonstrate without much difficulty that the number and nature of new actors have changed the conditions for the success of deterrence to the point where they are unrecognizable. It is no longer impossible, for example, to imagine a Korea reunified to China's benefit, with nuclear weapons. China could use that state of affairs for its own strategic purposes, as it uses Pakistan's weapon against India—a possibility Washington sometimes refuses to recognize, persuaded that it has the same interests as China on the question of a denuclearized Korean peninsula.[7] Those who argue that nuclear weapons will play a reduced role are right. But those who claim that the risk that nuclear weapons might be used is far greater are far from wrong.

The first camp recalls facts that we must keep remembering. When the new weapon appeared in 1945, what was at stake was ending the war with Japan and impressing Stalin, whose continued presence among the Allies was uncertain.[8] But Hiroshima and Nagasaki must continue to be seen as transforming events. Sixty years later, one of the great dangers lies in our having grown used to living in a nuclearized world whose dangers we no longer measure because we think we know them so well. If deterrence is preserved, nuclear weapons may still protect the world from greater and more frequent outbreaks of violence than those we are witnessing today.[9] Deterrence is contingent, however, on the refusal to tolerate nuclear blackmail—from China against Taiwan or from North Korea against Japan and the United States or from Iran against its neighbors—but also on determination to act in case of non-compliance with the Nuclear Non-Proliferation Treaty. And we may well ask: are both those conditions being met?

The second camp thus may be closer to the historical reality of this century than the first camp. The preservation of nuclear peace is largely in the hands of the five permanent members of the Security Council. Whether they like it or not, they are the ones responsible for the nuclear future. They are the officially recognized nuclear powers, and any conflict between them would have a nuclear shadow. The rivalry between the United States and Russia has given way to a Sino-American relationship that is a mixture of cooperation and confrontation. The true situation will probably become clearer in fifteen to twenty years, when Beijing has modernized its army. For the time being, the privilege of the permanent members of the Security Council still goes along with a twofold obligation: not to help new countries acquire the bomb, and to respond to any violations of the Non-Proliferation Treaty, to which three of the members are depositories. Considering the way they have dealt so far with the two nuclear crises in "slow motion" that started in 1992 (North Korea) and 2002 (Iran), their action look hardly responsible. History will tell.

On October 26, 1962, at the moment when the world was nearly plunged into the Third World War, Khrushchev sent Kennedy a remarkable letter. In it he compared relations between adversaries at a time of acute crisis to two individuals holding the ends of a rope in the middle of which is a knot:

> If the peoples do not act wisely, then in the end they will confront one another like blind moles, and mutual destruction will begin. If you have not lost all self-control, then, Mister President, neither of us should pull on the end of the rope in which you have tied the knot of war, because the more you and I pull the tighter the knot will grow. And a moment will come when the knot will be so tight that even the one who tied it will not have the strength to untie it. And at that moment, there will be no solution but to break it.[10]

Khrushchev's letter explains what actually happened—not in 1962, where wisdom prevailed—but in 1914, and what may again happen. The direct experience that the Soviet leader had of the Second World War probably played a decisive role in his determination to prevent another war and a nuclear exchange. World leaders of today have not had that kind of experience. But more than sixty years after Hiroshima and Nagasaki, it should not be forgotten.

The Human Soul Torn to Pieces

Consciousness seems to be a mirror
in which sometimes the sky, sometimes
the ground comes toward the spectator.

—PAUL VALÉRY

What is most peculiar about our age is the conviction that evil is installed at the core of history and our frenetic rejection of that conviction. Twenty-first-century man bears a strange resemblance to primitive man seeking to drive evil outside the known world and transform it into a taboo. For us as for him, evil brings misfortune, and we want it out of our sight. But the world no longer has any borders beyond which we might cast it. The experience of evil has such force in contemporary consciousness, and the disorder of minds and things is so evident, that what seems most pressing is restoring vigor to whatever might allay the ubiquitous anxiety. Fear of tomorrow and the inability to bear adversity not only threaten mental equilibrium but increase the instability of events. The most painful questions about the future are the ones raised by times that have seen natural or political cataclysms and are living in the expectation of metamorphosis or apocalypse. One can read just that in the gaze of our contemporaries: the expectation of something that does not yet have a name and that, as in 1905, has secret bonds with repressed memory and premonitions of the future. The history of the last century, that *hortus inclusus* of which we remain unconscious prisoners, is so full of misfortunes on which to meditate that we sometimes feel the weight of the dead mowed down by wars and revolutions, wandering like ghosts through our cities demanding justice. As for the future, it seems opaque or even obscure; all projects appear vulnerable, as peace appears precarious.

The "promise of the future" is what the contemporary world most lacks, having what can be called a crepuscular consciousness. Europe should understand better than any other part of the planet what is at stake in this twilight, for we are familiar with the signs of decline and have an age-old experience of catastrophe. Having long helped give the world its intellectual shape, we cannot be unaware that chaos in ideas—now ubiquitous—is particularly alarming when it is at work in our own societies. Those societies are no longer a model for the rest of the world. Full of confusion ourselves, we can hardly shoulder that role.

Advocating only a return to reason and rational activity is not without value, but one may fear that this appeal is doomed to failure for at least two reasons. The first is that reason has been disqualified in the twentieth century for allowing everything to be justified, including the unjustifiable, under every sky. Ideologies were products of the overdevelopment of rational activity—the first aberrations appearing in the eighteenth century in Europe—and it was rational activity that gave birth to the "monsters" announced a century later by visionaries like Nietzsche. The second reason is of a completely different order. What is most striking in the expressions of contemporary consciousness is not the demand for rationality but the need to find a new place for the irrational, an essential component of the human psyche. Early in the past century, Carl Jung worried about an evolution that condemned individuals to imbalance by frustrating what he called "the mythic side of man" and banning the expression of what the mind could not grasp rationally. Now, at a time when religion is making a spectacular comeback in violent and destructive forms, we should inquire into the spiritual void that is undermining our societies and the psychological disturbances that go along with it. If we do not succeed in discovering a new harmony between the rational and the irrational, the excesses of either—more likely the latter—may again produce collective catastrophes.

As for reason, it should rediscover the thread of a lost way of thinking. The questions that have stirred humanity for centuries—on human freedom, the meaning of history, political responsibility—have all become suspect. Nonetheless, they have not gone away. Since the end of the nine-teenth century, politics seems to have had no goal outside itself—that is, beyond the exercise of power—except for economic development. But Adam Smith had already warned of the dangers lying in wait for nations in which economic interests dominated: "Minds grow narrow, elevation of spirit becomes impossible ... and the heroic spirit comes close to dying out altogether," concluding that "It would be highly important to reflect on the means to remedy these defects." For there comes a time when weakness of intelligence and of will make it impossible to grasp one's responsibilities in world affairs or even one's own security interests. That time is here, with all its turbulence, and humankind should have been more startled by the realization. In all of human history there has been no period when the dangers of politics and the limits of the economy have been made so brutally manifest as in the past century. Nor has there been any when ethics, or their absence, have been more obviously at the core of public action.

The central question posed by totalitarianism was that of human free-dom—the negation of the individual versus the human capacity to resist terror and mass crimes. It is also the question posed today by international terrorism. In a world without direction, drifting at random and *operating in the void*, human freedom may not have much meaning. But if we evoke the new terrorists' paroxysm of violence or the incredible greed of the clandestine networks that sell the components of nuclear weapons to the highest bidder, everyone will understand that we are asking questions not only about the world for which those acts are laying the foundation but also about what has led the world into such dire straits.

Contemporary societies are riven by fear of the unknown, for human beings can no longer discern the fate of the species in the historical process. And if that is the case, it is difficult if not impossible to construct a project for the future. The sense of historical continuity seems to have been lost. Survivors of the Cold War resemble survivors of the French Revolution, who were conscious of finding themselves "amidst the debris of a great storm" but feared their memories and rarely spoke about themselves. Bal-zac has them say that they have "forgotten" themselves. That forgetful-ness, more devastating in 2005 than in the early nineteenth century, is part of the rising savagery of contemporary consciousness. It protects us from an unprecedented moral crisis that we should all experience, a crisis that would be particularly acute in countries such as Russia, China, or Cambodia, whose past tragedies are the least bearable. Historians will no doubt realize one day that an essential component of international relations may be found precisely in what that forgetfulness is covering up.

Guizot's old nostrum, "Get rich!" has been put back on the agenda worldwide by globalization. But those who do not reckon with the explosive power of collective emotions buried in memory and who think that all past misfortunes will be overcome by economic development understand neither the force of the unconscious nor the force of repression. Nor do they understand the strength of the truth concerning past crimes when it finally triumphs.

After going through a period of adjustment that has now come to an end, we have to clean the lens of the telescope turned on the past before turning it toward the future. Through it we see the conflicts that were not resolved in the last century and have become more complex and acute as time has passed. Such is the case in the Korean peninsula, in the Middle East, in South Asia, and in East Asia. The speed of events makes the consequences of the numerous crises hard to predict, and the interconnection of individual fates around the globe is extraordinary, far beyond what our forebears experienced a hundred years ago. The gravest danger, however, still comes from the messages that the twentieth century has left us but which have not been received. Here are a few. *Political, cultural, and moral regression is now part of our political landscape. The dehumanization of which we are the heirs is a threat to our survival. The memory of crimes is a condition of international security.* But also: *Resistance to terror is not doomed in advance, and in the century of lies, it sometimes happens that truth lifts up its head.*

Philosophers and scientists have agreed that one of the most important questions to resolve is the nature of time. How could something so deeply contradictory be the underpinning of our world and of human existence? The question has haunted thinkers in many forms and spawned countless works on first causes, genealogies, evolution, the aim of history, and the theory of relativity. In that determination to question and hypothesize there is an obvious search for meaning, whether concerned with the order of the world or the significance of human existence, at a time when many believe that religion no longer provides answers to such questions. What humanity is now experiencing with respect to time is the terror that

Pascal described on contemplating the immensity of space. We are terri-
fied by our powerlessness in the face of the universe while at the same
time greatly fearing our capacity to misuse what earthly power we have
acquired. Even more than the limited historical ambitions and the egocentrism of current Western societies, what is striking is their deep dis-
tress. Freud's *Herzelend* (heartsickness) still defines our age. If change has
become a public enemy, it is because of the expectation of new catastrophes, of the *great ax* of history that inhabits everyone's mind, perhaps the
minds of Europeans most of all.

Violence and the call to murder have taken up residence in the gaping
void at the core of a modernity that has too much room for new utopias.[1]
The emotions and fears provoked by images of violence and destruction
may have the effect of again plunging humanity into a period of troubles
in which reason, argument, and balance are overwhelmed by the exacer-
bation of passions. The individuals best adapted to such times are also the
most dangerous, and the new forms of terrorism that we have witnessed
in recent years can thus be interpreted as a warning. Freud was convinced
that there was something at the heart of civilization that defied any will
and any possibility of reform.

He may be right. But great artists have always offered another response
to the enigma of history, which Mozart expressed by saying simply that
humans were on earth not to regress, repeat, or agonize about their crimes
but "to always go further." For that to be possible again, ethics must be
rescued from the paralysis that has incapacitated it. The more violent,
chaotic, and incomprehensible the world becomes, the more that need
comes to the fore in our consciousness. The violence and disorientation of
our time may be signs of a form of backwardness and a prelude to new
misfortunes. But they also make clear the urgent need for renewal. As
Diderot remarked, with great insight:

> It seems in truth that all things, good as well as evil, have their time of maturity.
> When good reaches its point of perfection, it begins to turn to evil; when evil is
> complete, it raises itself toward the good.[2]

The fear that Tocqueville expressed for the twentieth century was
neither disorder nor injustice but the danger that equality would pose for
the highest human aspirations.[3] In this new century, one may also have

fears for human nobility and hence for freedom, but in a still more dramatic form. The moral stakes have in fact moved one more rung up the ladder, placing the bar very high with regard to the exploration of evil. And because of the unthinkable crimes committed all through the last century, that century remains in many respects *a century without forgiveness*. It is from that dark ground still accessible to memory that we must set out once more to find the promise of a future, in the absence of which no survival is possible. If the world is shaped in the image of the spirit, the capacity to rediscover belief in the spirit's power is of crucial importance. At the Nuremberg trials, the French chief prosecutor, François de Menthon, understood that he was to judge

> a crime against the spirit . . . a doctrine which, denying all spiritual, rational, or moral values on the basis of which the peoples of the world have attempted for millennia to move the human condition forward, is aimed at casting humanity into a conscious barbarism[,] . . . using for its purposes all the material resources made available by contemporary science.

More than fifty years later, those remarks are moving not only because they evoke the atrocities committed but because of the strangeness of the words used by the French prosecutor, particularly the deeply unfashionable expression "crime against the spirit." We no longer understand what it designates: the loss of that which constitutes humanity itself.

The feeling of no longer having any real grasp of events, of anxiety about change, the future, and time, is linked to that loss. For people functioning without freedom or ambition of spirit—without humanity—events will be dangerously in advance of our thinking and capacity for thought. The relationship of consciousness to the world has lost its axis: human freedom. Without it we can build nothing, defend nothing, and will lack the courage to confront what history holds in store. Rediscovering human freedom would not necessarily make the future more serene, but that future would at least be played out with responsible beings. As Gottfried Benn wrote with despairing humor: "We know all too well that men have no souls; if only they had some manners."

But the future was no more carved in stone in 2005 than it was in 1905. Of course, even more now than in the twentieth century, humankind has the capacity to serve the most destructive bent of the human psyche. But it can also overcome the fatal combination of advanced technology and acute nihilism that is now humanity's lot. That is the choice that must be made. And that is the choice that must guide future political action.

Notes

Prologue

1. Leo Tolstoy, *War and Peace*, trans. Anthony Briggs (New York: Viking, 2006), 1339.

2. He shares this view with Balzac, who thought that the horrors of the Revolution had had a greater impact than was generally recognized in the early nineteenth century. As for Napoleon, Freud, too, saw him not as the hero of a new era, but as a madman who had set Europe ablaze. The father of psychoanalysis may in fact have had a personal grievance against the Emperor, because the Code Napoléon had banned the "profession of divination, prognostication, or the interpretation of dreams."

3. The expression comes from Georges Perec, *La Vie mode d'emploi* (Paris: Hachette, 1978).

4. From this perspective, George Orwell's *1984* is a realist work: "War is Peace. Freedom is Slavery. Ignorance is Strength."

5. Paul Valéry, *Regards sur le monde actuel*, in *Œuvres* (Paris: Gallimard, Bibliothèque de la Pléiade, 1960), II, 1068.

6. Some see this as an explanation for the rejection by youth of the gradual and unspectacular approach followed from the outset by the European Union.

7. One of the best historians of the First World War, John Keegan, has a persuasive chapter on this point in *The First World War* (New York: Knopf, 1999).

8. On the same subject with respect to the Second World War, see a collection of anonymous articles written by French exiles in London between November 1940 and 1943, published under the title *La Guerre des cinq continents* (London: Hamish Hamilton, 1943).

9. The December 2004 tsunami that caused 300,000 deaths in a few hours, from Indonesia to the Somali coast, provided a macabre natural counterpoint to human violence.

10. Valéry, *Regards sur le monde actuel*, in *Œuvres*, II, 1068.

11. A demented experiment was conducted on the Internet in the summer of 2004 by an American, Benjamin Vanderford, who had decided to reproduce a fake execution modeled on the real ones carried out in Iraq by al-Zarqawi: "I wanted to show how easy

it is to fake this kind of video." The film was produced in 45 minutes with fake blood, and the staging of a decapitation, was reproduced on an Internet site, and was seen around the world. When the FBI questioned him, the producer did not understand what he was being criticized for.

12. See Peter Brooks, *Troubling Confessions* (Chicago: University of Chicago Press, 2000).

13. This was true of the speech delivered by Vaclav Havel, then president of Czechoslovakia, at the Charlemagne Plenary in Aachen, Germany on May 15, 1996.

14. See Balzac's *La Peau de Chagrin*, in which Moreau de l'Oise, son of a follower of Danton who was guillotined, challenges a republican with those words at a banquet.

15. Andrei Sinyavsky, "Matériau à débiter," introduction to Varlam Shalamov, *Récits de la Kolyma* (Paris: Fayard, 1986), 5. The most sinister aspect of the story is the indifference of the men unloading the cargo when it arrived in Great Britain.

16. Margaret MacMillan, *Paris 1919* (New York: Random House, 2002).

17. Peter Hennessy, *The Secret State: Whitehall and the Cold War* (London, Allen Lane/ Penguin Press, 2002), 2.

18. Michael Herman, former Secretary of the British Joint Intelligence Committee, claims that "the Cold War was essentially an intelligence conflict. . . . Never before in peacetime had relations between adversaries been so deeply influenced by intelligence analyses. Never before had the collection of information and its protection from the enemy played such a role in international rivalry."

19. Established in October 1989, this association attempts to preserve the testimony of survivors of the camps and the physical traces of the camps throughout the territory of the former Soviet Union, and to evaluate the effects of past policies on the current life of Russia. It was Memorial that made public in 1995 the atrocities committed by the Ministry of Internal Affairs (MVD) in the village of Samashki.

20. During the election campaign, displaying his features disfigured by dioxin, Viktor Yushchenko said, "You like my face? It is the face of Ukraine."

21. In *Death by Government* (New Brunswick: Transaction Books, 1986), R. J. Rummel has shown that between 1900 and 1986, governments killed 170 million people, a figure higher than the number of deaths caused by war between 1900 and 1995 (110 million). These figures are repeated in a 1999 paper, "The Failure of Politics: The Future of Violence and War," delivered by an American researcher, Barry Weinberg, at a conference in Saint Petersburg on the future of war.

22. According to a survey conducted by Euro RCDG, the results of which were published in October 2004, French society seems to be dominated by doubt, fear, violence, resentment, and victimization. Some participants in the survey used the expression "new obscurantism" to define a society that is suspicious of everything and no longer believes in anything or anyone.

23. Simon Sebag Montefiore, *Stalin: The Court of the Red Tsar* (New York: Knopf, 2004), 96. The anecdote provides an opportunity to point out the unintended humor supplied by Voroshilov, who interrupted Stalin to object that tanks were also "very important."

24. Erich Maria Remarque, *All Quiet on the Western Front*, trans. A. W. Wheen (1929; New York: Fawcett Crest, 1958), 134. Remarque is describing the dehumanization of a group

of twenty-year-old German boys. The experience of young Frenchmen who were in the trenches opposite was not very different.

25. Li Zhinsheng, *Le Petit Livre rouge d'un photographe chinois* (Paris: Phaidon, 2003), 139–40.

CHAPTER 1

1. Martin Wright, whose principal works were published in the 1960s and 1970s, maintains that political communities have moral obligations to their citizens, to the community of nations, and to humanity at large. Grotius and Kant would not have rejected that view.

2. Schopenhauer would have used *compassion* rather than *sympathy*.

3. The *Economist* has written on this question, referring, in an incisive formulation, to countries "that care, but do not share."

4. Here is Russell's reasoning, which might amuse the reader: the industrial revolution is due to modern science, which is due to Galileo, who derives from Copernicus, who comes out of the Renaissance, which is due to the capture of Constantinople, itself connected to the migration of the Turks, a consequence of drought in Central Asia. As for the consequences of the love life of Henry VIII, had the king not fallen for Anne Boleyn, England would not have broken with the papacy and thus would not have challenged the pope's gift of the Americas to Spain and Portugal.

5. Johan Huizinga points out that it is a salutary exercise to recognize in the past and the present various elements that would have made possible—or will make possible—different outcomes.

6. See Roberto Toscano, "The Ethics of Modern Diplomacy," in Jean-Marc Coicaud and Daniel Warner, eds., *Ethics and International Affairs* (Tokyo: United Nations University Press, 2001), in which the author shows that the relationship between ethics and war was changed by the Kosovo crisis.

7. This is the title of an excellent report published in 2002 on the subject of the conditions for and the obligation of the right to intervene.

8. Considering the unfavorable context, it is remarkable that the Group of High Level Experts appointed by the Secretary General in 2003, largely made up of figures who had held official positions in countries broadly representative of the diversity of today's world, submitted a report in December 2004 in which the responsibility to protect civilian populations was unambiguously recognized.

9. Known in his native Norway primarily for his role in the 1993 Oslo agreements.

10. The United Nations received more in one week for the victims of the tsunami than in the whole of 2004 for Darfur and the Democratic Republic of Congo.

11. Humanitarian organizations have also been urged to leave and journalists find it increasingly difficult to do their job.

12. Anna Politkovskaia's *Tchéchénie: Le déshonneur russe* (Paris: Buchet Chastel, 2004) must be read if one is to grasp the horrors the Europeans have tolerated to facilitate agreement with Russian President Vladimir Putin. Her recent assassination is most probably tied to her work on Chechnya.

13. A BBC film revealed the monstrous practices, justified as preparation for a conflict with South Korea, for which the quantities of chemical agents required to dispose of the population of Seoul had to be determined. Nothing has been done to halt them.

14. "If your heart turns to stone, your head into a cold thinking machine, and your eye into nothing but a camera, you will never more recover them" (Z. Gradowdki, *Rouleaux d'Auschwitz*, I [1944], from the French translation by M. Pfeffer, 24–25).

15. See Andrew Linklater, "The Problem of Harm in World Politics," *International Affairs* 78, 2 (2002), 319–38.

16. In June 2005, the proposed resumption was delayed not because of a better understanding of what was going on in the region, but because of the intensity of American, particularly congressional, pressure. At the end of 2006, no decision has yet been taken on this front.

17. A less charitable interpretation would emphasize the blinkered nature of societies huddled around their privileges, unable to understand the transformations taking place around them.

18. Alexis de Tocqueville, *De la démocratie en Amérique*, vol. 2, part 4, chapter 8 (Paris: Garnier-Flammarion, 1981), 402.

19. This is the case with Simon Sebag Montefiore's *Stalin: The Court of the Red Tsar* (New York: Knopf, 2004), in the very first chapters of which the author brings together the private life of Stalin's circle with the great famine raging in the countryside in the early 1930s.

20. Jacob Burckhardt discerned the seeds of a deadly malaise as far back as the eighteenth century, in the optimistic age of the Enlightenment: the perpetual and universal search for unattainable happiness that was soon transformed into an equally widespread desire for wealth and power.

21. It has often been pointed out that globalization intensifies questions of identity, which is true, but it is less often noted that it has provided even the most remote village with tools for comparison with the rest of the world that did not previously exist and that can provide support for the egalitarian enterprise. See Daniel Cohen, *La Mondialisation et ses ennemis* (Paris: Grasset, 2003).

22. The desire for equality may go hand in hand with increased demands for the recognition of one's identity, which constitute a response to the growing uniformity of cultures fostered by certain aspects of globalization.

23. The progression of democratic regimes has been real, as evident in Europe during the nineteenth century, the postcolonial world after the Second World War, Central and Eastern Europe after 1991, and in South America, Asia, and even Africa. It is estimated that the percentage of democratic countries in the world increased from 20 to 61 percent between 1974 and 1998. (These statistics would benefit from more refined analysis. Russia, for example, is included among the democracies.) The movement has now reached a portion of Central Asia and the Middle East.

24. Security Council reform was once again removed from the table in 2005, and the New York summit meeting on UN reform will stand as one of the institution's great failures.

25. The American experience in the Philippines can hardly be compared to that of the British and French colonial empires.

26. C. G. Jung, *The Undiscovered Self*, in *Civilization in Transition*, R. F. C. Hull, trans. (*Collected Works*, vol. 10) (Princeton: Princeton University Press, Bollingen Series, 1964), 304.

27. Anne Applebaum, *Gulag: A History* (New York: Doubleday, 2003).

28. The true historical origin of concentration camps can be found in the Boer War in South Africa at the end of the nineteenth century.

29. One of Stalin's favorite jokes told of an adolescent tortured until he confessed that he had written *Eugene Onegin*. He dies under torture and his parents are visited by secret police, who tell them, "Congratulations! Your son wrote *Eugene Onegin!*"

30. Quoted by Edgar Faure, assistant chief prosecutor at the Nuremberg tribunal. See Michel Dobkine, *Extraits des actes du procès de Nuremberg* (Paris: Romillat, 1992).

31. Karl Kraus, *The Last Days of Mankind*.

32. Boris Volodarsky, "The KGB's Poison Factory," *Wall Street Journal*, April 7, 2005.

33. On the contemporary dangers of technology, see Lloyd J. Dumas, *Lethal Arrogance* (New York: St. Martin's Press, 1999).

34. Speech by François de Menthon, French chief prosecutor at the Nuremberg tribunal, quoted in Dobkine, *Extraits des actes du procès de Nuremberg*, 44.

35. Note the comment by Simon Sebag Montefiore: "Most [Bolsheviks] came from devoutly religious backgrounds. They hated Judaeo-Christianity—but the orthodoxy of their parents was replaced by something even more rigid, a systematic amorality." See *Stalin: The Court of the Red Tsar*, 86.

36. See in particular Abdelwaheb Meddeb, *La Maladie de l'Islam* (Paris: Seuil, 2002), in which the author explains that traditional Islamic practice had preserved access to the text of the Koran and to the prophetic tradition, but that undisciplined readings by semi-literate men have had disastrous effects on both religion and politics. An equally severe critique could be made of some interpretations of the Bible presented by Christian fundamentalists, particularly in the United States.

CHAPTER 2

1. Some 60 percent of Americans, more than 145 million people, play video games, with the average age of the players being 28. In 2004, sales of consoles and game software reached more than six billion dollars, a figure that no doubt increased in 2005. After a period in which games employed fictional characters, we have witnessed the triumph of realistic games, treating conflict situations in particular.

2. George Orwell, *Homage to Catalonia* (1938; Harmondsworth: Penguin, 1962), 221.

3. We might add that France did not anticipate the disaster in Côte d'Ivoire, even though it was inherent in the unenforceable agreements that no one even tried to enforce.

4. That is also one of the messages of Hermann Broch in his novel *The Sleepwalkers*.

5. See Emmanuel Brenner, ed., *Les Territoires perdus de la République* (Paris: Mille et Une Nuits, 2002).

6. Holland has 900,000 Muslim inhabitants, 300,000 of whom are Moroccans.

7. The expression comes from Alain Finkielkraut in an article in *Libération*, March 26, 2005.

8. Freud's *Beyond the Pleasure Principle* was published in 1920.

9. To those who would accuse Alexander Solzhenitsyn of excessive pessimism here, he might answer that pessimists have done more for world peace than promoters of the radiant future.

10. We refer not only to the European origin of the two world wars, or to the doctrines—Marxism and nationalism—that justified countless massacres. There is also the intellectual training provided in Europe to the leaders of the Khmer Rouge and of the 1979 Iranian revolution.

11. The expression "Cold War," an inspired coinage, was first used by Walter Lippman in 1947.

12. The British historian John Keegan speaks of conflicts of have-nots against have-nots, which might also be expressed as conflicts between the dispossessed.

13. A recent, fascinating work on the causes of the First World War: David Fromkin, *Europe's Last Summer: Who Started the Great War in 1914?* (New York: Knopf, 2004), maintains that the German general staff had decided on a preventive war against Russia before the assassination of Archduke Franz Ferdinand in Sarajevo, and that the Kaiser was confronted with a fait accompli.

14. When the chancellor was still only Prime Minister of Lower Saxony, Volkswagen country, he had turned himself into a dauntless traveling salesman in China. After his accession to leadership of the German state, he traveled there every year, and it must be admitted that the economic results were impressive: Germany is the largest outside investor in China, especially in the chemical and automotive sectors. The leaders of the German economy—and many smaller companies as well—regularly accompanied him on his trips to Beijing, using them to thoroughly analyze ways of penetrating the market. Since the restoration of diplomatic relations in 1972, the volume of German exports to China has grown seventy-fold. In these circumstances, it is easy to understand that there is not much time left over to devote to strategic risks.

CHAPTER 3

1. Erich Maria Remarque, *All Quiet on the Western Front*, trans. A. W. Wheen (1929; New York: Fawcett Crest, 1958), 294.

2. Remarque, *All Quiet on the Western Front*, 132.

3. See the remarkable BBC film on Hitler and Stalin, combining documentaries made at the time and contemporary interviews. The most troubling aspect is the way some Germans and Russians interviewed still justify the crimes they committed 60 years earlier. *The War of the Century: Hitler-Stalin*, BBC 2, four 50-minute episodes.

4. *Die Reden am Reichsparteitag*, 1933.

5. The Soviet judges at the Nuremberg trials, justified by the horrors the Nazis committed on Soviet soil, provoked many comments in light of what had been happening in the Soviet Union since the establishment of the gulag.

6. The anniversary of the Cultural Revolution in 2006 might be the occasion for an effort of memory similar to that undertaken by the Germans, and to a lesser degree the Russians, long ago.

7. Zheng Yi, *Stèles rouges: Du totalitarisme au cannibalisme* (Paris: Bleu de Chine, 1999).

8. Zheng, *Stèles rouges*.

9. China, a signatory to the Convention on Political Refugees, does not grant political refugee status to North Koreans who manage to cross the border.

10. There is a memorandum on the subject from Lavrenty Beria to Georgy Malenkov, dated April 1953.

11. Greatly surprising Stalin, who was convinced that "the West would never accept such a large red spot" on the world map, as he confided to Marshal Tito's emissary in 1944. See André Fontaine, *La Tache rouge* (Paris: La Martinière, 2004).

12. On the program *Apostrophes*, broadcast on France2 on April 11, 1975, and very often referred to. *The Gulag Archipelago* had appeared in French in June 1974, and Solzhenitsyn had been expelled from the Soviet Union in February of that year. The unity of the left for the coming elections in France was more important than the truth about the millions of dead in the gulag.

13. Francis Fukuyama, *The End of History and the Last Man* (New York: Free Press, 1992).

14. Nuclear deterrence was established in 1949, while Stalin was still alive.

15. In his memoirs, Aron recalls that Herman Kahn, one of the major deterrence theorists, adopted this formulation in his book *On Escalation* (Washington, D.C.: Hudson Institute, 1965). See Raymond Aron, *Mémoires: Cinquante ans de réflexion politique* (Paris: Julliard, Presse Poche, 1983), II, 649.

16. The first major works on nuclear weapons date from 1946: Bernard Brodie, *The Ultimate Weapon* (New York: Harcourt, 1946), and Jacob Viner, "The Implication of the Atomic Bomb for International Relations," in *Symposium on Atomic Energy and Its Implications* (Philadelphia: American Philosophical Society, 1946). In 1960, Herman Kahn published *On Thermonuclear War* (Princeton: Princeton University Press). As for the evolution of Soviet thinking on nuclear weapons, one may consult Honoré M. Catudal, *Soviet Nuclear Strategy from Stalin to Gorbachev* (Atlantic Highlands, N.J.: Humanities Press, 1989), and Stephen Shenfield, *The Nuclear Predicament: Explorations in Soviet Ideology* (London: Chatham House Paper no. 37, 1987).

17. On the North Korean camps, see David Hawk, *The Hidden Gulag: Exposing North Korea's Prison Camps*, http://hnrk.org.

CHAPTER 4

1. Montesquieu, *De l'esprit des lois*, Book VIII, ch. 1.

2. George Orwell, "Looking Back on the Spanish War," in Sonia Orwell and Ian Angus, eds., *The Collected Essays, Journalism, and Letters of George Orwell* (New York: Harcourt, Brace & World, 1968), II, 259.

3. On this issue, see the confession of Vsevolod Meyerhold, who in a letter to Vyacheslav Molotov after his arrest in 1939 speaks of a division of his personality during interrogation: "Immediately after my arrest . . . I was cast into the deepest depression by the obsessive thought 'This is what I deserve!' The government thought, so I began to convince myself, that the sentence I had received . . . was not sufficient for my sins . . . and that I must undergo yet another punishment, that which the NKVD was carrying out now.

'This is what I deserve!' I repeated to myself and I split into two individuals. The first started searching for the 'crimes' of the second, and when they could not be found, he began to invent them. The interrogator proved an effective and experienced assistant and, working closely together, we began our composition … When my fantasy started running out, the interrogators took over." Quoted by Peter Brooks, *Troubling Confessions* (Chicago: University of Chicago Press, 2000), 35–36.

4. Why, then, did Aragon defend Lysenko in print? Lysenko had received personal con-gratulations from Stalin in 1935—"Bravo, Comrade Lysenko, bravo!"—reason enough to support his pseudo-doctrine. Aragon was probably drawn in by a conflict between Stalin and the Zhdanov clan that began when Andrei Zhdanov's son Yuri took the liberty of making fun of Lysenko. Lysenko appealed to Stalin, backed by Georgy Malenkov, and Yuri Zhdanov's apology subsequently appeared in *Pravda*.

5. Quoted by Simon Sebag Montefiore, *Stalin: The Court of the Red Tsar* (New York: Vin-tage Books, 2005), 89. He mentions another message, terrible in its brevity: "My son. We couldn't wait. God be with you."

6. These cases of cannibalism are included in official reports sent to the Kremlin. As early as 1930, the year in which the destruction of the kulaks was decided, when Stalin was not yet able to answer the question "What is a kulak?" despair among the peasants was so deep that they began to kill their animals to persuade the government to change its policy. The great famine began in 1931, and Stalin in this merely followed Lenin, who had asserted that the peasants had to be starved. In 1932, a Ukrainian came to see Anas-tas Mikoyan and asked him: "Does anyone in the Politburo know what's going on in Ukraine? If not, I can give you some idea. A train recently came into Kiev filled with the bodies of peasants who had died of hunger. It had picked up the bodies all along the way from Poltava."

7. The United Nations Development Program report, *The Arab Human Development Report*, a first version of which was published in 2002, with supplements in 2003 and 2004.

8. The expression is from Balzac, referring to the legacy of the French Revolution.

9. An assertion of Raymond Aron.

10. The Canadian general Roméo Dallaire, who commanded a UN assistance mission of 2,500 men in 1993, understood two months before he arrived that a genocide was about to happen. On January 11, 1994, three months before the most rapid massacre cam-paign of the twentieth century, he warned the UN that a census of the Tutsis had been taken in preparation for their extermination. The UN has at least recognized its wrongs in Rwanda. But France?

11. See Lunis Aggoun and Jean-Baptiste Rivoire, *Françalgérie: Crimes et mensonges d'État* (Paris: La Découverte, 2004), which presents an account of the violence that has ravaged Algeria since 2004 entirely different from the one the French public is used to.

12. For lack of any other argument, condemnation was justified by Iraq's violation of the 1925 Protocol, guaranteed by France, prohibiting the use of chemical and biological weapons. This protocol, which is part of the humanitarian law whose implementation is supervised by the Red Cross, is one of the achievements of the consultations that fol-lowed the First World War.

13. And yet, according to opinion polls, the question of security and the global political role of the Union is the most constant area of preoccupation for the 450 million Europeans.

14. The Dutch president of the Union first requested "explanations" from Moscow, then in the face of the insults this timid request provoked from the Russian Foreign Minister, he retreated, frightened by his own audacity.

15. See the article by Marie Jégo in *Le Monde*, November 6, 2004.

CHAPTER 5

1. Stalin opposed the 1905 war and rejoiced in the czarist forces' defeats, like all the revolutionaries. See also this statement by Trotsky in *My Life:* "My work during the years of reaction consisted in large part of commentaries on the 1905 revolution and a theoretical preparation for the next revolution."

2. The Russo-Japanese War was described by Russian Prime Minister Sergei Witte, who was opposed to it, in these terms: "the most disastrous of disastrous wars, then, as an immediate consequence, a revolution that had long been fostered by a regime ruled by police, court, and camarilla."

3. See Georges Sokoloff, ed., *1933 L'année noire: Témoignages sur la famine en Ukraine* (Paris: Albin Michel, 2000). The opening of the Soviet archives in the late 1980s provided access to the results of the 1937 census, publication of which Stalin had banned.

4. Vladimir Nabokov, who was so severe on Dostoevsky, considered this novel a masterpiece.

5. That phenomenon was already widespread in the 1880s, when the dreaded Okhrana had only 37 secret agents—that is, fewer than the revolutionary organization Narodnaya Volya. It was the period of the sinister Lieutenant Colonel Georgy Sudeikin, who had succeeded in thoroughly infiltrating the revolutionary movement. He finally fell victim to his own obsessive fondness for secret meetings and complicated plots when he fell into a trap set by the double agent Sergei Degaev. Shortly before his death, Sudeikin made plans to assassinate Interior Minister Dmitri Tolstoy to show the czar that the Okhrana was indispensable and that he deserved the rank of general. He did not have time to put his plan into operation and died a mere colonel.

6. There was something strange about this alliance between the French Republic and the greatest autocracy in Europe, especially in the scenes of popular jubilation that were unfailingly sparked by the most insignificant meeting between the two heads of state.

7. Isaiah Berlin, "Political Ideas in the Twentieth Century," in *Four Essays on Liberty* (Oxford: Oxford University Press, 1969), 16–17. See also the corrected version of this incident, which changes details without affecting its import, in the Appendix to that volume, 207.

8. Mass emigration had already taken place in the late nineteenth century, after the pogroms of 1881. In 1903, the Kishinev massacre, in conjunction with the pogroms in the aftermath of the defeat by Japan, resulted in a very large wave of emigration.

9. In 1918, one of France's requests was for all of Germany's rights in Morocco.

10. These details about school textbooks and the unionization of teachers were provided to me by Mona Ozouf, whom I am delighted to be able to thank.

11. Ivan Bloch was a Polish businessman who made a fortune in railroads in the nineteenth century. In 1897, he presented a voluminous report to the Russian government in which he asserted that the firepower now available made war suicidal for states and for societies as well. He published his work in Paris in 1898 under the title *La Guerre future, aux points de vue technique, économique et politique.*

12. Michael Howard, *The Lessons of History* (London: Oxford University Press, 1991), 99.

13. On the French side, 20,000 Russians who had enlisted in the army wanted to return home after the revolution. They were shot for "desertion."

14. Sun Yat-sen was removed from power by Yuan Shih-kai when the Chinese Republic was declared in 1912. He died in 1924, when China was in ruins.

15. Simon Leys, *Écrits sur la Chine* (Paris: Robert Laffont, Bouquins, 1998), 210.

16. According to the most recently published biography of Mao Zedong, his long reign caused 70 million deaths: Jung Chang and Jon Halliday, *Mao, The Unknown Story* (London: Jonathan Cape, 2005).

17. Leys, *Écrits sur la Chine*, 9.

18. The terms of the treaty amounted to a substantial weakening of Russian positions in East Asia.

19. The Treaty of Paris between Spain and the United States (December 10, 1898) gave independence to Cuba, ceded Guam and Puerto Rico to the United States, and allowed Washington to purchase the Philippines for 20 million dollars.

20. The first results confirmed Schlieffen's views: failure of the French offensive, German victories in Belgium, advance of the Kaiser's armies to the outskirts of Paris. It was the attack on the flank of General von Kluck's army followed by the battle of the Marne that changed everything. There was no longer any question of winning in six weeks as predicted. Four more years had to be wasted.

21. At this time, France was up to plan number XV, which dated back to 1903. It carried out plan number XVII.

22. As the lessons of the 1930s and the Cold War have been forgotten today.

23. Paul Valéry, *Regards sur le monde actuel*, in *Œuvres* (Paris: Gallimard, Bibliothèque de la Pléiade, 1960), II, 913–14.

CHAPTER 6

1. See John S. Ridgen, *Einstein 1905: The Standard of Greatness* (Cambridge: Harvard University Press, 2005).

2. This problem went back to Newton's time.

3. Einstein spent ten years developing the formulation of his principal thesis. Special relativity is based on the postulate that nothing can move faster than the speed of light. This is contrary to Newton's theory of gravitation. To resolve the contradiction, in 1916 Einstein proposed the theory of general relativity, asserting that masses in the universe mutually influence one another by curving the space around them and that gravitation is propagated at the speed of light, like ripples in water. It was not until 1994 that the first post-Einsteinian theory of gravity was published and subjected to experimental verification through the observation of neutron stars.

CHAPTER 7

1. Tocqueville's remark concerned the United States and Russia. There was no prophecy of communism, only an argument about the population and the resources of Russia, the sole country comparable to the United States.

2. Osip Mandelstam, *The Noise of Time: The Prose of Osip Mandelstam*, Clarence Brown, trans. (1965; San Francisco: North Point Press, 1986), 117.

3. Quoted by Simon Sebag Montefiore, *Stalin: The Court of the Red Tsar*, 27. Stalin's admiration for Hitler is well known. After the Night of the Long Knives in June 1934 he said to Anastas Mikoyan: "He's really something, that Hitler! That was really a stroke of genius." Stalin's only real rival, Sergei Kirov, was to be killed in December.

4. Hugh R. Trevor-Roper, quoted by Ron Rosenbaum, *Explaining Hitler* (New York: Random House, 1998), xv.

5. François de Menthon at Nuremberg in 1945: Dobkine, *Extraits des actes du procès de Nuremberg*, 37.

6. For example, the theologian Emil Fackenheim.

7. This reluctance led Alan Bullock, the Oxford historian, to exclaim in an interview with Ron Rosenbaum: "If *he* isn't evil, who is?" *Explaining Hitler*, xxi.

8. Heinrich Heine, *Histoire de la religion et de la philosophie en Allemagne* (Paris: Imprimerie nationale, 1993), 205. I thank David Yost for this reference.

9. Fritz Stern, *The Politics of Cultural Despair: A Study in the Rise of the Germanic Ideology* (Berkeley: University of California Press, 1961).

CHAPTER 8

1. Freud maintained that the species did not struggle for survival but to reach inertia and rest; an internal entropy was thus at work in history and in human nature.

2. We might note that Stalin, who left the seminary to embark on a career as a revolutionary, adopted the name of Koba, inspired by the hero of a novel entitled *The Parricide*.

3. Ivan Bloch in the late nineteenth century: "Those who are preparing for war and living only in the expectation of war are visionaries of the worst variety." The war he was speaking of was not the kind that broke out from time to time far from Europe or some punitive expedition of the colonial powers, but "the one that has haunted the imagination of the human race for thirty years, a war in which nations of major importance, armed to the teeth, hurl themselves with all their resources into a battle to the death"—in a word, world war, repeated twice in the twentieth century, which destroyed European civilization and "the world of yesterday" that Stefan Zweig spoke of.

4. Note the Russian plan to transform the Vorkuta gulag into a vacation resort for lovers of extreme sensations.

CHAPTER 9

1. Tocqueville worried about the break with past generations magnificently illustrated by the history of the French Revolution: "Everyone easily loses track of the ideas of his ancestors or barely pays them heed," *De la démocratie en Amérique*, vol. II, Part 1, chaps. 1, 10.

2. Edward Gibbon, *The Decline and Fall of the Roman Empire*, chapter LII (New York: Heritage Society, 1946), III, 1859.

3. Quoted in *Commentaire*, 106 (Summer 2004), 479.

4. Tocqueville, *L'Ancien Régime et la Révolution* (Paris: Gallimard, Folio, 1973), 50.

5. Paul Valéry, *Regards sur le monde actuel*, 937.

CHAPTER 10

1. Martin Rees, *Our Final Hour* (New York: Basic Books, 2003).

2. See Michael Kenney, "From Pablo to Osama: Counter-terrorism Lessons from the War on Drugs," *Survival*, vol. 45, no. 3, 187–206.

3. *Les Territoires perdus de la République*, edited by Emmanuelle Brenner (Paris: Les Mille et une Nuits, September 2002) provides frightening illustrations of this observation.

4. See the report by Inspector General Jean-Pierre Obin, *Les Signes et manifestations d'appartenance religieuse dans les établissements scolaires* (Ministry of National Education, Higher Education, and Research, June 2004). Inspectors were told the same story several times in the course of their investigations: an old working-class neighborhood changed into a "ghetto" housing development that the "French" and people with steady incomes had left. Families living there were increasingly at risk, property prices collapsed, "European" shops disappeared, and the further flight of inhabitants was precipitated by targeted violence. In the end the only people remaining were the most vulnerable.

5. Terrorist acts increased threefold in 2004, according to the annual report of the State Department published in May 2005.

6. One of the reasons for doubting that Pakistan has put an end to the activities of the criminal network of A. Q. Khan, the self-proclaimed father of the Pakistani bomb, is the fact that this network for the illicit sale of nuclear technology has also been used by Pakistan to purchase equipment and technology for its own nuclear program. In support of this argument, we should note that the United Sates has never had access to Khan for purposes of direct interrogation.

7. This is particularly true of Iran, one of whose classic texts is titled *The Book of Tricks*.

8. Syria and Egypt have both been in contact with A. Q. Khan's clandestine Pakistani network. See Gordon Corera's book *Shopping for Bombs* (London: Hurst, 2006).

9. The Ukrainian elections made Vladimir Putin drop his mask on this question.

CHAPTER 11

1. The case of Liberia clearly demonstrates the corruption undermining a large part of Africa. Beginning in the 1970s, rulers took control of the principal national resource, diamonds, which represented 70 percent of government revenue in 1970 and only 10 percent by the end of the 1980s because of the involvement of the ruling class in their private sale.

2. Earlier elections of Arafat to the presidency resembled those held in the so-called people's democracies, with majorities of greater than 90 percent.

3. From this point of view, France has a particularly hypocritical position, with the Constitution now requiring a referendum for any accession to the Union subsequent to those

of Bulgaria and Romania. It is commonly assumed that the enlargement of the European Union will stop after the accession of those two countries.

4. The most impoverished of the Pakistani provinces was the site of an uprising in the 1970s, and there is now talk of a new crisis, the strategic repercussions of which would be much more serious than those of thirty years ago.

5. That origin was identified by Martin Wight in an article titled "The Balance of Power and International Order," in Alan James, ed., *The Bases of International Order* (London: Oxford University Press, 1973).

6. See Irfan Habib, Bipan Chandra, Ravinder Kumar, Kumkum Sangari, and Sukumar Muralidharan, *Gandhi Reconsidered* (New Delhi: Sahmat, 2004).

CHAPTER 12

1. In Kyrgyzstan, the stakes were even higher because it is an Islamic republic and its example spoke to Muslims as well as all others living under repressive regimes.

2. They were only municipal elections and voting was limited to men, but this was a step that is important for being the first. It also shows how great the divide still is between the theocratic regime of Riyadh and the modern world.

3. He was of course still guaranteed a fifth term. The constitutional amendment was perhaps approved to deflect criticism of that fact.

4. Nearly a billion people suffer from malnutrition, and 15 million, 6 million of whom are children, die from hunger every year. A billion people lack access to potable water.

5. The president elected in June 2005, Mahmoud Ahmadinejad, is a man with a past: he is suspected of having participated in the assassination of three Kurdish opposition figures in Vienna in 1989. As mayor of Tehran, he prevented the normalization of relations with Egypt because he did not want to change the name of the street in Tehran named after the assassin of Anwar Sadat.

6. In April, UN Secretary General Kofi Annan informed Cambodian Prime Minister Hun Sen that financing for trials was now guaranteed, removing a final obstacle.

7. Chinese authorities seem to have understood that, because after three weeks of anti-Japanese demonstrations that they did nothing to prevent or halt, there was suddenly talk of a "plot" against the Chinese Communist Party.

8. Jung Chang and Jon Halliday, *Mao: The Unknown Story*, (London: Jonathan Cape, 2005) 230–31.

CHAPTER 13

1. Vaclav Havel, interview in *Le Monde*, February 24, 2005.

2. See Olga Krishtanovskaya, *Le Régime de Poutine* (Moscow: Pro et Contra), 7, 161.

3. Opinion polls in 2004 and 2005 show popular support throughout Ukraine for independence, though stronger in the west than the east. Ukraine has endured successive Polish, Russian, Nazi, and Soviet domination. It is a long-victimized country that began to revive in November–December 2004. Its evolution since July 2006 is much more confusing.

4. During the 2004 U.S. elections, observers from the OSCE were sent to the United States at the request of both parties, which feared challenges because of the circumstances in which George W. Bush had been elected in 2000.

5. See *Le Monde*, January 29, 2005, "Russian officers implicated in the killings in Beslan." In this article, Alexander Torshin, the president of the parliamentary committee investigating the Beslan tragedy, stated that Russian troops, including superior officers, helped the hostage takers in Beslan, and that these individuals were still serving in the Russian military.

6. Heads of state and government had decided at a previous meeting of the European Council, against the advice of France and Germany, that the agreement with Russia should be comprehensive and that it was not possible to agree on questions pertaining to the economy, education, and research without also reaching agreement on questions of freedom, justice, and external security.

7. That assassination took place just as Maskhadov had declared a unilateral cease-fire in Chechnya and stood clearly opposed to radical Islamism. He had also condemned the Beslan massacre.

8. This institution was established in the very first days of Belarus's independence by a group of professors and the Orthodox Church.

9. See Patrick de Saint-Exupéry, "Les 'siloviki,' garde prétorienne du président," *Le Monde*, December 2, 2003.

10. The head of the gigantic privatized energy corporation Yukos was taken into custody in Siberia on October 25, 2003, and accused of tax evasion and fraud. The oligarch's biggest fault, in the government's view, was to have broken the agreement that oligarchs were not to become involved in politics. Previously, the tycoons Boris Berezovsky and Vladimir Gusinsky had been forced into exile in 2000.

11. See Krishtanovskaya, *Le Régime de Poutine*. Her conclusion: "The machine is running. When everyone notices, it will be too late."

12. This was in a brief report presented on February 23, 2004, to the European Council, which also contained the following passage: "It is clear that the European Union has not been able to clearly define its objectives nor to promote its values or effectively defend its interests. Relations with Russia are in danger of getting sidetracked into procedural questions at the expense of any real progress on concrete questions of mutual interest." It would be hard to speak more clearly. We should recall that it was in 1999 that the European Union decided to define a common strategy toward Russia. The February 2004 report is an acknowledgment of failure.

CHAPTER 14

1. In the December 2004 legislative elections in Taiwan, the main trend the press detected was a decline in support for the Democratic Progressive Party of President Chen Shui-bian, which favors independence from China. Fewer observers pointed out that the worst defeat had been suffered by the most pro-Chinese party on the island, "The People First," which lost 12 of the 46 seats it had held. Thus there was thus no weakening in Taiwanese national feeling—quite the contrary.

2. Taiwan belonged to the Manchu Empire from 1644 to 1911, but it is unlikely that Chinese authorities will use that historical argument.

3. The expression "peaceful rise to power" is a favorite of Chinese diplomats reassuring neighboring countries and the rest of the world as China builds up its military power.

4. Jean-Baptiste Duroselle, *L'Europe de 1815 à nos jours* (Paris: Presses Universitaires de France, 1996).

5. During an official visit to Beijing in May 2006, French Prime Minister Dominique de Villepin expressed support for China's new anti-secession law aimed at Taiwan.

6. In March 2004, the French government presented to parliament a document titled "Reflections on the future of relations between the European Union and China," according to which a "strategic partnership implies going beyond a logic based on rewards and punishments."

7. Especially since the document that was leaked in February 2004 was a working draft making extensive use of the statistics in the UN report on the Arab world.

8. Remarks made by Prime Minister Wen Jiabao, directed at Japan.

9. See Pierre Haski, *Le Sang de la Chine: Quand le silence tue* (Paris: Grasset, 2004).

10. Francis Deron, "L'Année de la Chine," *Commentaire* 105 (Spring 2004), 61.

CHAPTER 15

1. When the diplomat, Georges Perruche, was freed, the Ministry of Foreign Affairs refused to pay his salary for his years of captivity on the grounds that he had been fed and housed. That ruling was reversed by the Conseil d'État in what is widely known as the Perruche decision.

2. There are about 5,000 North Korean refugees in South Korea, most of whom have arrived since 1999.

3. An inter-Korean dialogue, about which even the United States is not well informed, has been going on for several years, with China's blessing. Seoul in fact has understood that the reunification of the two Koreas is impossible without Beijing's agreement, and that it will not be lucky like Germany, whose reunification was accepted by Moscow even though it was obvious that it would join the Western camp.

4. Similarly, in 1992 China promulgated a law on territorial waters unilaterally granting itself four-fifths of the South China Sea, characterized as its "historic waters."

5. See Part One, chapter 3.

6. The study, titled *The Biological Standards of Living in the Two Koreas*, was conducted in 2004 and involved 2,384 adults and 283 children and adolescents.

7. See Kang Chol-hwan, "Moon over Pyongyang," *Wall Street Journal*, July 13, 2005, in which the author, a former inmate of the North Korean camps, fiercely criticizes this aid policy, which benefits only the regime.

CHAPTER 16

1. The Dutch authorities were a welcome exception.

2. Quoted from *The Responsibility to Protect*, a 2002 report by the International Commission on Intervention and State Sovereignty, which Secretary General Kofi Annan drew on in the proposals he offered in September 2005.

Chapter 17

1. Even though *European Security Strategy*, a European report published in December 2003, acknowledged that Europe is both a target of and a base of operations for terrorism.

2. See for instance Simon Serfaty, "One West or Two?" *Defense* 108 (November–December 2003).

3. An illuminating illustration can be found in Ian Buruma and Avishai Margalit's book, *Occidentalism: The West in the Eyes of Its Enemies* (New York: Penguin, 2004).

4. A statement by John Quincy Adams in 1793 went very far in that direction: "True independence requires separation from all European interests and all European politics."

Chapter 18

1. Success was not achieved without difficulties. Aside from the Cuban missile crisis, the superpowers, stirred by false alarms or mistaken perceptions, skirted nuclear annihilation on several occasions (November 1979, June 1980, and September 1983).

2. The conflict that broke out in 1999 between India and Pakistan in the Kargil region, one year after both countries tested nuclear weapons, persuasively illustrates this reality. If President Bill Clinton had not intervened with Pakistani Prime Minister Nawaz Sharif to make him respect the line of control between the two countries, there might have been catastrophic consequences.

3. In the Middle East, the potential nuclear powers are, beyond Israel: Iran, Saudi Arabia, Egypt, Turkey, and Syria; possible Asian ones would be, beyond India, Pakistan, and China: Japan, Taiwan, and Indonesia. In some of these countries—Japan, for example, or Taiwan—nuclear tests could be carried out with powerful computers, thereby avoiding attracting world attention to activities that violate international agreements. A succession of unresolved crises with North Korea could eventually lead to such results in Japan or Taiwan.

4. See Thérèse Delpech, "The Imbalance of Terror," *Washington Quarterly*, Winter 2001.

5. "Forty Years after 13 Days," *Arms Control Today*, November 2002. See also Robert Kennedy, *Thirteen Days: A Memoir of the Cuban Missile Crisis* (New York: Norton, 1971).

6. The idea in Moscow was to announce their presence in November 1962. Any discovery of the missiles before that announcement would have provoked a major crisis with no deterrence possible.

7. It is already possible that South Korea will play a double game with the United States. Seoul has sent soldiers to Iraq to serve in the U.S. mission there, but it is establishing closer relations with Beijing, which holds the reins of Korean reunification, as Moscow once held those for Germany. Seoul and Beijing are in agreement on a fundamental point: reunification must take time.

8. American statements at Potsdam about a new weapon of unmatched power hardly impressed Stalin, who knew the details of the work being done on the Manhattan Project through his spies.

9. In 1999, for example, the presence of nuclear weapons in India and Pakistan led the United States and China to put pressure on Pakistan to stop its aggression in the Kargil region.

10. Quoted by Robert McNamara in the minutes of a conference that brought together some of the participants in the Cuban missile crisis in 2002.

EPILOGUE

1. See Nikolay Berdyayev: "We were unfamiliar with utopias and we lamented too much about the impossibility of their being realized. But utopias turned out to be much more feasible than we believed. Now the question is to avoid their definitive realization. Utopias are easier to bring to fruition than what real politics wanted to do, which was only a rational calculation of men in their studies." ·

2. Denis Diderot, *Correspondence*, ed. Roth (Paris: Éditions de Minuit, 1955), XI, 21.

3. "I confess that I fear much less in democratic societies the boldness than the modesty of desires; what seems to me the most to be feared is that, in the midst of the constant small concerns of private life, ambition will lose its drive and its grandeur." Alexis de Tocqueville, *De la démocratie en Amérique*, vol. II, Part Three, chap. 19 (Paris: Garnier-Flammarion, 1981), 304.

Index

About the Author

Thérèse Delpech is currently director for strategic studies at the Atomic Energy Commission of France and senior research fellow at CERI (Fondation Nationale des Sciences Politiques). She is also the French commissioner at the UN for the disarmament of Iraq (UNMOVIC), and member of the IISS Council as well as of RAND Europe's Advisory Board. She served as advisor to the French prime minister for politico-military affairs (1995–1997). She also served as permanent consultant to the Policy Planning Staff, French Ministry of Foreign Affairs (1991–1995).

Thérèse Delpech is the author of five books: *L'Héritage nucléaire* (Complexe, 1997), *La Guerre Parfaite* (Flammarion, 1998), *Politique du Chaos* (Le Seuil, 2002), *L'Ensauvagement* (Grasset, 2005), and *L'Iran, la Bombe et la Démission des Nations* (Autrement, 2006), to be published shortly in English by Hurst, London). She has written numerous articles on defense and strategic issues in journals such as *Politique Etrangère, Commentaire, Politique Internationale, Foreign Policy France, Le Meilleur des Mondes (Fr), Internationale Politik (Germany), Survival (IISS), Global (Italy), International Affairs (UK), the Washington Quarterly,* and *the American Interest (U.S.).*

George Holoch has been a teacher and a lawyer. He is now a free-lance translator and has translated nineteen books.